JONATHAN SWIFT AND THE MILLENNIUM OF MADNESS

The Information Age in Swift's
A Tale of a Tub

BY

KENNETH CRAVEN

E.J. BRILL
LEIDEN • NEW YORK • KÖLN
1992

The paper in this book meets the guidelines for permanence and durability of the Committee on Production Guidelines for Book Longevity of the Council on Library Resources.

Library of Congress Cataloging-in-Publication Data

Craven, Kenneth.
   Jonathan Swift and the millennium of madness: the information age in Swift's A tale of a tub / by Kenneth Craven.
      p.   cm.—(Brill's studies in intellectual history, ISSN 0920-8607; v. 30)
   Includes bibliographical references and index.
   ISBN 9004095241 (alk. paper)
   1. Swift, Jonathan, 1667-1745. Tale of a tub. 2. Swift, Jonathan, 1667-1745—Knowledge and learning. 3. Literature and science—England—History—18th century. 4. England—Intellectual life—18th century. 5. Information science in literature.
6. Philosophy in literature. I. Title. II. Series.
PR3724.T33C7   1992
823'.5—dc20   91-43722
                                                                      CIP

ISSN   0920-8607
ISBN   90 04 09524 1

A knot of Fooles.

BUT,

Fooles, or Knaves, or both, I care not,
Here they are ; *Come laugh and spare not.*

Printed at *London* for *Francis Grove*, and are to be sold at
his shop on Snow-hil near the Sarazens Head without New-gate, 1658.

A Knot of Fooles ... 1657. By permission of the British Library.

JONATHAN SWIFT
AND THE
MILLENNIUM OF MADNESS

BRILL'S STUDIES
IN
INTELLECTUAL HISTORY

For Rosanne

CONTENTS

PREFACE

The study integrates for the first time the best evidence of literary and intellectual historians to show Jonathan Swift's unabated challenge to the seductive scientific millenarian myth enmeshed in our modern information systems. In his first masterpiece, *A Tale of a Tub* (1704), Swift juxtaposes optimistic Christianized Neoplatonism with freewheeling Epicurean atomism only to reject both philosophical systems by projecting the somber truth of Kronos-Saturn, the god of satire.

Swift holds historians accountable should they adhere more to modern myth than to the logic of their evidence. By offering this new evidence and new approach, this author too risks becoming vulnerable to Swift's savage indignation and Kronos's dread dismissal.

I have sorely needed and been divinely blessed with the constancy of my understanding wife Rosanne E. Bricker; of critically supportive colleagues Angus Ross, Frank T. Boyle, and John Irwin Fischer; and of an accomplished editor Joan Emma. My debt is also beyond measure to John S. G. Simmons and the Bodleian and Radcliffe Science Libraries, Oxford; P. M. Rattansi and the University of London Library; Marianne Winder, Roy Porter and the Wellcome Institute for the History of Medicine Library, London; Ian C. Ross, David Berman and the Trinity College, Dublin Library; Andrew Carpenter, Muriel McCarthy and Marsh's Library, St. Patrick's Cathedral, Dublin; Richard H. Popkin and The William Andrews Clark Memorial Library, University of California, Los Angeles; Mary F. Zirin and The Huntington Library, San Marino, California; the late Louis A. Landa and the Firestone Library, Princeton University; the late James L. Clifford and Butler Library, Columbia University; A. C. Elias, Daniel Traister and The Teerinck Collection, University of Pennsylvania; James A. Duran, Jr. and The Library of Congress; A. Owen Aldridge and the University of Illinois Library at Champaign; Hermann J. Real, Heinz Vienken and The Ehrenpreis Center for Swift Studies, Münster. I am also most grateful to Michael V. DePorte, Frank H. Ellis, Ruth Mathewson, J. G. A. Pocock, Irwin Primer, Claude Rawson, John P. Rumrich, William H. Sievert, Joel Weinsheimer, and Jeanne K.

Welcher, and the staffs of The British Library and The Warburg Institute, the University of London.

For their cooperation, encouragement, patience, and goodwill, I express gratitude to Elisabeth Erdman-Visser, Editor, and Arjo J. Vanderjagt, General Editor, Studies in Intellectual History, at E. J. Brill.

Permission has been granted by the *Eighteenth-Century Ireland* journal to reprint material in chapters two and three originally published in the article "*A Tale of a Tub* and the 1697 Dublin Controversy," 1 (1986): 97–110.

New York
August 1991

ABBREVIATIONS

Corr.   *The Correspondence of Jonathan Swift.* Ed. Harold Williams. 5 vols. Oxford: Clarendon, 1963–65.

Discourse   Swift, Jonathan. *A Discourse of the Contests and Dissentions between the Nobles and the Commons in Athens and Rome, with the Consequences they had upon both those States* (1701). Ed. Frank H. Ellis with an Introduction and Notes. Oxford: Clarendon, 1967.

Poems   *The Poems of Jonathan Swift.* Ed. Harold Williams. 2nd ed. 3 vols. Oxford: Clarendon, 1958.

PW   *The Prose Works of Jonathan Swift.* Ed. Herbert Davis. 14 vols. Oxford: Shakespeare Head Press, 1939–1968.

Tale   *A Tale of a Tub, To Which is added The Battle of the Books and the Mechanical Operation of the Spirit.* Ed. A. C. Guthkelch and D. Nichol Smith with an Introduction and Notes. 2nd ed. Oxford: Clarendon, 1973 (with corrections).

Diligently gleaned which proved to be a Work of Time.

Jonathan Swift

CHAPTER ONE

KRONOS: THE END OF ALL

> The *Person* [Time] to whose Care the
> Education of *Your Highness* [Prince Pos-
> terity] is committed, has resolved (as I am
> told) to keep you in almost an universal
> Ignorance of our Studies, which it is Your
> inherent Birth-right to inspect.
>
> *Tale* 31

Jonathan Swift based *A Tale of a Tub* (1704) on a well-documented complex
of historical facts that buoyed its persona then and has sustained a majority of
all of us living since. In our time, John Warwick Montgomery has dispassion-
ately summarized the dramatic turn of European events: "The years from
1500 to 1700 witnessed not one, but two, staggering revolutions of thought.
In cosmology, the Copernican revolution, culminating in the discoveries
of Brahe and Kepler, totally changed man's conception of the physical
universe. . . . Simultaneously with this cosmological revolution came a
theological revolution—the Reformation. . . . As [Philip S.] Watson well puts
it: 'Just as Copernicus started with a geocentric, but reached a heliocentric
conception of the physical world, Luther began with an anthropocentric or
egocentric conception of religion, but came to a theocentric conception'"
(Montgomery 1).

While the awesome twin pillars supporting the modern world lose none of
their staggering authenticity when seen through the *Tale*'s intricately crafted
lens, the satire invests them with comico-tragic foundations. Once upon a time
zealous reformers sprang up in Europe with illuminated visions of new
worlds. Having decided to concentrate learning on what could be measured,
they soon organized vast new knowledge in encyclopedias, compendiums, and
philosophical transactions. Reformers argued with one another over the
ascendancy of two inner lights: human reason or divine revelation. Paradoxically, either of these lights served wonderfully to remove the rough edges
from the human animal, perceived now as increasingly rational, likeable, and
benevolent, as well as more individual, communally urban, collectively

disciplined, and responsive to the general welfare. One may well imagine, therefore, how these reformers—some become revolutionaries—were uniformly incensed when anyone impertinently spread the word across Europe that the human in his native habitat was still mean, nasty, and brutish and required unremitting control. Because few listened, however, during almost two centuries of intellectual, religious, and political strife, the novel informational priorities of the utopian world changers gradually became bulwarks of our world.

Whether the reforms were sacred or secular, millennial or rational, or, as Swift would have it, a magical blending of all these, individualism and consensus would gradually supplant custom and hierarchies. Soon nearly everyone high and low—excepting an isolated mean-spirited reactionary or satirist here and there—joined the chorus welcoming the modern time of linear progress, freedoms and rights, goodwill abounding, rational information as the basis for assent, amelioration of the human condition, and unrelenting challenge to absolute tyrannies everywhere. Almost everyone lived happily ever after.

When we add up the dividends recounted above, even Swift's best twentieth-century interpreters have discounted his minority satiric voice as fine-tuned but futile to stem the modern tide. The consensus is that his works support a civic theology of controls at variance with modern evidence, inclinations, and myths. Swift might agree this far with his critics; but the question becomes what priest systems, in the broadest sense of that term, can best govern us. Both he and the twentieth century pose the same pertinent queries. How are esoteric belief systems to be formulated and exoterically promulgated—that is, mythologized and finally accepted as settled public lore? Who should be the leading oligarchs in learning, religion, and governance? If we no longer have European hegemonies, are we moving inexorably toward anarchy, fantasy, and mayhem?

However our environment is constituted, one could easily despair that Swift's discourse can find redemption—*except* that its deliverance may rest on the efficacy of modern information delivery systems, ironically one of the satirist's prime targets. Once combined, massive new evidence for conceptual frameworks in intellectual history and for understanding Swift's satire and mythology hoist moderns with their own petard. Let Swift thank his god Kronos, the grim reaper, for the harvest of new systems, concepts, and evidence that may restore his credibility at the expense of those attendant at his wake.

In search of ourselves, modern researchers now ask the same questions Swift raised about channel crossings of reformers and their ideas centuries ago. How did Calvinism and republican ideals in Geneva and Basel—absorbed by the Marian Exiles in the sixteenth century—lead, on the exiles' return to Elizabethan England and Scotland, to the literal truncating of the Stuart monarchy and the ascendancy of warring parties and myriad dissenting sects in Britain by the mid-seventeenth century? How did the Rosicrucian-sponsored Thirty Years War in the first half of the seventeenth century propel European reformers such as Hartlib, Comenius, and Andreae to flee the Continent, infiltrating and energizing the Royal Society with utopian dreams that permanently changed the face of European learning? Why did the empiricism and alchemical magic of Paracelsus rise to challenge the rational Galen and instigate conflicts still splitting twentieth-century medicine? Which philosophic system prevails today: Neoplatonism with its latitudinarian accommodations for Christian theologians and heterodox thinkers or Epicurean atomism describing a universe of kaleidoscopic chance, thereby providing *carte blanche* for dominant world changers and the obsessed to impose their own configurations on it? Of the two inner lights—revelation and reason—worshipped by moderns, to what extent may we place faith in either—or both?

Is it possible that a third mythical alternative that has been eclipsed by the other two categorically denies their pervasive theosophies? Classical satirists thought so. They found that third option personified in their god, the dreaming Titan Kronos/Saturn, the tyrannic god of night, harvest, mortality, and satire. In theology, Aristotle, Hesiod, and Plutarch gave precedence to the Kronos myth over Plato's soul of the world permeating our very being. Whether the god is called the Greek Kronos or the Roman Saturn or even Father Time, his is the presence in the *Tale* that Swift, and by allusion Horace as well, serves. Out of the Kronos myth, by way of Aristotle and Galen, come the allied humors traditions in medicine and literature, the golden mean, the Golden Age of Astraea, and the opposing psychic conditions of mad and divine melancholy: the aesthetic foundations of the *Tale*. The issue is balance—primarily in each individual's, or reader's, body natural but by extension also in the body politic. For the balancing Swift, Kronos-Saturn grants us an annual rich harvest, but surely returns as the grim and perennial annihilator of all our works and days. For Swift, harsh truth—Truth is the daughter of Kronos—requires Exantlation (67), that is, drawing up from the bottom of her well.

Wherein is the truth of the human condition? Private and public well-being depend on the viability of the myth prevailing. Truth and viability should be inseparable. Accordingly, Swift challenges Christianized Neoplatonism and Epicurean atomism, the conflicting myths we live by, by deploying the multifaceted Kronos myth. It is the golden thread that runs through the *Tale*.

Four elements of Kronos-Saturn have been studied in this century. Robert C. Elliott has traced all satire to this myth as it has come down to us from its prehistoric and primitive roots. Raymond Klibansky, Erwin Panofsky, and Fritz Saxl have concentrated on the psychiatric saturnine melancholy—both the divine and the mad—from Aristotle through Middle Eastern cultures to Renaissance Europe and beyond. From the lost dialogues, A. P. Bos has reconstructed Aristotle's meta-cosmic theology as it was woven around the dreaming god Kronos; the Kronos myth was suppressed in classical times just as it is now by proponents of the more seductive myths of Plato and Epicurus. Samuel L. Macey has examined the universal origins and modern disposition of the Kronos-Saturn myth finding, sources in the Indo-Iranian gods of time and in emasculating reconstructions in the modern period—with sickle and daughter discarded—in the Newtonian Watchmaker God and the Shaftesburian Father Christmas. Swift integrates all these elements in the *Tale*.

It is clear not only that his knowledge of the humors tradition in medicine and literature remains unsurpassed but that few literary artists have examined the cosmic sweep of modern history with the learning of Swift; and his unique experience only enhanced prodigious reading and reflection. His contemporary observation posts among the decision-makers in London and Dublin from the 1680s until well into the first decade of the eighteenth century provided unparalleled opportunities for a satirist to witness the final agonies of the Stuarts, the inaugural of William III's Glorious Revolution in 1688, and the overt renewal that began in the 1690s of the revolutionary programs and propaganda that had toppled monarchy and episcopacy a half century earlier. The jockeying for power among Anglicans, Protestant dissenters, and the heterodox, king and houses of parliament, and Whigs and Tories in this confrontational time was both unprecedented and pivotal in shaping establishment policies and revolutionary foment throughout eighteenth-century Europe and America. No less was the century-long struggle between chemical and physical-mechanical science ending with the Newtonian synthesis.

During these two critical decades at the end of the century shaping public opinion in all these areas became the vital new *modus vivendi* of power. Swift mocked the inundation of propagandists, labelling them *hacks, orators,* and *unquiet spirits;* but he staked his career as one of their motley tribe. It was for public and personal reasons that he kept an unflagging eye on John Toland, the most prolific and eclectic writer among his peers, a fellow Irishman, and his major epistemological adversary. Sometime protegé of John Locke, freethinker, deist, classical republican, "illuminist rationalist" (Pocock's label), and populist, Toland served John Lord Somers' Whig Junta and then Robert Harley's Tories as propagandist—as did Swift—without compromising his incendiary principles. Like Swift, Toland believed in a mixed government with power distributed equitably among the one, the few, and the many, but he tilted toward the many just as Swift did toward the few. Like Swift, he abominated priestcraft, but nevertheless opted for civic theology. And like Swift, he saw modern European history as a continuum with democracy growing from the early sixteenth century—although what he saw as a boon appalled Swift. Unlike Swift, he found salutary the heroic virtue displayed in the mid-century changers of social and political belief such as John Milton, James Harrington, and the more inflamatory revolutionaries.

Spiritual kin to James Joyce, both Swift and Toland rose out of their labyrinth in Ireland to participate extensively in the learned, religious, and political European ferment. But their Celtic roots were important for instilling in both a strong sense for the mythic and universal: what we live by. For Swift, in particular, Dublin served as an exceptional observatory to monitor the prime movers—*grandees,* he called them—as they enthusiastically experimented with modern innovations in university, church, and state in this provincial capital.

Thanks to Margaret Jacob, J. G. A. Pocock, Robert E. Sullivan, and Stephen Daniel, we now confidently consider Toland as a major intellectual and political bridge translating a wide range of ideas commending revolution and reform from the seventeenth to the eighteenth centuries and from Britain to the Continent and America. When we conjoin the impressive twentieth-century research on Toland, encompassing his intellectual ancestry and heirs, with the significant twentieth-century literary scholarship on Swift, encompassing his aesthetic—particularly satiric—and epistemological foundations, we discover for the first time in three centuries that Toland is Swift's major satiric victim and foil in the *Tale.* The *Tale*'s discourse systematically dissects, parodies, and satirizes Toland's major publishing prior to 1704: *Christianity Not Mysterious* (1696) on religion, his 1697 edition of James Harrington's *Works* on governance, his 1698 *The Life of John Milton,* and his pirated 1699 edition of Shaftesbury's *An Inquiry Concerning Virtue* on learning. While this finding may startle Swiftians and Tolandians, Swift purposely and enigmatically concealed the sources of the ideas he satirized and judged, thereby sponsoring such confusion and delay. Now before us, the unexpected harvest calls for some historical reassessments and revisions.

Felicitously, the multi-faceted *Tale* can yield new insights into conflicting forces that shaped its time and continue to shape ours. To begin with, although the *Tale* was a publishing success and Swift may have anticipated a positive reaction, the learned and the influential among the establishment and the heterodox uniformly damned it and he was shocked. Perhaps aware at another level that the deeper reality he presents might be inundated by the philistine modern tide, Swift dedicated the *Tale* to Prince Posterity. Within this witty context, it serves as a useful guide to those skeptics in the postmodern information age who at this late date may relish a retrospective on our formation and destiny. Three centuries after the *Tale* the European world continues along the optimistic path sketched out by Montgomery. Actually the epistemology underlying the European events that concerned the satirist has not changed much since 1500. If the diminished world Swift's humoral medicine diagnosed earlier approximates ours, we have been experiencing half a millennium of madness.

In Swift's view, since the sixteenth century moderns have allowed the surface facts of history to triumph over the depth of art. Finding our way in the half-light of simple facts and pinned down with the overload of possibly useful information, we are denied the illumination of art. But having come to another critical watershed in the human journey, we may wish to examine more intently the implications of our path described in the *Tale:* implications that still require drawing up Kronos's daughter Truth, the truth that can help us from the bottom of a well.

Swift's minority voice sees the modern world as having been constructed empirically of new sensibilities at the expense of immeasurable values and priceless standards. In the *Tale,* he identifies a major human problem that transcends the fantasies one wishes to believe. In 1704 his isolated and still unknown voice argued that the reduction of learning to the measurable and of the human only to virtues—*sans* vices—spelled the doom of art, the humanities, and the *consensus gentium* of the hard-won legacies of time. Swift was convinced that the reductive process had skewed scientific information to fit the optimistic parameters of its own myth, effectively burying other knowledge systems.

In place of a fragmented but flattering glass, he raises a holistic mirror truthful to the modern time and its failing condition. The modern pragmatic state, in the name of removing the figurative veil, cannibalizes art for the social and political purposes embedded in its synthetic myth. As a last defense, the Scriblerian satirists Swift, Pope, and Gay were to resort to mock epic to challenge the new myth as transparent, destabilizing, delusive, and ersatz. Coordinately, the modern universe that in the twentieth century many enthusiastically embrace has served as a pall for the satirist's epistemology of a larger reality based in classical wisdom, pushing keystones of societal harmony even further from human understanding. Notwithstanding timeless conspiracies of limitation, the great satirists from Juvenal and Horace to Thomas More and Swift have probed below contemporary surfaces for the profound and scanned the heavens for the sublime. With the modern world deconstructing, Kronos-Saturn once again seems ready to sweep away the waste products of history.

The modern objectives of wealth and power are granted at the cost of wisdom and virtue. Accordingly for Swift, ordering surface information into rational systems rather than mining for wisdom defines the modern conceit. Thus the title of *A Tale of a Tub* introduces its theme. The key metaphor, a tub, describes a systems program designed to keep moderns preoccupied with surfaces. Sailors throw out a tub from a ship in danger to divert the attention of meddlesome and threatening whales, thus rendering them harmless.

The conflict in the *Tale* is between a mad, modern persona and a keenly observant satiric voice. By the tub metaphor, the satiric voice means to protect the commonweal, the ship of state, from reforming moderns by throwing out to them the most universal program in learning, religion, and governance assembled by their most prolific and most meddlesome writer so that he may divert his own kind—and himself—by spinning out his newfangled information systems. Indeed this tub of systems purports to be the *magnum opus* of a supremely confident madman—"a most devoted Servant of all *Modern Forms*" (45)—bent on suppressing old tyrannies and vastly improving the human condition through an enormous outpouring of processed information.

Having recognized this ordering of information rationally as the vital learned engine generating the modern world, Swift transforms it into the self-replenishing energy that galvanizes the teeming *Tale*. Constantly stepping on each other's lines, both the zealous modern persona with his superficial optimism and the corrective satiric voice with its profound pessimism assure the reader in the subtitle that each of their interpretations of the future was *Written for the Universal Improvement of Mankind.* Each boasts a rational system that renders the other's unintelligible and mad. At every turn, the satiric voice simply transforms this optimistic surface information of the new world to a reversed plane of comprehension. His topsy-turvy tale constantly points to the empty flotation and the randomly fluctuating wave rotation of the modern tub.

Swift's tub metaphor is spiritually at one with François Rabelais's boxes of Silenus highlighted in the Prologue to *The Histories of Gargantua and Pantagruel* (1523). They are painted on the outside with gay, comical figures, "light-heartedly invented for the purpose of mirth," that distract attention from the rare drugs and other precious things hidden inside. Both Swift and Rabelais construct the outside-inside, superficial-profound, skin-anatomy, surface dross-hidden treasure, facade-reality dichotomies to set off the disparity in distinct planes of knowing. Rabelais's inspiration is Plato's Socrates.

On the outside, we can all see the ugly, absurd, bovine, idiotic, plain, boorish, impoverished, unlucky, unfit Socrates always playing the fool, always concealing his divine wisdom. Only a discriminating minority cherish the divine drug within: "superhuman understanding, miraculous virtue, invincible courage, unrivalled sobriety, unfailing contentment, perfect confidence, and an incredible contempt for all those things men [and women] so watch for, pursue, work for, sail after, and struggle for" (37).

The *Tale* has made a deluded fool, *a priori*, of every modern reader, to the extent that the reader subscribes to the modern rational information synthesis. To believe that everything necessary for the human to know can be rationally established seems impertinent pride and sure disaster to Swift. If one takes the modern world seriously on these terms, Swift recommends that true happiness for fools—that is, the *Tale*'s persona, the whales, the reader, and all moderns—consists in staying at the informational surface of things within the comforting purviews of credulity and self-deception. The rational pursuit of serene happiness "is *a perpetual Possession of being well Deceived*" (171); Swift has adroitly practiced this deception on his most discerning twentieth-century critics. His revelling in such artifice, described below, is hardly *de rigeur* for a modern or postmodern author hopeful of quickly improving human kind.

Scornfully, Swift scourges the modern synthesizers reputed for probing surfaces: Paracelsus, Calvin, Bacon, Descartes, Milton, Locke, Toland, Shaftesbury, and Newton; disdainfully, he dismisses their millennial mysteries in medicine, theology, natural philosophy, literature, and rational philosophy. Here the buoyancy and belligerence of the satiric voice matches the exuberance and cocksureness of the *Tale*'s modern persona. The inexorable mill of Kronos-Saturn, the god of mortality and satire, sustains the patient Swift to affirm the ancient truism that enduring breadth and breath belong ultimately to Time's sacred art, not transitory life.

Swift's major animus against the modern synthesizers derives from their tendency to mythologize and worship rational information systems. When Francis Bacon (1561–1626) decided to make all knowledge his province, he hoped to replace the constructs of Aristotelians and Paracelsians. However, as P. M. Rattansi reminds us, this "influential propagandist of a new vision of science . . . in giving the study of nature a central place in human knowledge . . . owed a great deal to the 'natural magicians' whom he attacked" (*Scientific Background* 213). Rattansi concludes that Bacon devalued humanistic learning and made natural philosophy dominant, extending it even to ethics. In the study of nature, compilation of the facts of nature from the experiences of the mechanical arts replaced memory and sense-experience (215–16). Swift reduces this Baconian program for the advancement of knowledge to the development of information systems. These systems in the *Tale* make the exact claims of late twentieth-century ones: widely disseminated, complete, up-dated, instantaneously accessible to the specialist and to the public, essential, useful, global, reductive, and programmed for transitory, disposable data.

Though Swift attacks Bacon for encouraging encyclopedic information systems, sometimes useful discoveries, and mechanical arts and for depreciating classical humanism, he agrees with Bacon's disparagement of the Paracelsians and Neoplatonists. Section X of the *Tale* ridicules the "scholiastic midwifry" of the "true illuminated" (186) and the Rosicrucianism of Thomas Vaughan for finding darker meanings in sixteenth-century learning than were intended. But in examining those faculties of the mind that lead to idea-fixation and obsessive publishing, Swift quotes the troglodyte philosopher (Bacon):

> 'Tis certain (said he) some Grains of Folly are of course annexed, as Part of the Composition of Human Nature, only the Choice is left us, whether we please to wear them Inlaid or Embossed. (183)

The editors of *The World's Classics* 1986 edition of the *Tale* note that this image derives from Bacon's *Idols of the Cave* in *The New Organum,* I.liii–lviii (216–17).[1] These idols "take their rise in the peculiar constitution, mental or bodily, of each individual (liii). . . . Men become attached to certain particular sciences and speculations, either because they fancy themselves the authors and inventors thereof [folly embossed], or because they have bestowed the greatest pains upon them and become most habituated to them [folly inlaid]" (liv). Thus Swift ironically borrows directly from his adversary Bacon to support his own antithetical theme: all so-called rational information systems—including Bacon's—come at us trailing clouds of built-in distortion.

Section V of the *Tale* presents the basic informational elements embedded in the Baconian program for the advancement of knowledge and reflected in the information overload of the late twentieth century. Yet in the *Tale* the Baconian information program suffers from the Paracelsian occult madness Bacon himself deplored—but covertly drew on. The persona

> cannot but bewail, that no famous *Modern* hath ever yet attempted an universal System in a small portable Volume, of all Things that are to be Known, or Believed, or Imagined, or Practised in Life. (125)

---

[1] The 1973 Oxford edition of the *Tale* is used for references to the text throughout this study. References to the 1986 *World's Classics* edition are to the editors' Introduction and Appendices.

But never fear, the persona has come upon some magical nostrum requiring the alchemical-medicinal-hermetic distillation popularized by Paracelsus, Robert Fludd, and Rosicrucians like John Heydon. After "infusing Quintessence of Poppy [opium]" and other alchemical magic, this nostrum

> will dilate it self about the Brain (where there is any) in fourteen Minutes, and you immediately perceive in your Head an infinite Number of Abstracts, Summaries, Compendiums, Extracts, Collections, Medulla's, Excerpta quaedam's, Florilegia's and the like, all disposed into great Order, and reducible upon Paper. (126–27)

Swift here joins the two emotional and physical sources of digestive overload in the world of the late twentieth-century: information in the brain and drugs in the body, with their common source the pursuit of some habit-forming euphoric fantasy of a prelapsarian paradise now accessible to everyone. This bootless fantasy has been subliminally implanted both in modern minds and in their information systems. The *Tale* devalues the millennial myth as hastening our inevitable mortality, tyranny, madness, and deconstruction. On the other hand, to say that Swift would not have applauded modern freedoms from arbitrary tyrannies is to miss his defense of liberty. For him, the issue is balance, restraint, and mature reflection.

With delusion widely disseminated in the modern world, Swift believes that information delivery must have achieved a much higher priority than informational substance. Thus the Introduction to the *Tale* contrasts two distinct auditory and visual delivery systems for useful information in the manner of Narcissus Marsh. Marsh—whose pervasive influence on Swift's life and the *Tale* will be treated below[2]—had both spoken and written on the use of the air waves, or transmitting medium, in his "Doctrine of Sounds" originally presented orally to the Dublin Philosophical Society in 1683 and subsequently published in the *Philosophical Transactions* of the Royal Society. Marsh is a major satiric victim in the *Tale*. Ironically consistent with the foolish role Swift assigns him as scientific handmaid to overweening demagogues, the ever-pompous and information-proud Marsh, in his "Doctrine of Sounds" lab report, first introduced the word *microphone* to the language. Coincidentally, Swift's *Tale* uses the rare seventeenth-century term *computer* satirically as the reckoner of exact quantities of scientific information delivered (146).

In considering Swift's satiric art in 1963, Edward Rosenheim discussed Swift's "stylistic and substantive parody of Marsh's writing" in the *Tale*'s Introduction (69–77). It is, he says, a parody on the mechanistic reduction of "abstractions (in this case, eloquence) to physical laws, and it reflects, at the

---

2 See below, pp. 39–55.

same time, on the meretricious orators whose arts can be successfully governed by such grotesque principles" (76–77).

Though Rosenheim has separated the myriad strands in the "many-faceted" Introduction to the *Tale,* he concentrates on Swift's "satiric preoccupation with the new science" and "deliberately simplistic acceptance of the physical properties of sound" (73). Commenting on the *Tale*'s appropriation of the pseudoscientific jargon of Marsh's acoustical science, he also notes its concern with Marsh's two major problems in transmission: to make the least sound as loud as the greatest and to propagate sound to the greatest distance.

Swift's satire of modern information technology extends, however, beyond Rosenheim's discerning analysis. The reader of the *Tale*'s Introduction is confronted with the three major issues in late twentieth-century information science—content formatting, data priority, and rapid delivery—joined with the three aims of Marsh's Royal Society and the Dublin Philosophical Society: advances in experimental natural philosophy, in medicine or chemistry, and in mechanics or physics. The *Tale*'s modern persona, Marsh, and the modern world—farewell publishing—are alike in assigning priority to the auditory over the visual delivery system. And though Marsh had introduced only the preacher and his pulpit, the persona adds two other dubious figures with their platforms: the criminal and his gallows, the mountebank-actor and his traveling stage. Creating this mechanical system directly from the *Philosophical Transactions,* Swift was able to devote five pages of the Introduction to "Physico-logical Scheme of Oratorical Receptacles or Machines," borrowing from Marsh's "Doctrine" such ponderous terms as "parallel to the horizon," "conveyance of sound," air and bodies "of much weight and gravity," and such communication hazards as the effects of bad weather (*Tale* 55–60; *Transactions* No. 156 (February 1683/4): 472–82).

To provide symmetry for the *Tale*'s information-delivery systems in the hands of unprincipled moderns, the Introduction moves from methodologies of the auditory system to methodologies of the visual system. Again the narrative involves three suspect moderns—three, of course, being a mystical number—this time Grub Street hacks in publishing, the scientists of Gresham College, and the poets of Will's coffee-house. Transported from oratorical systems to encyclopedic ones, the former auditor, now reader, submits to catalogues, complete abstracts, and other systems and codifications of knowledge, including various treatises, appendices, and annotations.

The separate information-delivery systems of three kinds of modern orators and three kinds of modern writers propagate the distorted modern myth. In the Introduction, Swift satirically pretends to weave the esoterica of this modern myth from a motley collection of Aesopian fables, folk tales, and lore of alchemy, cabala, and apocalypse, giving them newfangled "scientific" content. *The History of Reynard the Fox* is identified as "a complete body of civil knowledge, and the Revelation, or rather the Apocalypse of all State-Arcana" (68). *Tom Thumb* will contain the whole scheme of Metempyschosis. *The Wise Men of Gotham* presents "a just Defence of the modern Learning and Wit" (69).

In Section V, Swift returns to his references from other 1680s *Philosophical Transactions* contemporary with Marsh's; but here he raises questions surrounding the fundamental split between science and humanism even as he parodies the modern agenda and methodology of natural philosophy. Some of the parodies are direct echoes of his student years at Trinity College, Dublin in the 1680s. Miriam Starkman and R. C. Olson pay particular attention to the persona's treatment of this material. He judges Homer's "achievements" on the basis of philosophical and scientific, rather than literary and humanistic criteria.

Against the persona's rational standards, Homer's transcendent accomplishments literally—and, of course, figuratively—do not measure up to several subjects treated in the *Philosophical Transactions* for the three-year period 1683–86. Bacon had earlier argued for technologically useful discoveries and charged the contemplative ancient Greeks with having contributed hardly "a single experiment which tends to relieve and benefit the condition of mankind and which can with truth be referred to the speculations and theories of philosophy" (*Novum organum,* 1.63). In Section V of the *Tale,* the persona echoes Bacon's sentiments in evaluating Homer. According to Olson, he has specific Royal Society sources for the mock disparaging of Homer's greatness. Homer, it turns out, knew little about the spleen, the *opus magnum,* the *sphaera pyroplastica,* and salivation without mercury—all references to the Royal Society's attachment to Paracelsian medicine and the occult. And he knew little about mechanics. His deficiencies in the matter of flies and spittle make his powers suspect when contrasted with the Society's dedication to natural experiments. Finally, Homer's glaring ignorance of the art of political wagering is clearly exposed by Sir William Petty's article on political arithmetic in the 1686 issue of the *Transactions.* (Swift's library contained a copy of Petty's 1699 *Essays in Political Arithmetick.*) Olson quotes from a review of these essays in the 1685 *Transactions* that would have attracted Swift's attention. According to the reviewer, Petty

> made it appear that Mathematical Reasoning is not only applicable to Lines and Numbers, but affords the best means of Judging in all the concerns of humane life. (Quoted by Olson 461)

Mathematical reasoning, lines, and numbers efficiently exclude less precise, more malleable languages, humane discourse, aesthetics, and subject matters accessible on other planes of knowing. The *Tale*'s satiric discourse, therefore, uses the aims and discourse of the Royal Society to illustrate how poorly equipped modern science with its methodologies, myth, and intellectual pride will forever be to pass beyond measured matter and extracted information to reach a more profound and comprehensive understanding of human nature. The combined judgments of the Swiftians Rosenheim, Starkman, and Olson suggest that the modern aims of Marsh and Petty and their Dublin Philosophical Society accurately reflected those of its Royal Society model. Further, we may judge from their research that Swift had the material at hand in the 1680s to attack with parody and satire the attempt of modern science both to overthrow Aristotelian scholasticism and at the same time to inundate humanistic learning with experimental philosophy, Paracelsian medicine, Cartesian mechanics, Baconian information-delivery systems, and Marsh's—and the modern world's—complacent premise that man may be defined as an *animal rationale*. The false myth of Bacon's *Great Instauration* is very specifically the *Tale*'s and modern Europe's new Genesis.

By inversion the persona, who scientifically legitimizes ancient fables, folk tales, and myths in the Introduction, chooses to ignore the epic and mythic sweep of Homer in Section V and introduces occult medicine and fantastic drugs in Section X of the *Tale*. Swift persuasively suggests that the rise of modern science is based on false myths with esoteric sources characteristically obscured by the proliferation, packaging, and marketing of transitory, novel, and kaleidoscopic information in well orchestrated rational media systems that promise irrational progress back to Eden, the residual primitive fantasy of a restless and immature species. Ultimately diminished through this exercise, the modern scientist serves the three auditory mountebanks, or ultimate crowd manipulators as willing accomplice.

In offering a sophisticated understanding of modern information systems, Swift bares two esoteric agendas hidden in their exoteric seams: their transmission is managed by a power elite and they reinforce a delusive and beggarly mythological orientation. Both agendas self-servingly guarantee that other knowledge systems will either be denied transmission or charged with doubtful credibility. The esoteric principles and theory that determine mythic priorities govern covertly for the disseminators, but must be simplistically revised to insure efficient transmission of the exoteric message by avoiding complexity. Consequently, nursery tales "scientifically" adapted in the seventeenth century or a saturation of inane and psychically ruinous animated cartoons in the twentieth century suffice for mythic content. If the modern myth is indeed too seductive to be contradicted, then all attention may be safely focused on the information-delivery system, as it is now and was in the *Tale*. With delivery to the vulgar mass the goal, Swift keeps his modern persona occupied hopelessly, harmlessly, and endlessly spinning his tale of a tub. He attacks simultaneously both the ordering of socially and politically useful information and the low human priority and deleterious uses for which the systems to transmit it are meticulously constructed. He yokes his or her scientific epistemology with the scientist, like the information flood with the sorcerer's apprentice, eternally producing banality, from emotional and intellectual immaturity, for the amusement of the gods.

Swift had no love for subscribers to promising modern myths in his time or ever. He minimally unsettled the general reader of his time by undermining comforting rational myths, and he has been more successful in confounding his twentieth-century critics. Ironically, the contemporary figures most frequently alluded to at the surface of the text who have been most studied by recent critics pale into insignificance beside the *Tale*'s major victims: the Lockean disciples Toland, Lord Shaftesbury, and Peter Browne, the Roscicrucian John Heydon, the classical republican John Milton, and the natural philosophers Sir Isaac Newton and Marsh, none of whom are named in the text and who, consequently, have rarely been considered in critical studies of the *Tale*. Resurrecting these more influential victims from critical limbo transforms the slippery *Tale* from a work within a narrower topical focus to the saga of a continuing universal conflict pitting the myth makers of modern history and transitory processed information against the satirist of classical art and ancient wisdom.

It is part of Swift's sophisticated jest, shown in the warp and woof of his art, that he fully anticipated that the *Tale* would challenge friend and foe, contemporaries and latter-day scholars alike, to ransack its myriad contemporary allusions with little to show for their pains. Therefore, when literary historians of the *Tale* attempt to move from the "conjectures" and monographs Swift anticipated to the substantive evidence he hid, they must be exceedingly wary of his devious bent. Although Rabelais warned his readers with the Silenus metaphor of the treasures they might be missing, Swift, without fair warning, has seduced generations of learned critics to remain at the surface of the *Tale* even as they have professed as a given the received opinion of their evolving world. Wickedly, his Rabelaisian wit has contributed to burying the *Tale*'s treasure, thereby leaving deluded moderns happily bobbing with their private tub. Processing disposable information remains, in Swift's view, the easy escape from painful truth for scholars. Should they insist on lingering about the vacant surfaces of the *Tale*, let them remain there and be damned. Let them wander off on the wrong scent. Let them be overwhelmed, stranded in half light, by dank rational information and dark private conjectures.

Certain that modern commentators of the *Tale* would go helter-skelter in all directions, Swift even concocted a global information-analysis project of his own, a modern game plan, to insure that all modern critics, the putative commentators, would gather about the tub at its evanescent surface. Convinced that "this comprehensive discourse" would tempt modern pedants to come forward in droves, Section X of the *Tale* recommends that "seven of the deepest scholars" in every Christian dominion be shut up in separate chambers for seven years to write their ample commentaries. "I shall venture to affirm, that whatever Differences may be found in their several Conjectures, they will be all, without the least Distortion, manifestly deduceable from the Text" (185). Swift joins this time-wasting project for scholars to another of his personal conceits. His Apology, composed for the 1710 Fifth Edition, announces that the universal *Tale* will hold out to this bitter end: "The book seems calculated to live at least as long as our Language, and our Tast admit no great Alterations" (3). After the limited language of measurement is exhausted and the last transitory waste products are processed, the misguided heirs will shuffle off, modernism will self-deconstruct, and the *Tale* will be the only memorial left on the abandoned beach.

Three centuries of massive scholarly efforts sustain Swift's wayward game plan and his boast. The *Tale*'s persona initiated an era of relative truth. He claims to have written the book *An Universal Rule of Reason: or, Every Man his Own Carver* (*Tale* 130).[3] Right you are, if you think you are. And why not? Nothing any idiot needs to know is obscured from reason. When all the world succumbs to the relative mercies of time, place, and private eccentricities, then specialized reasoning in little corners becomes the modern forte while considering the work of art as an entity and truth as absolute becomes an unfashionable, obscure, unneeded mystery. Fittingly, Swift appended to the 1710 Fifth edition the pedantic notes provided by William Wotton, a ransacking modern to the core. With the scholarly assurance that this masterpiece can be fathomed "without the least distortion," many twentieth-century Swiftians circumscribe their findings about the *Tale* with such discrete categories as its theme and structure or the satirist's art or such specialized topics as its relation to learning, Anglican rationalism, the Puritan background, governance, scatology, madness, reason, ancients and moderns, language, experimental science,

---

3 Robert M. Adams discusses the *Tale*'s use of this metaphor, a possible borrowing from Shaftesbury, in terms of moral relativism, interest, and opinion. There are "lunatic assumptions" in making "each man his own measure of his own truth" (*Mood* 88–89).

and the occult. These thorough and rational projects have been made easier by a model of modern erudition, the 1973 Oxford Second Edition of *A Tale of a Tub to which is added The Battle of the Books and the Mechanical Operation of the Spirit*.[4] Perhaps to justify their methodical care and certainly to emphasize its critical importance, the Oxford editors record Samuel Johnson's keen insight that the *Tale* "exhibits a rapidity of mind, a copiousness of images, and vivacity of diction, such as he never afterwards possessed." Johnson's pontific literary assessment seems reinforced when the Oxford editors quote Swift's own humble-proud judgment in his old age. "Good God! What a genius I had when I wrote that book" (xix).

Embalmed since 1710 in its protective winding sheet of depending on tyrannic Kronos's reversal of perspective, offering unsavory truths and wild goose chases, and carrying idiosyncratic conjectures of confounded critics, the *Tale*'s discourse has awaited the recognizable correlation of a future time for its unraveling. Now that some correlation exists between late twentieth-century reality and the *Tale*'s dire warnings, probing beneath the surface has become a viable, if still discomforting option. With a delicious Swiftian irony, the metaphoric—and real—choice has inexorably come down at last to whether twenty-first-century Europe will live on with the irreplaceable legacy of Venetian art or the inundating pollution of Venetian commerce. If moderns insist on scientific progress to achieve the good life, Kronos will soon deny them enduring art and life itself.

---

[4] It should be noted that this definitive edition was reprinted in 1965, 1968, and 1973 (with corrections).

CHAPTER TWO

TOLAND: MYSTERIOUS REASON

> What little was left of the main Substance of
> the Coat [the Scriptures], he [Jack] rubbed
> every day for two hours. . . . but at the same
> time went on with so much Violence, that he
> proceeded a *Heathen Philosopher.*
>
> *Tale* 199–200)

When the Licensing Act expired in 1695, John Toland was waiting to publish his *Christianity Not Mysterious* (1696). Toland's intent was to submit all ecclesiastical authority and received opinion on Christianity to finite reason, giving the *coup de grace* to revealed religion. Outlining a theory of knowledge by analyzing the nature of reason and belief, he placed the origins of Christian mysteries in Levitical rites, pagan ceremonies, and philosophical pretexts. In the judgment of H. F. Nicholl, Toland's "evidences of vitality, of sincerity and of penetrating insight atone for" his exaggeration, wild accusations, imprecision, and lack of restraint (61).

The theological storm that swirled around the publication of Toland's treatise in due course awakened most of the priests in Britain and Ireland; no less than nine influential Anglican divines rushed to attack it in print.[1] As Ernest Mossner puts it, "this work opens the new propagandist era for Deism. First recapitulating Locke's theory of knowledge, Toland proceeds to make the application to Christianity" (53).

Toland clearly acknowledges his indebtedness to Locke, alluding to him as "an excellent modern Philosopher" and "great Man" (82, 85) In fact, a year before publication of Toland's book, Locke, who had earlier encouraged him, read it in manuscript. But since Locke was "designedly orthodox" though "effectually deist," Toland's unequivocally deistic work would prove a public embarrassment to him (Mossner 42). To counter its effect, that same year Locke quickly rushed into print with *The Reasonableness of Christianity* as a preemptive detachment from the work Toland would publish a year later

---

[1] Thomas Beconsall, Thomas Beverley, Edmund Elys, Jean Gailhard, John Norris, Stephen Nye, William Payne, Edward Stillingfleet, Edward Synge.

(Daniel, 42–3; Jacob, *The Newtonians* 214–15). Like the divines, Locke realized that Toland had entered the epistemological lists on the side of reason, using this evidentiary tool to proclaim to the Established Church, the Learned, and the Vulgar that the Christian mysteries were patently suspect and implicit faith was unreliable.

Locke and other keepers of the faith would not deny the test of reason, but exempted mysteries as above reason, though not contrary to it, thus accommodating the Anglican center. But Locke's deistic disciples Toland and Shaftesbury had used his empirical epistemology to move radically to his left, toward natural religion, and Peter Browne, a conservative Anglican disciple, used the same empiricism to buttress revealed religion.

Enjoying the consternation among the divines and savoring the divergences among the Lockeans, Swift victimized all four rationalists in the *Tale*. Just as lapsing of the Licensing Act opened the doors to voice deistic tenets for Toland, *Christianity Not Mysterious* opened the doors to respond satirically for Swift—who may yet prove to be the book's finest reader. Swift recognizes that much of Toland's objective Lockean reasoning subjectively offers religious and political mysteries necessary to John Milton and the Puritan Revolution.

The *Tale* dwells on mysteries. They include the real and suspect Christian ones, Toland's even more suspect mysteries presented as modern reason, and Swift's own career-protecting and privacy-guarding mysteries enabling him to conceal the identity of his parodied sources and satiric victims—at the same time that he universalized their behavior. The fallacies of modern reason, which Swift considers abuses in learning and religion, proved almost inexhaustible in the *Tale*.

Toland's attack on Christian mysteries attempts to remove the veil of obscurity in all useful matters of human concern for everyone from the learned to the vulgar. According to Joel Weinsheimer, Toland's work "inaugurates the epoch of universal hermeneutics" (11).[2] Glossing "If after all [our efforts] we should be at a loss about the Meaning of any Expression, we ought rather to charge it upon Distance of Time, and the want of more Books in the same Tongue, than to attribute it to the Nature of the Thing" (*Christianity Not Mysterious* 51–2), Weinsheimer's says, "We do not understand many things, of course, but there is nothing that we could not understand, with sufficient effort and opportunity. Toland's hermeneutics urges us to the task" (22).

---

[2] Weinsheimer's unpublished draft, "Toland on Reason," presented at the Northeast American Society for Eighteenth-Century Studies, Amherst, Massachusetts, November 2, 1990, represents a chapter of a forthcoming book on eighteenth-century philosophy in which the *Tale* will be discussed. He has kindly permitted use of his cogent analysis here.

The *Tale* provides ample evidence that Swift studied Toland's universal hermeneutics minutely. For Swift, Toland removes obscurities for the learned and the vulgar by limiting human concerns to the superficial and the mundane, by misnaming modern reason as wisdom, and by offering a theological system of his own that rivals the Christian mysteries in obscurity. Thus the *Tale's* Introduction distinguishes between superficial information and hard truth: "Readers of the present Age . . . will by no means be persuaded to inspect beyond the Surface and the Rind of Things; whereas, *Wisdom* is a *Fox*, who after long hunting, will cost you the Pains to dig out. . . . 'tis a *Nut*, which unless you chuse with Judgment, may cost you a Tooth, and pay you with nothing but a *Worm*" (66). In other words, some profundities and mysteries are critical for human life but are difficult to decipher—and therefore ignored—by modern reason.

The *Tale* critiques *Christianity Not Mysterious* in merciless detail, yet Swift concurs with Toland on the abomination of priestcraft and the essential simplicity of the New Testament. Critical indictments of priestcraft had had a popular ring from the earliest deists, Lord Herbert of Cherbury and Charles Blount, to Anthony Collins and Matthew Tindal; and on the matter, Swift agreed fully with Toland's dismissal of "the Gibberish taught in *Divinity Schools*," "litigious Disputes, and vain Subtilties" and "pompous Worship."(141, 154, 152).[3] He had smarted under Provost Narcissus Marsh's pontific discipline and text on logic at Trinity College, Dublin from 1682 on. On this score Swift welcomed the irreverent sallies in *Christianity Not Mysterious* since they provided satiric hints, parodic opportunities, and useful quotations to mock the priesthood generally and Marsh in particular. He also agreed with *Christianity Not Mysterious* in deriding both the false Christian mysteries that departed from "the plain Dress of the Gospel" and "all corrupt Clergy-men . . . who make a meer Trade of Religion" (152, xxx) to the extent of copying Toland directly. The *Tale* alludes to the "very plain" coat of the New Testament and concludes that "this Mystery of venting spiritual Gifts is nothing but a *Trade*" (82, 276). It is small wonder that William Wotton thought the unknown author of the *Tale* had copied from Toland or that Samuel Clarke accused the author of being an atheist.

Toland's idea of religion as a trade when yoked to his synoptic history of the corruptions of institutional religion, his implacable hostility to the Church

---

[3] In 1708, Swift found Matthew Tindal echoing Toland on the "miserable Gibberish of the Schools." Swift's rejoinder to the deist recalls his bittersweet agreement with Toland in the *Tale:* "We have exploded Schoolmen as much as he [Tindal], and in some People's Opinion too much, since the Liberty of embracing any Opinion is allowed" (*PW* 2: 97).

of Rome, and his replacing implicit faith with reason in *Christianity Not Mysterious* supply the satiric mainspring for the even-numbered sections of Swift's *Tale*. Essentially, these sections present the persona's exegesis on the temple of "sublime Mysteries" (54). In them, Swift utilizes Toland's synoptic and propagandistic history of priestcraft and adapts his imagery and ideas for the Allegory of the Coats. In wickedly borrowing his allegory from Toland's literal language, he purposely engages in what the rationalist abhors as a mystery—"a mad Liberty of Allegory [which] accommodate[s] the Scriptures to . . . wild Speculations" (xx).

Responding to Toland's generalized attack on priestcraft, Swift traces, with parodic fidelity to his source, the rise of institutionalized Christianity. These religious sections of the *Tale* employ an absurd allegory that equates the New Testament or Gospel—that is, God's Will—with a coat.[4] Swift uses Toland's notion of the Gospel as the simply "revealed Will" of God given to the Brethren (xiii, xiv, 42, 101, 131), but Swift adds nuances. *Will* has three meanings in his story: the Gospel, what God ordains, and God's stipulations on how His earthly priests are to preserve the divine inheritance. He names three priestly brothers as beneficiaries—Peter the papist; Jack the dissenter, and Martin the Anglican—each inheriting the same plain coat of the Gospel, God's Will. Here Swift borrows principally from Section 3.6 of the Second Edition, Enlarged, of *Christianity Not Mysterious*.[5] Replete with traditional clothing metaphors, the history of Christianity's suspect mysteries in Chapter 6 of Section 3 provides the frame story of the Allegory of the coats with its tailor worship. Toland suggestively argues that Jesus Christ "having stripped the Truth of all those external Types and Ceremonies. . . . rendered it easy and obvious to the meanest Capacities. His Disciples and Followers kept to this simplicity for some considerable time" (151), though later priests "engrossed at length the sole Right of interpreting *Scripture* . . . distinguishing themselves from other men in their Garb."(167). "Scandalized by the plain Dress of the *Gospel*" (152), they set themselves up with "*white linen Stoles, Mitres,* and

---

[4] Conventional wisdom on the religious allegory has been set forth in the 1973 *Oxford* edition (xxxi–xliii) and again by Irvin Ehrenpreis: "A magical legacy and the three brothers who fall out—are common in folk lore and literature" (*Swift* 1:186); recognition of the triparte Christian Church is also common after the Reformation. Speculation on sources include a sermon of Bishop John Sharp and the story of the three rings. The widely learned Swift like Shakespeare had no difficulty borrowing, combining, and transforming multiple sources. The trigger here is clearly *Christianity Not Mysterious* as associated with the 1695 lapsing of the Licensing Act and the 1697 outrageous and public Dublin Controversy involving Toland, Narcissus Marsh, and Peter Browne described in ch. 3.

[5] It is critically important to realize that these metaphors do not appear in the first edition of that year.

the like. . . . But indeed the design at bottom was to introduce Riches, Pomp, and Dignities" (152, 156):

> Thus what at the beginning was but only tolerated in weaker Brethren, became afterwards a part of *Christianity* itself, under the pretence of *Apostolick* Prescription or Tradition. (152)

Swift realized the satiric possibilities in Toland's sketchy history of the Church's early degradation and its three sordid motives. In the *Tale,* the brethren who inherited the plain dress observe the Gospel "for the first seven Years [centuries]" (74)—Toland had limited it to three—but then fall in love with three ladies: "The Dutchess *d' Argent* [riches], *Madame de Grands Titres* [pomp], and the Countess *d' Orgueil* [dignities]" (74). Then, because Peter, the "more *Book-learned*" brother (83)," encourages the other two to believe that the universe is a large suit of clothes, they come to worship the tailor's idol, an iron. (Toland had referred "to the pompous worship and secret *Mysteries* of Deities without Number" and ceremonies "not having the least Precedent . . . from the Gospel" [152–53]).

To further his tailor mysteries, Peter adds appropriate codicils to the Will and locks it up; he also acquires church lands through the conversion and accompanying generosity of emperors like Constantine (83–91). Peter's elaborations on Christianity in the *Tale,* including transubstantiation, match Toland's charges precisely, for Toland concluded that the Church had "augmented" the Bible, kept its mysteries secret, and "appropriated" all the endowments of zealous emperors (156, 158, 155).

Clearly Toland's *Christianity* and Swift's *Tale* agree on the simplicity of the Gospel; both also state explicitly that organized Christianity has perpetually been beset by priestcraft, a trade. And although the deist emphasizes ornate ceremonies while the satirist concentrates on his inside-outside reversal, the clothes' metaphor, it is Toland's chronicle of abuses that Swift uses in the coats allegory. Still, despite their anticlerical concurrence, Swift and Toland remained forever opposed on reason and faith. From the publication of *Christianity Not Mysterious* (1696), the two writers confronted each other over two basic epistemological issues: whether to choose implicit faith or reason in religion and whether the ancients or the moderns supplied the more reliable sources in learning. On both counts, Toland intended "to take up a new Road" (111). With respect to faith, he argued that it is "far from being an implicit Assent" (139). A man with implicit faith "is ready to be shaken, and *carried away with every wind of Doctrine*" (36). Faith should become assent only after knowledge (128, 139). In contrast, reason is "the Candle, the Guide, the Judge He has lodged within every Man" (140–41). It is "the only Foundation of all Certitude" (6). He asserts that Scripture, the self-evidently true text, and reason-the-rule, "I'm sure, agree very well together" (xv).[6]

Because of their fundamental epistemological split, Swift had no intention of exempting Toland from his blanket condemnation of moderns in the *Tale*. The Anglican divine grounded his own beliefs in implicit faith, which Toland had attacked fervently, submitting the Gospel, instead, to the dictates of reason. Equating reason with free will and the Church Fathers with venal authority, Toland had rallied the vulgar to make up their own minds about all Christian mysteries; so that they could exercise their God-given reason, he had traced these mysteries to heathen philosophers; he championed the moderns over the ancients; and he believed the carnal mind to be limited to a relatively few lewd, wicked men. Often by parody, Swift satirized every one of these positions in the *Tale*. He also satirized Toland's extensive use of Locke's philosophy, his excessive hostility to Papal Rome, his zeal for publishing, and his facile discourse on the history of the Christian mysteries, transubstantiation, allegory, Revelation, and the Mosaic veil.

Toland's works afforded Swift a wealth of materials to set against his own basic principles and convictions; but more than this, the heteroclite, heterodox, and ubiquitous man served, metaphorically and directly, as the quintessentially inventive modern writer on whom Swift modeled the angry, zealous, and mad Jack of the *Tale*. Who among his contemporaries so felicitously, and so publicly, embodied all that Swift satirized as abuses in modern learning and religion? Without coaxing, Toland conveniently smiled for Swift's portrait of a consummate modern. And since Toland operated within a multitude of revolutionary contexts, his writings provided a superabundance of allusions for parody and satire. With his works, Toland's persona was a satiric treasure, based on his own profession of being the moderns' most facile, ubiquitous, and prolific propagandist and prophet of the future.

Happily for this study, Louis A. Landa's "Swift, The Mysteries, and Deism" fully summarizes Swift's lifelong views on reason and faith, juxtaposing them contextually with Toland's. Swift's "fairly conventional" (242) sermon "On the Trinity," first published in 1744 though probably written before the 1726 *Gulliver's Travels*, reflects orthodox reaction to Samuel Clarke and others who from the turn of the century vigorously opposed the anti-Trinitarian views of deists like Toland. To deploy latitudinarian rationalism against the rational deists, as Clarke did, seemed to Swift and

---

6 Weinsheimer elucidates Toland's complex understanding of reason: "Using reason-the-instrument consists in accommodating the text to reason-the-rule. When the text conforms to the rule—that is, when the text is rationalized—we understand. . . . Rationalizing the text—discovering how it makes sense—is not subsequent to understanding, but understanding itself" (13).

other conservative Anglicans to lend credence to the authority of reason over faith. In *A Letter to a Young Clergyman* (1720), Swift pointed out "that nothing in the canons or articles of Christianity warrants the attempts of divines to explain the mysteries and that such attempts serve no useful purpose" (Landa 243); and the Trinity sermon supports Swift's consistency by asserting that divines who attempted "farther Explanations of this Doctrine of the Trinity, by Rules of Philosophy . . . have multiplied Controversies to such a Degree, as to beget Scruples that have perplexed the Minds of many sober Christians, who otherwise could never have entertained them" (Landa 243; *PW* 9:160). Landa argues that Swift's anti-intellectualism in this instance, also "discernible at other points in his works," is accounted for by "the fundamental tenet of the sermon, the incomprehensibility of the divine nature" (244–245). He characterizes Swift's epistemological clash with Toland as centering on whether the Christian mysteries are within the compass of reason or above it. Swift ascribes to humans only a measure of reason; voicing a conventional skepticism, he asserts, "How little do those who quarrel with Mysteries, know of the commonest Actions of Nature?" (*PW* 9:164). Landa summarizes the thrust of his qualified antirationalism in "On the Trinity" as follows:

> Swift's defense of the mysteries rests upon the reasonableness of faith—the view . . . that faith is itself a higher form of reason. . . . The crux of Swift's position is evident in his definition of faith: "a Virtue by which any Thing commanded us by God to believe, appears evident and certain to us, although we do not see, nor can conceive it.". . . This conception of faith is . . . called implicit faith, that is, assent to a doctrine on authority, even though the doctrine is not fully comprehended. (Landa, 252; *PW* 9:164)

In other words, Swift's orthodox views in "On the Trinity" are within the framework "of contemporary reactions to these fashionable [deist] heresies" and Swift's earlier antideist tracts (Landa 255).

Swift did not reject reason; but like Bishop Berkeley he recognized its severe limitations and applied the same skepticism to the supreme faith in reason of the deists, the natural philosophers, and the classical republicans that each of them in turn had applied to orthodoxy, learned authority, and absolutism. Geoffrey Cantor's "Berkeley's *The Analyst* Revisited" finds areas of agreement between Berkeley and Swift that extend from 1700 through the 1730s. Cantor points out that the *freethinker*, a term Locke introduced to the language in 1697 to describe Toland, "championed natural above revealed religion [and thus] contributed to the moral decay of Great Britain" (673). For Berkeley and Swift, the loss was not to revealed religion but to governance. Modern thinkers sometimes charge that reason brings ultra conservatives to obscurantism, overbearing authority, and absolutist positions. Berkeley and Swift similarly charge that reason is the instrument that causes freethinkers, latitudinarians, and other moderns to create a priesthood of their own devising, rife with old tyrannies.

Swift's contemporaries accused the author of the *Tale* of irreverence and impiety and believed he had copied Toland's ideas approvingly. Flowing with the eighteenth-century tide and with a majority of twentieth-century Swiftians, Landa has excluded the *Tale* from what he defines as Swift's orthodox framework and asserts that "Certainly it cannot be denied that *A Tale* lends some support to the charges of irreligion" (239). The evidence we have seen of Swift's and Toland's agreements, as they are reflected in the *Tale,* tends to reenforce these judgments. Yet the judgments are fragmented and distancing: they caused Swift's clerical career to suffer when he was alive and contribute to a mistaken understanding of his satirical intentions now.

Reading the *Tale* whole supports the priority of Swift's satiric concerns over his Anglican ones. The *Tale*'s defense of implicit faith is as decidedly secondary as the fate of Brother Martin. Yet the misunderstanding of its priorities has made it easier for the modern world to bury the *Tale*—and then bury Swift as an obscurantist High Church Anglican anxious over the crisis of atheism rather than heed him as a prescient satirist. He is not the benighted, panicky "atheist hunter" that Roger Lund contends (54). The evidence that follows below moves in the opposite direction, explicating the epistemological clashes in the *Tale* that Landa finds in other works of Toland and Swift.

Swift's classical theological principles as a satirist prevail in his art over any narrow Anglicanism. He is the votary of Kronos-Saturn. In the *Tale,* he engaged in an epistemological discourse with Toland over *Christianity Not Mysterious*—and, by extension, with Locke. The mad persona and mad Jack, the dissenter, alternate in carrying the burden of representing Toland's so-called rational positions that Swift labels mysteries in their own right. The emphasis is less on defending Christian mysteries than exposing modern rational ones. If we ask how Swift could link the deist Toland with the fanatic sects, we note that he uses Toland's reliance on reason (deism) and the Gospel (dissent) as the twin pillars of Jack's Christian faith. The *Tale* has Jack marshal "many of the *Fox*'s arguments . . . for bringing *Martin* to *Reason,* as he called it; or, as he meant it, into his own ragged, bobtailed Condition. . . . In a few Days it was for certain reported, that he had run out of his Wits. In a short time after, he appeared abroad, and confirmed the Report, by falling into the oddest Whimsies that ever a sick Brain conceived" (141).

The modern mysteries are shown to be life-threatening, and the satiric foreboding extends to all European learning, religion, and governance. At this depth of concern, Swift sets about to undermine secular, modern reason as it spawns its own priestcraft—with seemingly rational modern mysteries increasingly seductive and tyrannic. This universal satiric mission, at once classical and spiritual, cost Swift a bishopric, but unfolds for his readers the growing dangers of an intellectually rudderless, spiritually leaderless modern European world. That world and the *Tale* itself are delivered, by the learned and the crowd, into the mechanically dexterous hands of the zealous persona and raging Jack—both mad, power-oriented, confident, and ascendant.

We are "absolutely ignorant" of real essence says Toland (83). No, counters Swift. Using Locke's notion of nominal as opposed to real essence as his theme and Toland's *Christianity Not Mysterious* as his source of satiric inspiration, Swift cannily opposes the seductiveness of nominal secular reason to its terrifyingly real essence: subjective interest and opinion, ingrained anger and prejudice, enthusiasm for fragmenting causes, and propaganda for discipleship. In the *Tale*, Swift presents what passes for modern reason as the facade of all facades. When one looks beyond the rational surface, the agendas of the persona, Jack, and *Christianity Not Mysterious* suffer from three demonstrable flaws: private, egoistic invention, relentless hostility to Rome, and a converting zeal.

Swift demonstrates the first flaw—that nominal objective reason is nothing more than subjective invention—by drawing on Toland's writing. Toland quoted the latitudinarian Tillotson on his Title Page and lauded Locke as "an excellent modern philosopher" (82). But Swift points out that though *Christianity Not Mysterious* praised these modern rationalists, it warned of ancient philosophical systems and sophistries that mixed "their old Opinions" (121) with Christianity, confounding "the Inventions of men with the Doctrine of God" (121). Swift uses his attack on the ancients as a boomerang against Toland. The *Tale* charges Toland with private invention masquerading as reason. For Swift, ancient or modern private invention is a snare, a delusion, and a vice. He illustrates the careening progress and descent of the modern rationalist from pride in his own reason to expansion of his private invention, then to creation of his own set of mysteries, and finally to founding a sect. The progress is swift from pride to invention to mysteries to the creation of an absolutist and irrational priesthood. Browne's *A Letter in Answer to a Book entitled Christianity Not Mysterious* (1697) in fact accused Toland of intending to found his own sect; and Toland's later pantheism and illuminist meetings on the Continent seemed to confirm Browne's suspicion. In creating the Aeolist sect in the *Tale*, Swift used the idea of mad moderns bound together in radical association—and literally feeding from the private invention of their leader.

To define modern rationalism—deistic and latitudinarian—as purely private invention, the *Tale* sets up a dichotomy between memory and invention:

> BUT, here the severe Reader may justly tax me as a Writer of short Memory, a Deficiency to which a true *Modern* cannot but of Necessity be a little subject: Because, *Memory* being an Employment of the Mind upon things past, is a Faculty, for which the Learned, in our Illustrious Age, have no manner of Occasion, who deal entirely with *Invention,* and strike all Things out of themselves, or at least, by Collision, from each other. (134–35)

Robert M. Adams has noticed that this passage reflects the heated and protracted exchanges between Locke and Edward Stillingfleet, the Bishop of Worcester, over Toland's *Christianity Not Mysterious.* Swift refers to the conflict in the *Battle of the Books.* It is one of his many obscure clues to his purposes to confirm that what he alludes to tangentially in the *Battle,* he pursues substantively in the *Tale.* Here Adams sums up Stillingfleet's argument—the one Swift adapts—against Locke's "the way of ideas":

> It is this [Socinian] controversy to which the Hack alludes when he says buoyantly that the learned in his illustrious age have no occasion for memory because they "deal entirely with *Invention,* and strike all things out of themselves, or at least, by Collision, from each other" (135). The first alternative refers to Locke's statement that his *Essay Concerning Human Understanding* had been "spun out of his own coarse thoughts,"[7] a phrase recurring again and again in the controversy, usually at the instance of Stillingfleet, who used it to impeach the philosopher of complacency and presumption. The second alternative alludes to the collision, not of authors, but of ideas; it is by reconciling conflicts among ideas, by forcing the ideas to clarify themselves, that Locke believes we can improve our understanding. The whole view of modern authorship as the spinning of insubstantial cobwebs out of one's own bowels, under the influence of self-sufficiency and contempt for others, finds an expression, so obvious that it is unnecessary to explore its details, in the spider-and-bee episode in *The Battle of the Books.* (Adams, *Mood,* 86.)

To exalt private and collective inventions as the budding mysteries of all rational modern sects, Swift again uses Toland's text as boomerang. *Christianity Not Mysterious* asserts that the Church hierarchs securely placed "sublime mysteries" above the reach of "the profanely inquisitive LAITY" (169). Not so Toland, whose private sublime mysteries are simplified for all. In the Preface, he defends his plain writing as "of considerable Advantage to the Vulgar, which I'm far from neglecting" (xvii) especially as it is the writer's very business "to serve the Vulgar, and spare them the Labour of long and

---

[7] See the "Epistle to the Reader" preceding the *Essay Concerning Human Understanding* (Oxford, 1894), I, 11.

painful Study" (xviii). Here Toland's confidence derives from his philosophy of the accessibility of reason: everyone, high and low, has common notions that serve as standards of truth. But the brahmin in Swift could not resist parodying Toland's patronizing and demagogic quotations in the *Tale*'s Preface as the solicitous persona opens the curtain on the *Tale:*

> Yet I shall now dismiss our impatient Reader from any farther Attendance at the *Porch;* and having duly prepared his Mind by a preliminary Discourse, shall gladly introduce him to the sublime Mysteries that ensue. (54)

Swift has no doubt what Toland's and the persona's sublime mysteries are: exalting individual reason at the expense of institutionalized faith; secularizing Milton's latter-day Calvinism; reestablishing Harrington's republican commonwealth; and translating modern esoteric invention to exoteric propaganda—that is, sponsoring a publishing frenzy.

After relabeling Toland's nominal reason as real invention leading to mysteries and sects, Swift attacks the two other flaws—that is, realities or essences—in what is passed off as modern rationalism: blind rage against tyranny and a zeal for change, both leading to madness.

During the period of the *Tale*'s gestation from 1696 to 1704, the young Toland's checkered career was the subject of scandalous rumors, often preceding him in Glasgow, Edinburgh, London, Oxford, Leyden, and Dublin. In this gossip, rage and zeal seemed the blots on Toland's escutcheon. His unsettled life, hostility to Rome, and reforming zeal contrasted with Swift's quest for stability in church and state and in his own life and career. Born on Inishowen in 1670 and raised a Roman Catholic, Toland had left Ireland in 1687 for Scotland.[8] During a time of civil and clerical strife, he allied himself first with episcopacy and then with the Presbyterians. After receiving his M.A. from the University of Edinburgh, he was welcomed in influential dissenting circles in London; in 1692, he studied theology with leading Dutch thinkers at the universities of Leyden and Utrecht. In politics, he became a throwback to the classical republicans of the Long Parliament dissolved in 1653 by Cromwell—men who counted Harrington and Milton as their prime intellectual and literary spokesmen and the Rome of Tacitus as their focus.[9] He was allied in religion with the Socinians, forerunners of English deism. By 1696, this modern Mercury—Janus to his enemies—had established his reputation as deist and freethinker and reflected an interest in the Renaissance naturalist Giordano Bruno whose investigations bordered on the occult. Sullivan finds

---

[8] For critical biographies of Toland and understanding of his epistemology, see Robert E. Sullivan, Stephen H. Daniel, and F.H. Heinemann.

[9] For the Republican background, see Blair Worden.

him "assiduous in studying and discussing the philosophy of Giordano Bruno for almost half his lifetime" (15–16).

Christianity Not Mysterious—like the parodying *Tale*—spoke reasonably of the simplicity of the Gospel but flung emotionally charged rhetoric at Mandarin "popery." Reiterating its attack on implicit faith, *Christianity Not Mysterious* accused the Fathers of teaching the faithful "*to adore what we cannot comprehend*" (26):

> This famous and admirable Doctrine is the undoubted Source of all the *Absurdities* that ever were seriously vented among *Christians.* Without the Pretence of it, we should never hear of the *Transubstantiation,* and other ridiculous Fables of the Church of *Rome* . . . this *Western Sink.* (26–27)

Just as *Christianity Not Mysterious* refers to the rites of the Lord's Supper as making "the plainest things in the World appear *mysterious*" (165), so raging Jack in the *Tale* recalls that Peter had earlier (117) "palmed his damned crusts upon us for Mutton" (138). The consistent hostility to "popery" (xii) of *Christianity Not Mysterious* Swift assigns to Jack, who goes about the Calvinist business of divesting himself of every remnant of papal control:

> Having thus kindled and enflamed himself as high as possible, and by Consequence, in a delicate Temper for beginning a Reformation, he set about the Work immediately" (138).

Mad Jack's hostility because of his association with Rome before the Reformation matched Toland's aversion to Rome because of his Irish Catholic rearing. To be sure everyone in the British establishment except the Stuarts was hostile to Roman Catholicism; but the intensity of mad Jack's rage and Toland's demonstrated virulence are akin.

If private invention and blind rage are Swift's synonyms for nominally deliberative modern reason, so is fanatic zeal. Again a parallel exists: Toland's zeal for his theological position is equated with Jack's in the *Tale*. At the outbreak of Jack's rage against Peter, the persona announces that Brother Jack's "Adventures will be so extraordinary, as to furnish a great Part in the Remainder of this Discourse" (137):

> For, the Memory of *Lord Peter*'s Injuries, produced a Degree of Hatred and Spight, which had a much greater Share of inciting Him, than any Regards after his Father's Commands. . . . (137)

At this juncture, the satirist skillfully blends Brother Jack, the persona, Toland, and *Christianity Not Mysterious* under the rubric of zeal. The hack persona proceeds to defend Jack's zeal while exposing his own zeal for

Locke's reason. Swift moves from rage to zeal by parodying Toland's illustration in Section 3.2 of *Christianity Not Mysterious* that explains Locke's distinction between nominal and real essence: "Whoever hears the Word *Sun* pronounc'd, this is the Idea he has of it. He may conceive more of its Properties" (82). In *his* two sentences, Swift not only parodies this illustration but satirizes Toland four ways: for zeal and for his sketchy history of Christianity, his simplistic exegesis of Locke on ideas, and his self-advertisement in the manner of Milton:

> As, I think, I have fully proved in my excellent *Analytical* Discourse upon that Subject; wherein I have deduced a *Histori-theo-physiological* Account of *Zeal,* shewing how it first proceeded from a *Notion* into a *Word,* and from thence in a hot Summer, ripened into a *tangible Substance.* This Work containing three large Volumes in Folio, I design very shortly to publish by the *Modern* way of *Subscription.* (137)

What Swift has done is to offer a Tolandic exegesis for the vulgar on the matter of Lockean nominal and real essence. The Lockean progress is from a notion or idea, in this instance, "zeal," into a word "ripened" into a tangible substance "a hot summer." He collapses *zeal* and *sun* as interchangeable ideas or words (nominal essence) with the same properties or substance (real or tangible essence): ripeners and providers of a tangibly hot summer. Even the persona's design to publish three large volumes on zeal derives from *Christianity Not Mysterious.* Indicative of the untiring publishing activity parodied by the persona's zeal, Toland had promised unflagging sequential efforts:

> I have expressly written of this Matter [the faults of holy Penmen] in an Epistolary Dissertation, now lying by me, entituled, *Systems of Divinity exploded.* In the following Discourse, which is the first of three, and wherein I prove my Subject in general, the Divinity of the New Testament is taken for granted. . . . In the next Discourse . . . I attempt. . . . and in the third, I demonstrate . . . (xxiv)

Toland's Lockean exegesis, his breathless puffery, his indefatigable publishing zeal, and his finding of other writers' faults qualify him, along with the *Tale's* persona, as that "most devoted Servant of all Modern Forms" (45).

Having dispatched the Lockean philosophy of ideas to his own, if not his reader's, satisfaction, Swift addresses another modern formula. If the *Tale's* discourse resolves its first epistemological issue by reducing Toland's, and by extension, Locke's and Tillotson's, notion of nominal reason in religion to its real essence—idiosyncratic invention, mad rage, and fanatic zeal—the discourse also addresses the second epistemological issue with equal contempt: Toland's, and by extension, C. Perrault's and M. Fontenelle's, conceit that the moderns have surpassed the ancients as authors and critics.

Section 3.3 of *Christianity Not Mysterious,* on the ancient Christian writers, provides grist for both the persona and the satiric voice in the *Tale*'s odd sections (III, V) on modern critics and authors. In *Christianity Not Mysterious,* for example, Toland linked the opinions of Perrault and Fontenelle to proclaim the superiority of the moderns and quoted Perrault, whose ideas he considered "no less ingenious than they are just and solid" (113), on the weakness of Antiquity:

> For if we consider the Duration of the World . . . as we do that of Man's Life, consisting of Infancy, Youth, Manhood, and old Age; then certainly such as lived before us were the Children or the Youth, and we are the true Antients of the World. . . . The experience of such as come last into the World must be incomparably greater than of those that were born long before them: for the last Comers enjoy not only all the Stock of their Predecessors, but to it have likewise added their own Observations. (112–13)

In response, as he did in the Locke-Stillingfleet debate, Swift develops an idea from the *Battle of the Books* more cogently in the *Tale.* In the *Battle* he had yoked the moderns Perrault and Fontenelle against Homer. "He [Homer] took *Perrault* by might Force out of his Saddle, then hurled him at *Fontenelle,* with the same Blow dashing out both their Brains" (246). The persona of the *Tale* lists Perrault in the direct genealogical line of his heroic, *true* critics, "the Noblest Sort" (93). Puffing himself up as a modern author, the persona paraphrases Toland's quotation by Perrault: "When I consider how exceedingly our Illustrious *Moderns* have eclipsed the weak glimmering Lights of the *Antients,* and turned them out of the Road of all fashionable Commerce, to a degree, that our choice Town-Wits of most refined Accomplishments, are in grave Dispute, whether there have been ever any *Antients* or no" (124–5). If Perrault believes that "we [moderns] are the true Antients of the World" (*Christianity Not Mysterious* 112), the satiric voice would accept this novel twist and assign "the proper Employment of a *True Antient Genuine* [Modern] *Critick.* . . . He is a *Discoverer and Collector of Writers Faults*" (95).[10]

To establish the links with antiquity of this True Antient [Modern] Critic, the satiric voice adopts a ridiculous animal allegory, mainly because Toland has rejected just such symbolism as ridiculous in Section 3.3:

> Every one knows how the Primitive *Christians* [writers], in a ridiculous imitation of the Jews, turned all the Scripture into Allegory; accommodating the Properties of those Animals mentioned in the *Old Testament* to Events that happened under the *New.* (115)

---

10 There is a congruence here of positions drawn from Fontenelle and Perrault—hardly lost on Swift—which Toland whole-heartedly supports and William Temple's *Essay upon the Ancient and Modern Learning* (1696) strongly rejects. See Roberta F. S. Borkat.

Since Toland hates all figuralism as an impediment to reason, the *Tale*'s satiric voice "cunningly shades" (98) his own ridiculous "Allegory" (98) by comparing the qualities of antiquity's so-called *true* critics to the properties of asses to find both odious and, at the same time, consistent with the reputation of their modern descendants. In the sixteenth century, Bruno had equated assinity with the priesthood and, despite his objection to allegory, Toland, admiring Bruno, had translated his *Spaccio della bestia trionfante* (Sullivan 198–99). Quoting Pausanias, Herodotus, Ctesias, and Diodorus randomly—in the manner of a Tolandic exegesis—the far-fetched satire "establishes" that the ancestors of the *true* modern critics were like asses who cropped what was already dead and worthless and frightened "a Legion of Authors" with their braying (98–99).

To recapitulate: Swift's late Sermon would conclude that humans have at best only a measure of reason, certainly insufficient to comprehend God's universe and plan; his much earlier *Tale* concludes that those moderns who prided themselves on their reason mistook its nominal for its real essence. For Swift, modern reason is just that—a name, a facade, a pretense for its reality: egoistic invention, uncontrollable rage, and misplaced zeal. All are real essences of the modern world epitomized in Toland, the modern satirically honored in the *Tale*. Swift would conclude in his climactic Digression on Madness that these realities are reaching their apocalypse in a millennium of madness.[11]

Swift uses Locke's original distinction of object essences, recorded by Toland in Section 3.2, to develop a satiric system to do no less than destroy faith in modern reason. He also makes a striking distinction between Toland's nominal and his real essence of modern reason.

Modern reason confidently programs surface information into demonstrable, universally verifiable "truth" in the apparent belief that the simplest mind can critically and felicitously examine the information and evidence relevant to it to arrive at valid judgments without correcting for emotional or other cultural biases. Preceding discussion has shown that Swift punctured one of these biases: the notion that change, by definition, surpasses tradition. Further to mock the proud givens of modern reason, Swift again found Toland apt— although any latter-day rationalist would have served as well.

For rationally organizing information, Toland's history of the Early Church confidently traces, with copious notes, the infiltration of heathen philosophers, the incorporation of their dubious pagan rituals into doctrine, and hence the origin of suspect Christian mysteries. His confidence in his organized information finds reenforcement in believing that the zealous critical mind will

---

[11] See below, pp. 85–108 and 159–78.

operate free of emotional or prejudicial contamination. Put differently, Toland separates mind and sense as Browne, another Lockean disciple, would soon join them to attack Toland. Swift attacks both positions in the *Tale*.[12]

Toland was not unaware, however, that the modern contention that the rational organization of information without emotional bias was itself a suspect and challenged tenet of modern reason. Thus, in *Christianity Not Mysterious,* he set up a fictitious dialogue between a priestly adversary and a parishioner:

> Pray, Doctor, says one of his Parishioners, what think you of such a Book? it seems to make things plain. Ah! dear Sir, answers the Doctor, it is a very bad Book; he's a dangerous Man that wrote it; he's for believing nothing but what agrees with his own purblind, proud and carnal *Reason.* (109).

Several pages later, in answer to this vicious imputation against his treatise, Toland dissociates the sensual mind from God and reason. The carnal mind "is not Reason, but the carnal Desires of lewd and wicked Men; whose Practices, as they are contrary to the revealed Law of God, so they are to that of sound *Reason* too" (124).[13]

Swift finds merit neither in the presentation of organized historical evidence on the origins of the Christian mysteries nor in Toland's assertion that modern reason can operate free of the species' carnal nature because sound reason is somehow mysteriously yoked with God. (We shall see that Browne's *Answer* to Toland that carnality promotes faith by analogy carries no weight with Swift either.[14]) In the satirist's reality, information systems skew the assembled evidence to satisfy private needs, ends, prejudices, and fantasies; among these ends, reason can distinguish no higher or more urgent priority than satisfying the reasoner's perpetually aroused carnal nature. While Swift and Toland agree on suspect mysteries, the satirist sees absolutely no way to prevent universal erotic nature from contaminating divinely sponsored reason at every turn.

Simultaneously to undermine the two key pretensions of modern reason— that its version of the origin of suspect mysteries is valid and that reason can be devoid of carnality—Swift presents his own condensed history of religious

---

12 For Browne, see below, pp. 39–55.

13 Weinsheimer shows this refutation of the priest to be Toland's rational interpretation of Romans 8.7: "The carnal mind is enmity against God; for it is not subject to the law of God, neither indeed can be." Weinsheimer explains that "Here the symmetry of Toland's hermeneutics is clearest: a true interpretation is that which discovers the truth of what it interprets" (15); and Toland's interpretation is, "If these words be spoken of Reason, there can be nothing more false; because Reason does and ought to subject itself to the divine Law" (124).

14 See below, pp. 45–48.

fanaticism in the *Mechanical Operation of the Spirit,* the *Fragment* of the *Tale* to be referred to as *Mechanical Operation.* His satiric aim is to make plain that the real essence of modern reason is fanaticism: fanatics—whatever their logics—organize their demagogic systems around carnality. He develops his history of fanaticism to parody, dispute, revise, and enlarge upon Toland's exegesis on the schematic history of the false mysteries in *Christianity Not Mysterious.* Toland had limited his history of the false mysteries to the pre-Christian Dionysian rites in Egypt and Greece and to Christianity in the first three centuries. Swift's history traces the same periods, but, with a purposeful thrust at Toland, adds a third, the time of the Puritan Commonwealth— enabling him to yoke Milton and Toland with their own false modern mysteries of typology and apocalypse.[15]

What ties together Toland's *Christianity Not Mysterious* and Swift's *Mechanical Operation* is Chapter 17 of the book of The Revelation of Saint John the Divine. Katharine R. Firth's *The Apocalyptic Tradition in Reformation Britain 1530–1645* demonstrates that John Foxe, John Knox, Nicholas Ridley, and Joseph Mede, Milton's tutor at Cambridge, use this particular scriptural passage to establish the Whore of Babylon as the Church of Rome and the antichrist (272).[16] Both Toland and Swift refer to the Whore of Babylon as the Scarlet Whore in the following apocalyptic context:

1 And there came one of the seven angels which had the seven vials, and talked with me, saying unto me, Come hither; I will shew unto thee the judgment of the great whore that sitteth upon many waters;
2 With whom the kings of the earth have committed fornication, and the inhabitants of the earth have been made drunk with the wine of her fornication.
3 So he carried me away in the spirit into the wilderness: and I saw a woman sit upon a scarlet coloured beast, full of names of blasphemy, having seven heads and ten horns.
4 And the woman was arrayed in purple and scarlet colour, and decked with gold and precious stones and pearls, having a golden cup in her hand full of abominations and filthiness of her fornication:
5 And upon her forehead *was* a name, written, MYSTERY, BABYLON THE GREAT, THE MOTHER OF HARLOTS AND ABOMINATIONS OF THE EARTH.
6 And I saw the woman drunken with the blood of saints, and with the blood of the martyrs of Jesus: and when I saw her, I wondered with great admiration.
7 And the angel said unto me, Wherefore didst thou marvel? I will tell thee the mystery of the woman, and of the beast that carrieth her, which hath the seven heads and ten horns.

---

[15] See below, pp. 69–72, on Milton and Toland.
[16] In her "Index of Images," Whore of Babylon (*Revelation* 17) references appear in discussion of the millenarian exegetes Foxe 99; Knox 116, 120, 130; Mede 217; Ridley 72.

18 And the woman which thou sawest is that great city, which reigneth over the
kings of the earth. (Rev. 17)

This critical, prophetic chapter fascinated Protestants in the seventeenth
century and provided the apocalyptic underpinning for belief in Rome as the
antichrist and for the importance of the mystical number seven in reading the
millennial signs. The optimistic expectations in northern Europe following the
Reformation hinged on overthrow of the antichrist as a pre-condition to the
millennium. Consequently, Revelation 17 is at the core of Cromwell's,
Milton's, and the utopian visionaries' belief in Britain as Albion, the New
Jerusalem, Paradise Regained, and the coming modern age. Paradoxically, it
is a central mystery explicated in Toland's *Christianity Not Mysterious.* Since
he feels obliged both to affirm and to deny this Christian mystery, Toland
encounters profound exegetic difficulties that Swift fully exploits in the *Tale.*

Toland, the illuminist rationalist unable to decide whether to call Revelation a Book or a Vision, settles obscurely for "a Prophetical History of the
External State of the Church in its various and interchangeable Periods of
Prosperity or Adversity" (106). Saint John—and hermeneutic scholars—
would never have accepted this narrow, rational interpretation of a deeply
figurative and nigh unfathomable prophecy. Yet Toland wants Revelation to be
simultaneously about the history of the antichristian Roman Church that
believes in mysteries and also about the history of the universal Christian
Church of reasoning souls. He selectively quotes Revelation 17.5,7 so that the
angel appears to reaffirm both necessities of his discourse—the Church of
Rome as the antichrist and mysteries as no part of a rational Christian religion:

Another Passage is in *chap.* 17.5,7. *And upon her Forehead was a Name written,*
MYSTERY, BABYLON THE GREAT, &c. *And the Angel said, I will tell thee the*
MYSTERY *of the Woman.* This he performs too in the following Verses, which
you may consult. Nor is it undeserving our particular Notice, that *Mystery* is here
made the distinguishing Mark of the false or *antichristian* Church. *Mystery is a*
Name written on her Forehead; that is, all her Religion consists in *Mystery,* she
openly owns, she enjoins the Belief of *Mysteries.* And, no doubt on't, *as far as any*
Church allows of Mysteries, so far it is ANTICHRISTIAN, and may with a great
deal of Justice, tho little Honour, claim Kindred with the *scarlet Whore.* (106–7)

It would be hard for reason to become more far-fetched. Here Toland in a
work purportedly refuting all Christian mysteries employs the metaphoric and
mysterious language of Revelation to support and link his own rational beliefs
incredulously with the Protestant mysteries of the optimistic, apocalyptic
tradition. As he moved toward his deistic and pantheistic positions over the

next decade, he would continue to construct modern myths from the reorganized, rationalized, and increasingly secularized material of ancient theological ones.

Swift, for his part, introduces his own selectivity when quoting Revelation 17.2,4,5 in the *Mechanical Operation*. He reduces these three verses to "(say some) the *Scarlet Whore*, when she makes the Kings of the Earth drunk with her Cup of Abomination, is always sober her self" (284). In the original text, "her cup of abomination" is fornication, that is, unsanctioned sexual intercourse. Swift gleans from the biblical text that drunkenness, sex, and idolatry are the three major supports of "artificial enthusiasm"; and therefore they figure prominently in the *Mechanical Operation*'s history of fanaticism. But this synoptic history is essentially parody and satire of Toland's false history of the false Christian mysteries in *Christianity Not Mysterious*. Thus Swift's interpretation of the Scarlet Whore contradicts Toland's interpretation by putting that rationalist in the position of defending the midcentury Protestant mysteries: the Church of Rome as the antichrist in the apocalyptic tradition, which Toland indeed does, and—by wittily stretching Toland's histories of the mysteries—the Scarlet Whore as the figurative antitype of Bacchus in the typological tradition.

The *Mechanical Operation* parodies Toland's exegesis of Christian history, its patronizing air toward the untutored reader, and, in contrast, Toland's claims of indefatigible research. *Christianity Not Mysterious* insists that the vulgar reader can clearly comprehend his simple exegesis since it is free of the "Gibberish taught in *Divinity Schools.*" According to Toland, to present the history of mystery, "we must trace the Original of it as far back as the Theology of antient *Gentiles*" (67):

> The most famous [mysterious initiations] were the *Samothracian,* the *Eleusinian,* the *Egyptian,* and those of *Bacchus,* commonly known by the name of *Orgies;* tho the word is sometimes put for any of the former. (71,72).

Swift's mocking parody, prepared for the unlearned, covers the same material. Toland had repeated "Bacchus" twice in succeeding paragraphs. To outdo him in making things simple for the vulgar, the satirist even more laboriously repeats "Bacchus" three times in one paragraph. The satiric voice also displays his "infinite reading" with copious footnotes from ancient authors—pretending to impress his superficial readers—in the manner of Toland:

> THE most early Traces we meet with, of *Fanaticks,* in antient Story are among the *Aegyptians,* who instituted those Rites, known in *Greece* by the Names of *Orgya, Panegyres,* and *Dionysia.* . . . These feasts were celebrated to the Honour of *Osyris,* whom the *Grecians* called *Dionysius,* and is the same with *Bacchus.* (283)

In introducing Toland's Scarlet Whore and Toland's Bacchus, the satiric voice invokes the worlds of typology and apocalyptic tradition. First Swift informs the curious reader that "the *Bacchanalian* Ceremonies were so many Types and Symbols" (284). Bacchus, we learn, is the type of "the *Scarlet Whore*" [The Church of Rome] (284). Neither of them gets drunk, although "she makes the Kings of the Earth drunk with her Cup of Abomination," and although Bacchus invented the mitre the Scarlet Whore has invested herself with a *Triple* Mitre (284).

But Swift goes further with Toland in the *Mechanical Operation.* There is a tortured, fundamental principle of fanaticism that the satiric voice means to get at in the manner of Toland and Milton by employing circumlocutions involving mysteries, types, and symbols. Having satirically established Bacchus as the type of the Scarlet Whore, Rome, and Peter, the satiric voice checks its symbols further to uncover "the great Seed or Principle of [the Mechanical Operation of] the *Spirit*" (283); and, by interpreting Revelation symbolically, the satiric voice concludes that the Scarlet Whore's encouragement of fornication must be at the root of fanaticism. This voice of the *Tale* may therefore triumphantly introduce an array of Bacchanalian symbols to echo Swift's interpretation of Revelation 17 and establish fornication, or obsessive sexuality and phallic symbol worship, as the generator of fanaticism: "Certain Circumstances in the Course of their Mysteries" have to do with "an entire *Mixture and Confusion of Sexes*" (285). Among the "many Shadows and Emblems of the whole Mystery," the satiric voice finds the sexual images of cleaving ivy and clinging vine, of satyrs, goats, and asses, "all Companions of great Skill and Practice in Affairs of Gallantry" (285). The Dionysians bore the *Virga genitalis* upon long Poles. "In a certain Town of *Attica,* the whole Solemnity stript of all its Types, was performed in *puris naturalibus,* the Votaries, not flying in Coveys, but sorted into Couples" (285). In contrast with the *Mechanical Operation,* Toland's interpretation of Revelation 17 is chaste, Puritanical polemic. That the carnal mind, not mysterious, holds the highest priority in information systems, including one's own, simply eluded Toland in his zealous service to modern reason, the self-evident truths of scripture, and modern man.

Swift uses *Christianity Not Mysterious* to accuse Toland of the very charges Toland had leveled against popery and episcopacy: making a trade of religion and creating false mysteries out of apocalypse, typology, and other symbolism. But it is important to distinguish between his parodying of Toland with variations on his adversary's own words and rhetorical instruments and the burden of his central arguments against his contemporary. That the mocking parody and the deeper satiric thrust of Swift's argument appear simultaneously complicates matters.

For example, *Christianity Not Mysterious* records the fate of uninitiated Athenians who pried into the mysteries of their priests because Toland wishes to show how the fiendish priests wickedly exclude and viciously massacre the masses: "And many were torn in pieces at the *Mysteries* of *Ceres,* and the *Orgies* of *Bacchus,* for their unadvis'd Curiosity" (70). To mock Toland and argue against him, Swift decides to introduce the same situation between the secretly initiated priest and the curious uninitiated horde. He uses Toland's phrase, "torn in pieces," but his intention is to contradict Toland. In furtherance of his satiric exegesis that obsessive sexuality is the real mystery that undergirds fanaticism, Swift parodies Toland. The *Mechanical Operation* describes "the Death of *Orpheus,* one of the Institutors of these Mysteries, who was torn in Pieces by Women, because he refused to *communicate his Orgyes* to them" (285). In Toland, the priestly few murder the curious many, whereas in Swift the lustful many annihilate the beleaguered sexual object. Adroitly Swift has reversed the roles here: the vicious, secretive priests dissect the harmless mass of uninitiated in *Christianity Not Mysterious,* but the lustful, anarchic, sex-crazed mob of women dismember the priest in the *Tale.* In Swift's view, hierarchical power may be honeycombed with carnality, corruption, and priestcraft, but rational consensus as its modern political alternative breeds populist fantasies, crowd rage, zealots for causes, sexual anarchy, social disorder, mob violence, and insane leadership. We are back arguing the Harringtonian balance. Which is worse: tyranny of the few or of the many?

Having used the figurative types, symbols, and emblems of Milton and Toland to discover the sexual basis of fanaticism in ancient times, the satiric voice moves his history confidently forward to the Protestant world they exalted. His last fanatics include John of Leyden, David George, Adam Neuster, the Family of Love, and the Sweet Singers of Israel. These sects and their founders flourished from the Reformation into the seventeenth century. Their "Vision and Revelations, always terminated in *leading about half a dozen Sisters, apiece,* and making That Practice a fundamental Part of their System" (286). Swift concludes his condensed history of fanaticism and his disassembling of the Protestant mysteries of Milton and Toland with a little sermon on confusing spirit and matter. Since the root of "spiritual intrigues" is in the earth, "too intense a Contemplation is not the Business of Flesh and Blood; it must by the necessary Course of Things, in a little Time, let go its Hold, and fall into *Matter*" (288).

Certainly Swift savors his jests at Toland's, Milton's, and the dissenters expense by reducing religious enthusiasm to sexual opportunity and spirit to its mechanical operation: The inflamed mind merely serves the inflamed body.

The superficial or ignorant reader might leave the matter there. But it stands as no mean accomplishment in historiography for Swift to have seized on the political magic wrought by the unbroken continuity of typological and apocalyptical interpretations of the Bible. The modern continuity extended from the sixteenth-century Marian exiles through Milton, Cromwell, and the Puritan Commonwealth to the deist and "heathen philosopher" Toland; and, in Swift's estimation, the suspect Protestant mysteries, typology and apoca-lypse, would have far more deleterious effects on modern European states than the papal ones decried by the dissenters. In modern Europe they had already been translated from a theology of fallen man to the secular ideology of a return to Eden—a modern, material utopia. Using the Janus-like *Christianity Not Mysterious,* Swift allowed the progress of his *Tale* to move from the extremes of Peter's traditional Christian mysteries, scourged by Jack, to the extremes of Puritan Jack's own mysteries of apocalypse and typology leading to anarchy, chaos, and madness.

CHAPTER THREE

MARSH AND BROWNE: ASS AND RIDER

> For, towards the Operation already mentioned,
> many peculiar Properties are required, both in
> the *Rider* and the *Ass;* which I shall endeavour
> to set in as clear a Light as I can.
> *Mechanical Operation of the Spirit* 265

The furor in Britain over John Toland and his priest-baiting book precipitated a more intense controversy in Dublin. The irrepressible Toland arrived there in March 1697 with confident expectations of serving as Secretary to the new Lord Chancellor John Methuen.[1] After a twelve-year hegira, he believed he was returning triumphantly to his native country to introduce a radical new religious and political system as essential to the Irish as it was to the British and other Europeans. Like a modern revolutionary, Toland was poised to spread his universal hermeneutics throughout the land; and on arrival he launched a vigorous campaign among Irish intellectuals, in their homes and in coffee houses, to publicize his startling positions.

What ensued illustrated for Swift how surely the lapsing of the Licensing Act would encourage ambitious moderns to engage in vicious dialectical combat that promoted civil unrest. The young man's natural enemies, bishops in the Church of Ireland, immediately initiated a brutal campaign against him. In particular, he aroused the implacable enmity of Narcissus Marsh, the Archbishop of Dublin, and his disciple Peter Browne. Browne had been Swift's classmate while Marsh was their Provost at Trinity College, Dublin, in the early 1680s when Marsh's antipathy to Swift and cosseting of Browne began—attitudes that would continue well beyond publication of the *Tale* in 1704.

Within a month of Toland's arrival, Archbishop Marsh, outraged at the heretic's infiltration of his See, dispatched Toland's book to Browne with a clear imperative: "It is no neglect in a shepherd to leave his feeding of the lambs and go aside for a while to beat off anything that comes to devour or

---

[1] Alan D. Francis 358; Robert E. Sullivan 8–9; David Berman 121.

infect them."[2] Browne's own purposes and temper coincided with Marsh's, since throughout the decade he had been ambitious for preferment at Trinity College and in the Church of Ireland. He now seized the occasion to adapt the Archbishop's earlier writings on logic and sense analogies to Anglican rational apologetics; and in joining the fray against Toland, he also was eager to enter the dialectic with Locke on reason and Christianity. Browne's hasty *A Letter in Answer to a Book entitled Christianity Not Mysterious,* to be referred to as *Answer,* accordingly appeared in May 1697 under Marsh's *imprimatur.*[3] His preferment was assured—while the career-impoverished and infuriate Swift was forced to languish at Moor Park.

Thus in 1697 the Dublin Controversy pitted the heretical freethinker Toland against the Anglican sensationalist Browne—and ultimately the classical satirist Swift ridiculed both of them. Swift used what he observed in the clash of his contemporaries to condemn the rising modern consciousness, its antecedents, and its predictable consequences. Because he knew its three principals all too well, the Dublin theosophical donnybrook not only generated and nourished the *Tale* but provided three major satiric victims. The preceding chapter detailed Swift's satire of Toland in the even-numbered sections of the *Tale;* and the exasperating pomposity of Marsh and Browne provoked him to satirize and parody them as ass and rider in the *Mechanical Operation,* appended to the *Tale.* Swift had both epistemological and personal reasons for attacking each man—and suddenly the unparalleled occasion to mock all three simultaneously for symbolizing the modern invasion of Ireland by Continental ideas.

Swift's assertion—in the Apology preceding the 1710 edition of the *Tale*—that "the greatest part" of the book had been finished in 1696 is not accurate. Though the work indeed germinated from extensive reading and active reflection over a long period and includes satire based on Swift's experience as an undergraduate at Trinity College, Dublin in the early 1680s, two controversies energized the shaping of the book but required time to be fit into its developing thought structure. The Temple-Bentley-Wotton and the Toland-Marsh-Browne affairs, in 1696 and 1697, provide bookends for the *Tale: The Battle of the Books* and the *Mechanical Operation.* Had the *Tale* appeared in 1698, just after the controversies reached climaxes the year before, the Dublin Controversy over Toland might have been counterbalanced by the Ancients-Moderns Controversy over Sir William Temple,[4] Swift's Church of Ireland

---

[2] Quoted by Arthur Robert Winnett 11.

[3] For useful biographies of Marsh, see Muriel McCarthy and George T. Stokes; for a sound biography of Browne, see Winnett.

[4] For the Swift-Temple relationship see below, pp. 109–35 and 137–57.

adversaries by Temple's academic foes, and the *Mechanical Operation* by *The Battle of the Books,* altering the character of the ultimate integration of the events and actors in the 1704 *Tale.*

Swift viewed his Dublin and London milieu within the context of the earlier and more encompassing European intellectual drama of revolution and reform that had been played out in Britain over the course of the seventeenth century. In the last decade of that century, Swift's career brought him into intimate contact and conflict with the leading advocates and exemplars of the modern world. It was a critical time when gains striven for since the sixteenth century in Europe were being consolidated, regularized, and urbanized. The satirist used his two urban centers as unique observation posts for examining the schemes and repertoires of emerging modern man.

Swift's millennial mock epic of modern Europe is therefore his tale of two cities, Dublin and London; two modern power brokers, Archbishop Marsh and the diplomat Temple; two decades, the 1680s and 1690s; and two controversies, the one played out in Dublin and the Ancients-Moderns controversy.

At the heart of the 1697 Dublin controversy, one of the two pivotal occasions of the *Tale*—given full attention, for the first time, in this study—was Archbishop Marsh. As Swift's *bête noire* in Dublin from 1682, he put Swift's career in the Church of Ireland into indefinite stalemate, keeping posts from him for two decades as effectively as in mid-1697 he banished Toland, another rude and incorrigible intruder, from his See. At the heart of the 1696 Ancients-Moderns Controversy, the *Tale*'s other occasion—carefully examined by previous scholarship—was Temple. As Swift's employer and English connection at Moor Park from 1689, he enlisted his Irish protegé in editing and other tasks related to his own moral commentaries, diplomatic memoirs, Epicurean philosophy, utopian ideals, and enduring fame.

Just as the *Battle of the Books* pales alongside the *Tale,* so Temple is a minor satiric victim alongside Marsh, as definitively a modern as Toland. Swift's contempt for Marsh's modern learning in the *Mechanical Operation* and the Introduction to the *Tale* is based in part on his scorn for studies dear to Provost Marsh at Trinity. A modern in every sense of that pejorative to Swift, Marsh had come to Dublin in 1679 with extreme piety and a reputation for vast scholarship. In 1682, the same year Swift matriculated at Trinity, Marsh with Sir William Petty, the utilitarian of Oxford's "invisible college," and William Molyneux founded the Dublin Philosophical Society. Marsh and Petty, each renowned for useful experiment, had thus formed an influential Dublin cell; it mirrored their marvelous midcentury years at Oxford with the Hartlib Circle, concerned with the Paracelsian-mechanist alternatives and ideas of the Rosicrucian visitors Andreae and Comenius.[5] According to R. T. Gunther's *Early Science in Oxford,* "it was largely due to the research of these early fellows (Marsh, Joseph Glanvill, Branker, Moyle, Borlase, Nicholls) of the Royal Society in Oxford that the Oxford Philosophical Society was founded in 1683" (9: 92). In addition to his reputation as natural philosopher, mathematician, Orientalist, and musician, Marsh produced *Institutiones logicae in usum iuventutis academiae Dubliniensis* (1681), also known as the *Provost's Logic.* The satirist's early reactions to Marsh's extensive learning, philosophical elitism, and other biases have been capsulated in Lord Orrery's remarks on Swift at Trinity. The young genius held logic and metaphysics in "utmost contempt and scarce considered mathematics and natural philosophy unless to turn them into ridicule" (11). His modern biographer, Irvin Ehrenpreis, has confirmed that Swift "did poorly in what he would always dislike—abstract philosophy and formal rhetoric" (1: 62). The epistemological abyss and temperamental antipathy that alienated Swift and Marsh at Trinity undergird the *Tale* even as they account for Swift's early travail in the Church of Ireland and contribute to his lifelong indignation with modern learning.

More than 25 years ago the Chicago Swiftians R.S. Crane, Louis Landa, and Edward Rosenheim perceptively and precisely recorded specific allusions to Marsh in Swift's *Gulliver's Travels,* his Sermons, and the *Tale* respectively. Though many other Swiftians have been preoccupied with Temple's more apparent influence in the *Tale* and the *Battle of the Books,* what needs emphasis here is that, in contrast with his love-hate toward Temple, Swift displayed no ambivalence toward Marsh while the autocrat lived—being only occasionally deferential to his temporal power.

As evidence of his indignation, Swift has left a character sketch of Marsh in manuscript of "unremitting severity" (Ehrenpreis 1: 49). In this savage portrait, Swift thrust his rapier at Marsh and attentive men like Browne, who served him: "He will admit a governor, provided it be one who is very officious and diligent, outwardly pious, and one that knows how to manage and make the most of his fear" (*PW* 5: 212). The sketch reveals Swift's view of the pontifical nature characteristic of the union of Anglican rationalism with modern learning. Marsh sat without budging one psycholgical inch for this portrait from 1682 until 1710. During that quarter-century he rose from Trinity College Provost to Dublin Archbishop to Primate of Ireland, with the recalcitrant Swift trailing dependently at his mercy all the way from unruly

---

[5] In forming his cosmologies Petty, like Robert Boyle and Isaac Newton, wrestled with the Paracelsian-mechanist split in natural philosophy.

student to penitent candidate for the priesthood to unrewarded parliamentary lobbyist.

An excerpt from Swift's unpublished piece attributed to 1710 will suffice:

> Marsh has the reputation of most profound and universal learning; this is the general opinion, neither can it be easily disproved. An old rusty iron chest in a banker's shop, strongly locked, and wonderfully heavy, is full of gold; this is the general opinion, neither can it be disapproved, provided the key be lost, and what is in it be wedged so close that it will not by any motion discover the metal by the chinking. Doing good is his pleasure; and as no man consults another in his pleasures, neither does he in this; by his awkwardness and unadvisedness disappointing his own good designs. His high station has placed him in the way of great employments, which, without in the least polishing his native rusticity, have given him a tincture of pride and ambition. But these vices would have passed concealed under his natural simplicity, if he had not endeavoured to hide them by art. His disposition to study is the very same with that of an usurer to hoard up money, or of a vicious young fellow to a wench: nothing but avarice and evil concupiscence, to which his constitution has fortunately given a more innocent turn. (*PW* 5: 211)

In the same year the Apology appended to the fifth edition of the *Tale* referred slightingly to "the weightiest Men in the weightiest Stations" (6). Already Swift was answering his severest contemporary critics who castigated satiric anti-intellectual insolence and exalted the scientific epistemology. As Swift foresaw, their brand of tyranny has achieved the status of sacred ritual among the high priests of the modern European world, whatever their institutional affiliation. What Marsh exhibited, Swift applied equally to all modern learning, religion, and governance—and *in perpetuo.*

Until his death in 1699, Temple, a retired diplomat and elegant essayist who cherished his retreat at Moor Park, was renowned among the powerful in London, for his diplomacy, social position, style, and taste. He also cherished the concept of a secular-dominated modern utopia modelled after a priest-free ancient China.[6] Lacking the sustained power, scholarly precision, and progessive expectations of his modern adversaries, Temple had called Swift to serve him during most of the 1690s. But he proved as disappointing to Swift's career in England as the forbidding Marsh did in Ireland. As these urban locales, modern men, chaotic decades, and publicized controversies became welded in Swift's mind and then in the *Tale,* they account for Swift's resentments against both Bishop Marsh, astride the Church of Ireland and the Dublin Philosophical Society, and diplomat Temple, still enjoying some access to English power. In both settings in the decades when they prevailed, these influential

---

6 See Frank T. Boyle's new light on Temple and China.

men who could have greatly advanced him instead contributed to the bleakness of Swift's career prospects in the Irish Church and among the Court Whigs. On the other hand, both men provided Swift with enough visible and combustible material in their own persons, associations, works, and critical public roles to stoke the fires of his fecund wit and classic satire.

Throughout the *Tale,* Swift concentrated on the matched pairs of Milton and Toland, Marsh and Browne as incomparable exemplars of the left and right wings of the modern world. The *Tale* attacks the post-Reformation system exemplified by the classical republican and rebellious mythmaker Milton,[7] but it also attacks the rise of science and Anglican rationalism exemplified by the Anglican divine and virtuoso Marsh. For Swift, all of the reformers compounded the abuses of the sixteenth and seventeenth centuries in learning, religion, and governance. In the 1690s, when the bulk of the *Tale* was composed, he knew Toland and Browne at first hand. Both "unquiet spirits" (*Tale* 41) had entered the lists of Irish and European philosophy committed jointly to Locke's methodology and respectively to the revisionist systems of Milton and Marsh. But whatever individual motives and satiric opportunities the public occasion served, the Dublin Controversy proved the crucible for Browne and Swift to contribute originally to Irish thought and engage with Toland and Locke over an epistemological issue of major European significance.

The Dublin humiliation of Toland did not go unnoticed in England. An implicated party, Locke himself monitored every stage. William Molyneux, a founder of the Dublin Philosophical Society, corresponded all of the spring and summer of 1697 with his friend Locke on nothing but Toland's awful fate in Ireland. Molyneux would never forgive Browne for his foul language and the opprobrious names he heaped on Toland. As the published letters show, he also castigated Browne for "calling in the aid of the Civil Magistrate, and delivering Mr. Toland up to secular punishment. This indeed is a killing argument" (227). Later, Swift's correspondence expressed contempt for Browne on similar grounds: "What dogs there are in this world" (*Journal to Stella* 2:596). By September 1697, the Irish House of Commons had decreed Toland's arrest and the burning of *Christianity Not Mysterious* by the public hangman. Shaken, Toland fled Ireland.

As for the aftermath, the Dublin Controversy indeed launched Browne. He became Provost at Trinity; and in 1710 Swift lost out to Browne for the Bishopric of Cork when Primate Marsh probably—and Queen Anne surely—exercised influence. Toland would later boast that he had made Browne a bishop, just as in a letter to the Reverend Thomas Sheridan in 1725 Swift

---

[7] See below, pp. 57–84.

could not resist ironic recall of the 1697 source of Browne's preferment at his and Toland's expense. "If you are under the Bishop of *Cork*, he is a capricious Gentleman; but you must flatter him monstrously upon his Learning and his Writings; that you have read his book against *Toland* a hundred Times . . . (*Corr.* 3: 66–67).

Swift's scorn for Browne and Marsh early and late is an important reason that the *Tale* concurs with *Christianity Not Mysterious* on abuses of the clergy. Both Toland and Swift attacked the notion of priestcraft generally, but Swift knew, at first hand, two specimens of the evil in Dublin. Consequently, he could move from Toland's priest-baiting, designed to incense the clergy and edify the vulgar (141), to more personalized satiric attacks on Marsh and Browne.[8]

Swift had more significant satiric uses for his clerical foes than simply implicating them in priestcraft. On one level, they provided an apposite contemporary gloss on Toland's theme of "the craft and ambition of priests and philosophers" (163), having used their craft to help bring about Toland's downfall. But more universally, his Anglican adversaries seemed to Swift to be superb examples of modernism—like Toland himself. Finding them guilty not only of priestcraft but of modern craft, he attacked them, with sophistication, for their newfangled, mechanical-mystical mysteries manufactured from the whole cloth of Anglican rational apologetics and the Dublin Philosophical Society. Swift classifies Marsh and Browne as Anglican rationalists, mechanic virtuosi, mystical Paracelsians, and modern adepti—finally at one with their extremist enemies, the fanatic dissenters. Emphasizing the kinship among all modern practitioners in religion and learning, he identifies all priestcraft with modern craft and his two victims with each other.

It is because Swift finds an integral connection in their twin philosophical doctrines of sense analogies that he binds Marsh and Browne as "ass and rider" and "enlightened teacher" (seeing) and "fanatic auditory" (hearing) in the *Mechanical Operation* (265). Because of their paired scientific-political-religious systems, he parodies and satirizes these Anglican purveyors of suspect modern mysteries, religious and secular, making the *Mechanical Operation* turn on their twin doctrines of sense analogies.

As Toland's *Christianity Not Mysterious* provides keen satiric opportunities for *A Tale of a Tub* proper, so Browne's *Answer* inspires the *Mechanical Operation*, its appendage. Swift opens the *Mechanical Operation*

---

8 "The uncorrupted Doctrines of *Christianity* are not above their [the common People's] Reach or Comprehension, but the Gibberish of your *Divinity Schools* they do understand not." (Toland 141). At Trinity College, Dublin in the 1680s, Swift had had his academic problems with Provost Marsh and the *Provost's Logic*.

by parodying the *Answer*'s hastily conceived format, with its abrupt epistolary style. He closes the *Mechanical Operation* with a brief history of fanaticism, parodying the pedantry of both Toland and Browne. (Browne had ended his *Answer* with ostentatious and labored quotations from the Church Fathers.)

More critically, Swift moves from parody of Browne's style to exposure of his epistemology. Like Toland, Browne begins his arguments with Locke's theory of knowledge—as coming ultimately from the senses. Sense experience leads to empirical validation; but in the area of spiritual matters, we are blind and must be skeptical about our capacity to deal with spiritual things— revelation, for example. Our only way into the spiritual world is through analogy with what we know and what is familiar through sense experience. In this manner, Browne's *Answer* to Toland propounds a brand new doctrine of analogies that found its way into both right-wing Irish philosophy and the mainstream of eighteenth-century European philosophy (Mossner 80, 82).

David Berman has noted Browne's original contributions to Lockean thought on sensationalism (119–40). For Browne, following Marsh, all ideas are derived from sensations; but from this empirical premise he excludes the Lockean idea of reflection:

> For Browne, we have no idea of a purely mental mind in a corporeal body; therefore, except by analogy or representation, we cannot understand things divine and supernatural. To answer Toland's challenge on the mysteries, Browne employed a key illustration: a man born blind who is told about light and colors. The blind man must understand light in terms of some other sense; thus he might think that light is 'wondrous soft and smooth' . . . We must trust that such representations are answerable to the things they are supposed to represent, even though we know that the two are of totally different natures. (Berman 122)

Berman further points out "Swift's lack of sympathy with Browne's theological representation" and with what Berman calls "the root metaphor of Irish philosophy," the blind man trying to deal with the visible. In *Gulliver's Travels*, Swift ridicules "the idea that a blind man can effectively deal with colors by means of touch or smell" (123, 135–36).

But what Swift ridiculed in *Gulliver's Travels* he had earlier scourged as a philosophical absurdity in the *Mechanical Operation*. Browne had categorically insisted that the Christian mysteries, remaining above sense and reason, might be understood only by analogy with material objects, and he had hung all his analogical arguments on the blind man's use of analogy to understand light. If the blind man can "see" light analogically, blind mankind can see into the Christian mysteries by analogy with mundane sense experience. At this point, where Toland had categorically denied that carnality interfered with reason, Browne embraces human sexuality as an empirical Christian boon:

> We affirm that all things of another World, even after they are *revealed* are totally
> obscured both from our *Senses* and our *Reason* as the real Nature and *Properties*
> of them are in themselves . . . That since we have not capacities for them [*i.e.,*
> mysteries], there is no other way of revealing any thing to us relating to another
> life, but by *Analogy* with the things of this world. Thus . . . the *Generation* of the
> Son of God under the notion of one Man proceeding from the Loins of another.
> (Berman 124–125)

Taken literally, the most pleasurable of sensual experiences—sex—enables
man to glimpse analogically the divine mysteries. But when Browne includes
sensual pleasure in the catalogue of helpful analogical experiences, he has
fallen into Swift's deep satirical trap. To introduce notions of the blind man's
inner light bordered on the metaphysically outrageous, but to introduce further
the sensual pleasures, the dark glass, as the analogical means to comprehend
Christian mysteries seemed morally degenerate. In the *Mechanical Operation,*
Swift recapitulates Browne's doctrinal position:

> THE Practitioners of this famous Art, proceed in general upon the following
> Fundamental; That, *the Corruption of the Senses is the Generation of the Spirit:*
> Because the *Senses* in Men are so many Avenues to the Fort of *Reason*, which in
> this Operation is wholly blocked up. (269)

When humans suspend sense and reason, do their thoughts naturally ascend to
divine mysteries and the stars? Swift thinks not.

> Let That be as it will, thus much is certain, that however Spiritual Intrigues begin,
> they generally conclude like all others; they may branch upwards toward Heaven
> but the Root is in the Earth. Too intense a Contemplation is not the Business of
> Flesh and Blood; it must by the necessary Course of Things, in a little Time, let go
> its Hold, and fall into *Matter.* (288)

Browne's analogies, which supposedly directed thoughts heavenward, remind
Swift of the ancient jest about Thales who, while contemplating the constella-
tions, "found himself seduced by his *lower Parts* into a *Ditch*" (289).

For Swift, Browne's philosophical speculations in the cause of defending
the faith had given birth to a new Christian mystery: "Inward Light" or vision
(278)—the blind man's analogical gift. Swift also saw other possibilities.
Melding the disciple Browne's inner light or vision with his mentor Marsh's
equally mysterious doctrine of sounds or cant, he binds Marsh and Browne,
"ass and rider" in the *Mechanical Operation,* with their twin doctrines of
sense analogies to implicate both Anglicans in the purveying of suspect
modern mysteries. This satiric conceit seemed highly appropriate to Swift for
making specific Toland's general charge that religion is a trade and his own
charge that modern learning is a false craft. In Swift's more basic view,

ambitious moderns achieve mutual elevation when they align outrageous and superficially learned notions in the lucrative game of oligarchic power.

As discussed earlier, Marsh had originally presented his theory on sense experience to the Dublin Philosophical Society in 1683 in "An Introductory Essay to the Doctrine of Sounds":[9]

> I shall, I say, omit these things, and apply myself wholy to the *usefulness* of the Theory, that we are now falling upon; which I think cannot better be discovered, than by making a comparison 'twixt the Senses of *Seeing* and *Hearing* as to their improvements, I mean, by shewing, that this later of *Hearing,* is capable of all those improvements which the Sense of *Seeing* has received from Art, besides many more advantages, that the Ear may enjoy, by the help of our Doctrine, above the Eye; all which moreover will be of as great benefit to mankind, as anything that Opticks have yet discovered, if not of greater. . . . (472)

> As *Spectacles* and other *Glasses* are made to help the *Purblind* and weak *Eyes,* to see at any competent distances: So there are *Otacousticks* (and better may be made) to help weak *Ears* to hear at a reasonable distance also. (481)

In Section II of the *Mechanical Operation,* Swift's virtuoso abruptly considers "by what kind of Practices the Voice is best governed" (277). The virtuoso at once reaffirms Browne's cardinal principle that spiritual contemplation remains above sense and reason; the spiritual mechanic cancels them out as summarily as Browne, solely to replace them here with his own doctrine of sounds, the fanatic's art of generating spiritual inspiration. For Marsh's "sounds" read Swift's "cant":

> For, it is to be understood, that in the Language of the Spirit, *Cant* and *Droning* supply the Place of *Sense* and *Reason,* in the Language of Men: Because, in Spiritual Harangues, the Disposition of the Words according to the Art of Grammar, hath not the least Use, but the Skill and Influence wholly lye in the Choice and Cadence of the Syllables. (278)

For Swift "this Mystery, of venting spiritual Gifts is nothing but a Trade, acquired by as much Instruction, and mastered by equal Practice and Application as others are"(276).

Swift intentionally confounds the art of canting with inward light, as Marsh in his doctrine had found recurring analogies between the use of the voice and the idea of vision. Further, Swift mocks Marsh's list of sounds requiring "the Art of Imitating," such as *Speaking, Whistling, Singing, Hollowing,* and *Luring* by inserting his own list of sounds requiring "the Art of Canting" such

---

[9] His Doctrine received wider currency in the *Philosophical Transactions* 14 (February 1683/4): 472–88.

as *Droning, Nose-blowing, Hawking, Spitting, Belching,* and *Snuffling* (Marsh 476; *Tale* 278–80). Marsh's "Doctrine of Sounds" has become the art of canting, a new mechanical Christian mystery, joined to Browne's own mechanical modern mystery—inward light or enthusiasm. Both modern arts, avoiding substance in favor of sense mechanics or clerical machinery, fit Toland's debasing notion of religion as a trade and Swift's of modern learning as a false craft. The "enlightened teacher" Marsh inspired the "fanatick auditory" Browne in the art of canting, the extended use of sense analogies, and the techniques of esoteric logic.

Parenthetically, Marsh's "Doctrine of Sounds" suits both the persona and the satirist in the Introduction to the *Tale:* the persona can expound on the demagogic efficacy of edifices in the air while the satirist can parody Marsh's sober science. Marsh himself had defined the media requirements well and the Plate in the Fifth Edition (1710) of the *Tale* conforms to Marsh's technical specifications. "Hence in a Church," as Marsh had explained, "the nearer the Preacher stands to the wall (and certainly 'tis much the best way to place Pulpits near the wall) the better is he heard" (477). In the Plate (following 56 in the 1973 *Oxford* edition), the preacher stands in a pulpit placed not only near the wall but above the heads of the crowd. In the *Tale*'s palace of learning, positioning above the heads of the crowd supersedes the need for credibility in the demagogue's new exoteric systems. Exaltation above the crowd in Swift's satire depends on Marsh's mechanics—his information-delivery system.

Swift's contempt for moderns like Marsh indeed had grave consequences for his clerical career. In 1694, the year that Browne had been honored to present the centennial oration at Trinity and the good offices of Temple had helped Swift's despised cousin Thomas receive a living in England, the satirist's famous "Penitential" letter to Temple gallingly described the one-sided encounter between the bitter suppliant and the unbending ecclesiastical authority:

> Above half the Clergy in this Town being my Juniors, and that it being so many Years since I left this Kingdom, they could not admit me to the Ministry without some Certificate of my Behavior where I lived; and my Lord Archbishop of Dublin [Marsh] was pleased to say a good deal of this Kind to Me Yesterday; concluding against all that I had to answer. . . . (*Corr.* 1: 17)

Undoubtedly, no apology from Swift would have erased Marsh's remembrance of those "rude and ignorant" young men in "lewd and debauched" Dublin, as he phrased it, whom he had endured as Provost from

1679 until 1683. With these distractions, he recalled, "I had no time to follow my always dearly beloved studies."[10]

Swift apparently had seemed one of the Trinity motley to Marsh, but the future Archbishop and Primate embraced Browne early on as a favored disciple. The sycophantic Browne, following Marsh's bidding to purge Ireland of Toland, in his *Answer* both vilified Toland and sought his incarceration. Swift, with no great fondness for Toland, saw his satiric chance for a more telling *ad hominem* thrust against Marsh's underling and pitted his own morality, his sense of justice, his position on the Christian mysteries, his biblical knowledge, and his righteous wrath against Browne's meanness and fraudulent, self-serving reasoning. He juxtaposed his own sensitive wit against Browne's crude storm of vituperation.

Browne's *Answer* delivered Toland "up into the hands of our *Governours*":

> They only can suppress his insolence. . . . They alone can hinder the *Infection* from spreading farther (139). And therefore . . . I would deliver him into the hands of the Magistrate, not moved by any heat of Passion, but by such a Zeal as becomes every Christian to have for his Religion. . . . I hope there is no Toleration for Blasphemy and Prophaneness. (144)

Browne even likened Toland to St. Paul's character of Elymas, the sorcerer in the Book of Acts—

> O full of all subtilty and all mischief, thou child of the devil, thou enemy of all righteousness, wilt thou not cease to pervert the right ways of the Lord? (Acts 13:10)

And he speculated:

> Upon his [Toland's] Principles we have no way, from the nature of the thing, of distinguishing between the *Delusions* of the devil, *those celebrated Feats of Goblins, and Witches, and Conjurers* which he speaks of; and those which are wrought by the *Finger* of God. . . . The Devil indeed may delude mens senses, so as to make them think that *Real* which is only an Appearance. . . . When they [devilish philosophers] endeavoured to imitate *Moses,* in the instantaneous production of any real thing with *Life,* there the Divel failed them, and they were forced to own it was the Finger of God. (153–54)

Swift responds to these passages in Browne's *Answer* at the beginning of Section II of the *Mechanical Operation.* He first contrasts the perspicacity of the wild Indians in distinguishing between good and evil, God and the devil, faith and reason, with the modern European tendency to blur these distinctions.

---

[10] Marsh's Library, Dublin, Diary of Archbishop Narcissus Marsh from 1690–96, transcript of the original. 15. See Muriel McCarthy 13, 28 fn. 1.

> Not so with Us, who pretending by the Lines and Measures of our Reason, to extend the Dominion of one invisible Power [the devil], and contract that of the other [God], have discovered a gross ignorance in the Natures of Good and Evil, and most horribly confounded the Frontiers of both. (274)

He then asserts that modern man, in this instance Browne, has equated the principle of good with his own behavior and that of evil with Toland's:

> After they [i.e., Browne specifically] have sunk their *Principle* of *Evil*, to the lowest center, bound him [i.e. Toland] with Chains, loaded him with Curses, furnished him with viler Dispositions than any *Rake-hell* of the Town [Dublin], accoutered him with Tail and Horns, and huge Claws, and Sawcer Eyes; I laugh aloud, to see these Reasoners, at the same time, engaged in wise Dispute, about certain Walks and Purlieus, whether they are in the Verge of God or the Devil, seriously debating, whether such and such Influences come into Mens Minds, from above or below or whether certain Passions and Affections are guided by the Evil Spirit or the Good. (275)

In a final profound thrust, Swift invents his own analogy to dispose of Browne's doctrine of analogies—his ill-nature and his ambition for clerical preferment.

> Thus do Men establish a Fellowship of *Christ* with *Belial* and such is the Analogy they make between *cloven Tongues,* and *cloven Feet.* (275)

Swift here juxtaposes his own sublime quotation from the second chapter of the Book of Acts concerning Christ and the cloven tongues of fire at Pentecost five pages back in the *Tale* (270) with Browne's hellish reference from the 13th chapter of Acts pronouncing anathema on the cloven-footed Toland. Within the Book of Acts Swift found a use of "cloven," identified with a Christian mystery, in contrast with Browne's metaphor for excommunication and hanging.

Clearly, Swift examined Browne's *Answer* to Toland as meticulously for satire as Browne had searched *Christianity Not Mysterious* for heresy. In the *Mechanical Operation,* his satiric wit and creative energy may have drawn their impetus in the bitterness of forced proximity and subjugation to his proud and power-grabbing epistemological adversaries. But, significantly, he subordinates his personal fortunes to his indignation against the modern age itself. If domestic concerns led him to satirize Marsh and Browne, it is their modernism combined with their knack for priestcraft—pious dissembling with material corruption—that casts a pall over the Ireland he sees reflecting a rising European consciousness.

The 1697 Dublin Controversy over Toland provided Swift with a wealth of material for the *Tale,* but in that hectic year he continued to remember Provost

Marsh from their years at Trinity College in the early 1680s. Their basic epistemological disagreement over reason had its origin then and became emblematic of Swift's distrust of the reason vaunted in all modern learning systems throughout his life. R.S. Crane pinpoints the source and, at the same time, answers critics who dismiss Swift as a misanthrope. While some modern scholars have softened the invective of Swift's satire by claiming it outdated and irrelevant to today's world, others defend against his savage indignation by calling him a misanthrope. But Crane makes it clear that his misanthropy was of a special kind:

> [Swift] looked upon man's nature as deeply corrupted by the Fall but thought that self-love and the passions could be made, with the help of religion, to yield a positive though limited kind of virtue; that he held reason in high esteem as a God-given possession of man but distrusted any exclusive reliance on it in practice or belief, and ridiculed the Stoics and Cartesians and made war on the Deists; and that he tended, especially in his political writings, to find the useful truth in a medium between extremes. (237)

Crane cites an oft-quoted letter Swift sent to Pope, September 29, 1725, concerning *Gulliver's Travels:*

> But principally I hate and detest that animal called man, although I heartily love John, Peter, Thomas and so forth. . . . I have got materials towards a treatise proving the falsity of that definition *animal rationale,* and to show it should be only *rationis capax.* Upon this great foundation of misanthropy (though not in Timon's manner) the whole building of my Travels is erected. (*Corr.* 3: 103)

Crane believes that the source for the three names—John, Peter and Thomas—and the definition *animal rationale* came from Marsh's *Institutio Logicae in Usum Juventutis Academicae Dubliniensis,* also known as the *Provost's Logic.* It is somewhat hard, then,

> not to conclude that Swift was remembering Marsh's logic as he composed the sentence, in his letter to Pope, about "John, Peter, Thomas, and so forth." But if that is true, can there be much doubt, in view of the Porphyrian context in which these names appear in Marsh, as to what tradition of ideas was in his mind when he went on to remark, immediately afterwards, that "the great foundation of misanthropy" on which "the whole building" of his *Travels* rested was his proof—against Marsh and the other logicians he had been made to study at Trinity of "the falsity of that definition *animal rationale*"? (252–53)

The vast distinction raised in Swift's letter to Pope between the prideful *animal rationale* and the more humble *rationis capax* is fundamental for understanding the *Tale* as well as the *Travels* and for fathoming Swift's philosophical melancholy and his dedication to balance.

At Marsh's feet, the *Provost's Logic* taught Swift to distinguish between our prideful expectations and our limited capacities for reason. As he learned to distrust modern reason at Dublin, ironically Marsh as model also taught him about modern agendas that threatened humane learning. If Marsh is Swift's test case of an overconfident rationalist, a tyrannical pre-Restoration influence returning to haunt modern learning, then the prelate's Dublin Philosophical Society enlarges that specter. Founded in August 1683, the organization by January 1684 became officially known as "The Dublin Society for the improving of Naturall Knowledge, Mathematicks, and Mechanics." According to K. Theodore Hoppen, it intended vigorously to "promote experimentall philosophy, medicin . . . [and] mechanicks."[11] One of its original members, Dudley Loftus, rejected this exclusively scientific emphasis and resigned, charging that "the Society of the mechanicks of fresh philosophers of Dublin is various in its names and titles, (being sometimes called a society of usefull learning, sometimes a shop of useless subtelties, but most commonly termed the Petty-Mulleneuxan meeting)."[12]

While Hoppen shows that Loftus's attacks represented "a mixture of intellectual opposition and sheer pique" (162), both Loftus and the Society he rejected faithfully reflect seventeenth-century traditions meshed with controversial issues beyond the parochial and contemporary. Writing at the end of the nineteenth century, S. P. Johnston called the ridicule by Loftus "the Dublin echo of the great controversy then general in Europe . . . between the literary and scientific spirit."[13] It is, of course, the same fundamental split and epistemological controversy that the *Tale* addresses.

From his Trinity days in the 1680s Swift learned to understand that events in the local context of Dublin totally correlated with major transitions in learning in Europe. Dubliners, in fact, did more than reflect these changes. As their works and correspondence show, men like William Molyneux and George Berkeley were to become key figures in the European discourse. More immediate to Swift, St. George Ashe, his tutor at Trinity and an active—but critical—member of the Dublin Philosophical Society, "most intimately affected [Swift's] evolving character" (Ehrenpreis 1: 51). In this local crucible for change, the losses for humanism, classical learning, moral philosophy, and literature may well have seemed alarming and threatening to the young Swift—as indeed they were.

---

[11] The Society's rules are printed in *The Petty Papers*. Ed. Marquis of Lansdowne. 2 vols. London, 1927. 2: 88–90. See Hoppen 84, 249.

[12] Hoppen 162. Hoppen notes that "Loftus's criticisms of the Dublin Society are contained in King's Inns Library Dublin MS No. 33." 264.

[13] "Additional Note to Lecture VI. The Dublin Philosophical Society," in George T. Stokes, 138–41.

The affinities between the Dublin Philosophical Society in the 1680s and midcentury developments in natural philosophy in England and Ireland run deep. T. C. Barnard tells us that "by the 1650s there was a small group of enthusiastic supporters of the new learning in Ireland, united by a common outlook and by their friendship with Hartlib" ("The Hartlib Circle" 61). As Samuel Hartlib had provided direction for the Royal Society in the 1650s, William Molyneux supplied "the driving enthusiasm" for the Dublin group in the 80s. The Dublin Society cultivated contacts with the Royal Society of London and the Oxford Philosophical Society in the way the Hartlib group had earlier kept in touch with intellectual developments in England and on the Continent. Barnard finds "most remarkable resemblances" between inquiries of the 50s and 80s.

> The Hartlib circle was active in medicine, husbandry, astronomy, mathematics, public finance and trade, in composing a universal language, in natural history and even in Celtic studies: all spheres in which members of the Dublin Philosophical Society later interested themselves. (63)

These beginnings of modern science lent themselves to satire by their novelty, grand designs, problematic performances, far-fetched experiments, and ultimate threats to humanistic learning. Writings by William Stubbe, Meric Casaubon, and Joseph Glanvill, like Thomas Shadwell's *The Virtuoso* and Samuel Butler's *Hudibras,* provided models for Dublin attacks by Loftus and by Ashe, Swift's tutor. As with Glanvill's work in England, their attacks reveal ambivalence. Loftus believed, for example, that the Petty-Molyneux clique "was impeding the grand Baconian design of the 'advancement of learning'" (Hoppen 162). Ashe criticized "those virtuosi interested only in the bizarre and unusual," believing that the true philosopher should study "the natural world by means of its most rounded and beautiful works."[14]

That Swift had access to goings on at the Society through Ashe seems undeniable. His poems mention members of the Society including Dr. Thomas Molyneux, the brother of William. One poem, "Mad Mullinix and Timothy," alludes to these

> Choice spirits, who employ their parts,
> To mend the world by useful arts. (*Poems* 3: 780)

The Dublin Philosophical Society's combined interests in medicine, Paracelsus, and air may have supplied very early inspiration for the *Tale*'s Digression on Madness. Hoppen mentions the Society's "considerable

---

14 Hoppen, 165–66. Also see Walter E. Houghton, Jr.

enthusiasm" for chemistry: it was preoccupied by Paracelsian alchemy and stimulated by the work of Robert Boyle. Sir Richard Buckeley and Allen Mullen, who read papers dealing with the nature of digestion and acid-alkali fermentation, depended on the theory of the Paracelsian Van Helmont (Hoppen 100). In 1690, Boyle himself wrote a treatise on air. Further, Ashe's "A Discourse of the Air" argued for "experiments and demonstration over empty speculations and spruce hypotheses"[15]. But if Swift had access to Loftus's paper, he would have found in it a distrust of the new learning as useless and little more than "a nimble kind of windage."[16] Since the Society's discourse smothered humanistic learning, Swift's animus against its enterprise could not but reflect his sense of personal and intellectual isolation. At the same time, with Marsh, Petty, the Molyneuxs, Ashe, and Loftus publicly active in this local scientific laboratory in the 1680s, Swift could examine at close range its origins, influences, possibilities, pretensions, and personalities. He could watch the irrational modern myth as it took shape from seemingly rational experimental inquiry.

In Swift's final cosmology, the species *rationis capax* has traded in its capacity for sound judgment because of pridefully aspiring to be *animal rationale,* with the restless, egoistic obsession to use knowledge and reason to return to Eden, the ultimate happiness. In this fantastic endeavor, the learned moderns literally distributed arrested self-knowledge and stunted spiritual growth.

---

[15] Hoppen, 77. Hoppen note: B.M. Add. MS 4811, f.54. Copy, R.S. MS Early Letters, A.34 and R.S. MS Copy Letter Book, 10,94–114. 248.

[16] Hoppen, 163. Hoppen note: This paragraph is based on a passage in King's Inns MS No. 33, pp. 220–5. 265.

CHAPTER FOUR

MILTON: CONSCIENCE FREE

> Is not . . . Conscience a *Pair of Breeches*,
> which, tho' a Cover for Lewdness as well as
> Nastiness, is easily slipt down for the Service
> of both."
>
> *Tale* 78

On November 23, 1644, by protesting Parliament's Licensing Order of June 16, 1643, John Milton's *Areopagitica* became the first sustained essay devoted primarily to freedom of the press. Just as Swift's *Tale* (1704) was to use the negative claim that information tends toward superficiality and distortion in an attempt to dismantle the modern synthesis, the *Areopagitica* used the positive claim of the need for liberty of conscience to help create that synthesis. In the process, Milton successfully undermined absolute monarchy and episcopacy. In his later works Milton heroically defended regicide in 1649 and extolled the republican commonwealth over monarchy in 1659, even on the eve of the Restoration.[1] And nearly thirty years later John Toland's *The Life of Milton* (1698) asserted that licensing in the 1690s bore some resemblance to licensing in the 1640s.[2] In 1695 the Licensing Act had lapsed for "practical reasons" (Siebert 263). Thus Toland could freely advance liberty of conscience, reason, and a host of republican principles that had inspired Milton's attacks against the earlier Act administered by Archbishop Laud.[3]

Acutely conscious of the dependence of the revolutionary alliance of Milton-Toland on unlicensed publishing to kindle what he considered incendiary programs, Swift set about to shatter the alliance by making its modern

---

[1] *Commonwealth* (and *res publica*) can be used neutrally, to denote any kind of government, monarchies included. Or it can steer in a kingless, classical direction. It can also denote a mixed government including a component of monarchy.

[2] Toland's *Life of Milton* was first published as an introduction to *A Complete Collection of the Historical, Political, and Miscellaneous Works of John Milton* (Amsterdam, 1698). It was republished without Milton's prose works one year later. *The Life of John Milton, Containing, besides the History of his Works, Several Extraordinary Characters of Men and Books, Sects, Parties, and Opinions* (London, 1699). The 1699 edition is used here.

[3] For other resurrection of Milton in the 1690s, see George F. Sensabaugh, "Adaptations of *AREOPAGITICA*."

ramifications the putative excuse for his persona's creating the *Tale*. All three reformers—Milton, Toland, and the *Tale*'s narrator—wish to be remembered by posterity for heroism in cultivating civic virtue. And between Milton and Toland, the *Tale* accessed enough quotable material to ballyhoo publishing mania with its self-puffery of heroic virtue.

Liberty of conscience is the principle that binds Milton and Toland. Since reason and freedom of choice will lead to the New Jerusalem, Albion, and the regaining of paradise, the individual and his civil society stand or fall on inward liberty or freedom of conscience. Although Milton's concerns about freedom of conscience were eschatological, their political implications are profound because inward liberty supersedes political stability. His argument for free speech in the *Areopagitica* places obedience to conscience—that is, to the voice of reason and the indirect voice of God in the New Testament—above the civil law and earthly powers. Toland approvingly focuses on Milton's "Give me the liberty to know, to utter and to argue freely according to conscience, above all liberties" (107).

But liberty of conscience and absolute monarchy cannot co-exist. Natural law enters the political equation to challenge civil law. The divine right of absolute monarchs must yield to the individual's need to follow natural law's commands. Publishing will subvert kingship even as it exalts God's—that is, nature's—goodness. With universal goodness immanent in the state of nature, men seek regeneration through reason. Books further the work of conscience and strengthen man's ability to choose good over evil; and human rights should not be subverted by legal encumbrances. It becomes the height of virtue for the heroic few who have attained inward liberty to broadcast its necessity and lead the many along the right pathways.

In his *Life*, Toland uses the new freedom to applaud its original sponsor and review Milton's argument in the *Areopagitica* (62–70). Had not "the liberty of Unlicensed Printing" prevailed in the Republics of Greece and Italy and survived "the most rigid Purgers, Corrupters, or Executioners of Books" in the dark ages,

> [to] what a degree of Ignorance and meanness of Spirit it would have reduc'd the World, depriving it of so many inimitable Historians, Orators, Philosophers, and Poets, the Repositories of inestimable Treasure, consisting of warlike and heroic Deeds, the best and wisest Arts of Government, the most perfect Rules and Examples of Eloquence or Politeness, and such divine Lectures of Wisdom and Virtue, that the loss of CICERO's Works alone, or those of LIVY, could not be repair'd by all the Fathers of the Church. (62–64)[4]

---

[4] As J. G. A. Pocock reminds us, "This is an Enlightenment, not a Christian, argument for

Toland concludes his *Life* with a sweeping condemnation of Licensers—"those sworn Officers to destroy Learning, Liberty and good Sense" (138)—even though, as Frederick S. Siebert explains, the Licensing Act had lapsed in 1695 becaause of the difficulties of administering it (263). But no matter how incidental the cause, expiry of the Act had profound repercussions that J. A. Downie makes clear:

> The combined effect of the triennial act [passed in 1694] and the abandonment of the licensing system was a tremendous growth in the production of political literature.
>
> Understandably enough, contemporaries were bewildered by the development of a 'fourth estate'. They were astonished by the sheer volume of political propaganda that the party presses managed to turn out. (*Harley* 1)

Swift mocks this revived freedom of the press as opening the floodgates for the heroic Toland and a host of other unquiet spirits. In the Preface, the *Tale*'s satiric voice beneath the persona's self-serving naïveté decries the modern publishing frenzy: "Mean while, the Danger hourly increasing, by new Levies of Wits all appointed (as there is Reason to fear) with Pen, Ink, and Paper which may at an hour's Warning be drawn into Pamphlets and other Offensive Weapons, ready for immediate Execution" (39–40).

By linking the satiric attack on the influx of hack writers with Time's (Kronos's) scythe, Swift leads the *Tale*'s persona in wild swings from proclaiming a Tolandic triumph over the publishing mania to sounding defensive about this dubious information explosion to quoting Milton's despair at the Restoration. In the Epistle Dedicatory, To His Royal Highness Prince Posterity, the *Tale*'s persona is hard put to defend the burgeoning, but ephemeral, productions of his age:

> 'Tis true indeed, that altho' their Numbers be vast, and their Productions numerous in proportion, yet are they hurried so hastily off the Scene, that they escape our Memory, and delude our Sight. When I first thought of this Address, I had prepared a copious List of *Titles* to present to *Your Highness* as an undisputed Argument for what I affirm. The Originals were posted fresh upon all Gates and Corners of Streets; but returning in a very few hours to take a Review, they were all torn down, and fresh ones in their Places. (34)

Ten pages later, the enthusiastic persona remains on the defensive "far from granting the Number of Writers, a Nuisance to our Nation" (45–46); and Swift brings him in stages to Miltonian despair.

---

liberty of expression. What it gave us was the ancient philosophy, and the *prisca theologia,* which the Fathers would have condemned." Correspondence, April 6, 1987.

In the *Life,* Toland empathizes with his subject and quotes from Milton's *Readie and Easie Way to establish a free Commonwealth* (1660).[5]

> He [Milton] endeavors to set before the Eys of the Nation the folly and unreasonableness of all they had so valiantly don for several years, if they at last readmitted Kingship; that they would be the shame of all free Countrys, and the Laughingstock of all Monarchies. "Where is this goodly Tower of a Commonwealth, will Foreners say, which the English boasted they would build to overshadow Kings, and be another Rome in the West? The Foundation indeed they laid gallantly, but fell in to a worse Confusion, not of Tongues but of Factions, than those at the Tower of Babel; and have left no Memorial of their Work behind them remaining, but in the common laughter of Europe." (119)

Swift leaves his persona with the same public embarrassment. Since Toland directly quotes Milton, who has borrowed from Luke 14:28–30 and Genesis 11:1–9, Swift has his aping persona use the identical sources in order to echo Milton's apocalyptic despair over the prospect of scornful laughter as the only memorial:

> I enquired after them [the vast daily outpourings in print] among Readers and Booksellers, but I enquired in vain; the *Memorial of them was lost among Men, their Place was no more to be found:* and I was laughed to scorn, for a *Clown* and a *Pedant* . . . (34–5)

Here is one of many instances when Swift selects his Milton citations directly from Toland's study and refines them.[6] The parody is precise, the satire apt; yet in recalling Milton's despair at the very beginning of the *Tale,* Swift has larger purposes and themes. To be sure, he wishes to yoke Toland with the lapsing of the Licensing Act and present him as a prime mover in the revival and revision of midcentury causes espoused by Milton, Harrington, Cromwell, and the Puritan utopians. His more critical concern is Milton's jeremiad, on the eve of the Restoration, that speaks heroically to the future and finds Toland heroically responding.

Swift's parody of these devotions asks for a full analysis of his Dedication to Prince Posterity since it extends Milton's and Toland's messages to a distant future, our present. Fortuitously, James Holstun's *The Rational Millennium* (1987) provides a comprehensive analysis of Milton's *Easie Way* and serves unintentionally as a gloss on the *Tale*'s Dedication to Prince Posterity. The

---

5 Second Edition, April 1–10, 1660. Cf. Milton's *PW* 7:422–23.

6 Unaware of Swift's parody and boomerang of Milton's Biblical allusions, the editors of the 1973 Oxford *Tale* nevertheless have found these sentences reminiscent "of Biblical phrases, e.g., Deut. xxxii.26; Zech. x.10; Rev. xii.8, xx.11; 1 Mac. xii.53" (35). "All memory" lost appears in their first, fourth, and fifth references and also in Psalms ix.6. But Luke and Genesis with their references to laughter and Babel are the critical ones for both Milton and Swift.

very mid-seventeenth-century political changes which Holstun, like Milton, sees as salutary in replacing centralized custom with the rational reorganizing of the modern state, Swift challenges as mad.[7] While Holstun's conclusions move approvingly from Harrington, Milton, Comenius, and the Puritan utopians directly to the twentieth century, these same early modern influences on the continuously evolving Information Age are filtered in the *Tale*—and correspondingly in this study—through the discerning but diametrical spectacles of Toland and Swift. Their retrospective discourses on the European intellectual and political revolution are within a half-century of the key players and events, and both participate in its development.

Because the Second Edition of the *Easie Way* was written six weeks before the Restoration, it had, as Holstun establishes, "no real audience" and the quotations from Jeremiah were "spoken only to trees and stones" (259). Still, Holstun says that Milton offers his "autobiographical voice of prophetic authority" (260). Since England has failed him, he has two messages for the future (262).

Milton's first message is "a retrospective view of the birth and backsliding death of the Commonwealth" (Holstun 255). He looks to the origins of the commonwealth wherein he had played a pivotal role. Just before referring to "no memorial except a new tower of Babel," Milton asks, "Where is this goodly tower of a commonwealth, which the English boasted they would build to overshadow kings, and be another Rome in the west?" (7.422–23). Swift's wry comments on the commonwealth use Milton's Babel image and glance at Milton as hangman.

Section XI of the *Tale* refers to Puritan Jack as "having introduced a new Deity. . . . by some called *Babel,* by others, *Chaos*" (194). Swift recalls the time "while this *Island* of ours, was under the *Dominion of Grace*" (201) when "in all Revolutions of Government, he [Jack] would make his Court for the Office of *Hangman* General" (195).

The second message is addressed to posterity; Holstun finds that the phrases in question from the *Easie Way* had appeared as early as 1654, in *A Second Defense of the English People:*

> Be sure that posterity will speak out and pass judgment: the foundations were soundly laid, the beginnings, in fact more than the beginnings, were splendid, but posterity will look in vain, not without a certain distress, for those who were to complete the work, who were to put the pediment in place. (4.685–86)

Holstun explains that

---

[7] The titles, illustrations, and conclusions of James Holstun's study (1987) and this one (in manuscript since 1985)—coincidentally, but independently arrived at—become antithetical discourses on identical sacred and secular forces developing in the seventeenth century.

Milton attempts to destroy himself and pass down his own resolute opposition to monarchy as an example to future times. In the passage . . . on the foolish tower builder, he fears that the English will have "no memorial of their work behind them remaining, but in the common laughter of Europe" (7.423); but even Milton doubts that this will be altogether the case, for his career as a prose writer has left behind a series of heroic memorials. (260)

In other words, Milton sees the failure of his free commonwealth as "a foregone conclusion" but understands that

In the act of their utterance his words memorialize themselves, and they will find their true, fit and few audience—and Milton his vindication—only in the future. . . . Milton as Jeremiah pleads almost suicidally for his own execution, which will verify his prophecy about his nation's expiring liberty, and so also his own authority as a prophet. (262)

With appropriate irony, the satiric voice in Section IV of the *Tale* facetiously urges heroes in the Miltonian and Tolandic mold to follow Hercules, who after great deeds and before encomiums committed suicide.

In his ambivalent "On Mr. Milton's *Paradise Lost*," Andrew Marvell had written, "What was easie he should render vain." The word *vain* draws on two sour meanings—*bootless* and *prideful*—as the *Tale*'s Dedication to Prince Posterity expands on Milton's jeremiad and introduces the *Tale*'s self-propagandizing persona. In the presence of Prince Posterity, Milton had blamed leaders and the multitude alike for failing to come apace with him in suppressing monarchy and building a commonwealth; the *Tale*'s vain persona blames Father Time (Posterity's governor and Swift's god Kronos) for having buried the outpourings of a newly free press. The villain Time has likewise rendered bootless the productions of prideful seventeenth-century poets:

WE [poets] confess *Immortality* to be a great and powerful *Goddess*, but in vain we offer up to her our Devotions and our Sacrifices, if *Your Highness's Governour*, who has usurped the *Priesthood*, must by an unparallel'd Ambition and Avarice, wholly intercept and devour them. (34)

The linkage between posterity and heroic virtue in Milton, Toland, and the *Tale* is secure. In Milton's *Of Reformation* (1641), he exhorts the English and the Scots to unite in the Contest for Liberty. Toland's quotations of Milton would have inflamed the Scot-hating Swift: "Be the Praise and the heroic Song of all Posterity. Merit this; but seek only Virtue, not to extend your limits" (29). In 1648, Milton lauds Cromwell's "perpetual renown to Posterity" (94); at another time he wishes great things to "be transmitted to Posterity" (80). Toland does not lag in seeking immortality for himself. In an epistle to his friend at the beginning of the *Life*, he announces that he undertook the work "to inform Posterity" (9), and parenthetically, in the same epistle, he insists that he is "neither writing a Satyr, nor a Panegyric upon MILTON, but publishing the true History of his Actions, Works, and Opinions" (8). In Section III of the *Tale* on TRUE Critics, Swift uses Milton as his prime example. His modern persona denigrates the Ancients who resorted to "*Satyr,* or *Panegyrick* upon the *TRUE Criticks*" (97)

Even as Milton and Toland use and abuse the term *posterity,* they usually join it, as does the parodying *Tale,* with the overworked phrase "wisdom and virtue." Two of the *Tale's* scant fourteen references to *virtue* appear in the Epistle Dedicatory to Prince Posterity, their source the fertile ground of Toland's *Life of Milton.* At the outset of the Epistle, Prince Posterity is appealed to as one "whose numberless Virtues in so few Years, make the World look upon You as the future Example to all Princes" (30–31). At the conclusion of the Epistle, the persona desires "that *Your Highness* may advance in Wisdom and Virtue, as well as Years, and at last out-shine all Your Royal Ancestors . . ." (38).

Wisdom and *virtue* are the Miltonian-Tolandic shibboleths Swift is mocking here. In the *Life,* Toland quotes liberally from Milton's *The Reason of Church-Government urg'd against Prelacy, in two Books,* an argument larded with the word *virtue.* In the second book, Milton speculates "on his design of writing an Epic Poem . . . whether his Hero should be some Prince" (31). This princely paragon or the author of the epic—both Milton and Toland leave his identity ambiguous—would instill "the Seeds of Virtue," describe "Virtue amiable or grave," and teach "Sanctity and Virtue" (32). The treatise goes on to propose that magistrates in his mythical happy Commonwealth

> may civilize, adorn, and make discrete our Minds by the learned and affable meeting of frequent Academies, and the procurement of wise and artful Recitations, sweeten'd with eloquent and graceful Inticements to the love and practice of Justice, Temperance and Fortitude, instructing and bettering the Nation at all opportunities, that the voice of *Wisdom and Virtue* [italics added] may be heard every where. (33–4)

Elsewhere Toland, supporting the arguments of *Areopagitica,* informs us that a Carthaginian Council resolution of 400 A.D. would have deprived the world of "the divine lectures of wisdom and virtue" (64) by heretical and heathen authors.

The Miltonian-Tolandic media program assures the *Tale's* Prince Posterity that "the voice of Wisdom and Virtue may be heard every where." Indeed, Milton asks rhetorically,

> Whether this [inculcating wisdom and virtue] may not be done, not only in Pulpits, but after another persuasive method, at set and solemn Paneguries, in

Theaters, Porticos, or what other place or way may win most upon the People to receive at once both Recreation and Instruction, let them in Authority consult. (34)

In response, the persona calls on "the Wisdom of our Ancestors" in erecting wooden machines "for the Use of those Orators who desire to talk much without Interruption. These [propaganda platforms] are the *Pulpit,* the *Ladder,* and the *Stage-Itinerant*" (56). As alluded to above, Swift glued these wooden machines together not only with proposals in Toland's *Life of Milton,* but also with scientific experiments from Narcissus Marsh's "Doctrine of Sounds." This technique of multiplying the satiric victims in a single passage anticipates Section III of the *Tale,* in which Swift attacks the cause of heroic virtue espoused with equal vehemence by Milton, Toland, and Temple.

From Milton to Temple to Shaftesbury to Rousseau to Jefferson to Paine to Lenin, the credo is the same. Virtue is something that humans come by naturally—a logical outgrowth of liberty of conscience and reason. Private good leads to public good. When suitably cultivated by a small learned vanguard, a band of professional revolutionaries with a virtuous cause are entitled to ascendant political power over outmoded and vicious absolutism.

In Swift's view, however, no one in his right mind could extrapolate virtue and wisdom from man's restless nature, let alone regenerate the beast through the cocksure efforts of a dedicated modern aristocracy acting as exemplars and claiming human reason or some other mystical form of inner light. Yet Swift is aware that Milton's theological and philosophical arguments have a seductive appeal for modern secularism. They have now helped spawn revolutions in England, America, France, and Russia. But the counterrevolutionary *Tale* exposes them. Swift systematically attacks the heroic virtue of modern authors gratuitously bringing benefits to mankind—Toland's avowed aim in the *Life.* "Writings of this nature should in my opinion [Toland's] be designed to recommend Virtue. . . . and for the benefit of mankind to know" (6–7). Conforming to Toland's agenda, the full title of the *Tale* proclaims that it is *Written for the Universal Improvement of Mankind.* Swift satirizes the toleration of dissenting sects by moderns, their rage against all hierarchical priesthoods, and their covert and overt attempts in the name of the people to establish a republican commonwealth; he suspects Toland's and the Whigs' pretense of resting content with the Williamite compromise of a mixed government and the Protestant succession.

Yoking Milton and Toland proved a satirist's delight. During the period of Toland's prodigious publishing activity and Swift's sporadic composition of the *Tale,* Toland published not only *The Life of John Milton* (1698) in a new edition of Milton's prose works but also *Amyntor: or, a Defence of Milton's*

Life (1699). It would be difficult to overestimate either the influence of Milton on Toland or Swift's abundant use of republican influence in the *Tale*. Milton had a comprehensive revolutionary program dependent on virtue; and Toland in the 1690s attempted to reestablish it. His deistic heterodoxy not the same as Milton's Christian heterodoxy, nonetheless, Toland in the 1690s attempted to align his ideas with Milton's—and Swift's satire followed suit. Toland's Milton provides for every major satiric theme directed against dissenting Jack in the *Tale:* liberty of conscience and unlicensed publishing, heroic virtue triumphant over vice, dedication to the public good, classical republicanism and the utopian commonwealth, inner light and the enthusiasm of dissenting sects, typology and apocalyptic vision, and learning from dark authors. Whatever his oppositions to the mysteries, Toland himself—and not merely by his earlier asociation with Presbyterians in Edinburgh and London—could not escape direct identification with all these Miltonian causes.

In 1699, an anonymous pamphlet noticed this mirroring of subject and biographer:

> It is storied of the *Italian* Painters, That they Compliment their Mistresses by drawing the blessed Virgin according to their Features; and in truth I am of Opinion that the Author [Toland] designed the like Compliment to himself in forming Mr. *Milton*'s Character; for his natural and acquired Parts, Estate, Publick Post, Great Reputation and Universal Esteem excepted, the Parallel seems to be drawn as near as may be. (2)[8]

The pairing of thought and quotation of master and disciple in Toland's *Life of Milton* allows Swift in the *Tale* to borrow from each. The path is clear from twentieth-century commentary on Milton back to Toland's slavish quotations and echoing textual appraisals and to Swift's parodying commentary in the *Tale*.

Much of what modern scholarship has deduced about Milton's ethical and political thought, Toland offered earlier in his *Life of Milton* with equal thoroughness. Considering his method, it would have been difficult for him to miss the mark. Almost half (48 percent) of his *Life* consists of direct quotations from Milton's work; the balance is commentary, often redundant.

The *Life* obligingly makes possible the *Tale*'s mock formula for the treatise of a modern: "transcribing from others, and digressing from himself, as often as he shall see Occasion" (148). Immediately following this passage in A Digression in Praise of Digressions, Swift makes it clear that he had in mind not only Toland's *Life of Milton*, but the wedding of Milton's and Toland's thoughts. Such a modern treatise would be preserved

---

8 *Remarks on the Life of Mr. Milton, As published by J.T. with A Character of the Author and his Party. In a Letter to a Member of Parliament.* London: J. Nutt, 1699.

for a long Eternity, adorn'd with the Heraldry of its Title . . . nor bound to everlasting Chains of Darkness in a Library: But when the Fulness of time is come, shall haply undergo the Tryal of Purgatory in order *to ascend the Sky*. (148)

The 1973 *Oxford* edition of the *Tale* noted seven allusions to Milton's *Paradise Lost* in the *Tale* and *The Battle of the Books;* the 1986 *World's Classics* edition cites one more.[9] These glancing allusions belong to a host of Milton and Toland references, hitherto unrecorded, that give unity to Swift's structural attack on modern mysteries. While the *Tale* alludes to *Paradise Lost* throughout, in the lines quoted above Swift concentrates on three separate phrases from *Paradise Lost* and *Paradise Regained*. As Toland transcribes from Milton, so does the *Tale*. And to leave no doubt of the identity of his target, Swift incorporates directly from Milton: "chains of darkness" (*PL* vi.739); "fulness of time" (*Paradise Regained,* iv.380); "ascend the sky" (*PL* vii.287). Eight other words in the sentence enjoy wide usage in *Paradise Lost: eternity, adorn'd, heraldry, title, haply, undergo, trial,* and *purgatory.*

Hermann J. Real has shared a transcript of Swift's marginal notes on *Paradise Lost:* "The gift of Dr. Jonathan Swift to Mrs. Dingley and Mrs. Johnson [Stella]. May 1703." These annotations, mostly identifying classical allusions, are localized to certain passages such as The Infernal Council in Book I. William Monck Mason objected to Walter Scott's conclusion that these notes "convey information useful only to persons of very indifferent education." Mason believed the "evidence, ill authenticated and vague" and not "sufficient to set aside all direct testimony in favour of Stella's literary character" (Mason 372). None of the annotated passages coincide with those documented by the Swift editors or this study as material for parody in the *Tale*. Swift referred to the *Tale* as "the you know what" in correspondence with Stella in 1710[10] and he may well have discussed finishing touches with her in 1703, a year before its publication. His note at the end of these annotations (*PL* x.896 [xii.6 in later editions]) does mirror his own situation at that moment: "From hence the Poet [Milton] flags very much to the end of the Book." After his climactic Section IX, the Digression on Madness, Swift too encountered the same difficulties in sustaining the *Tale* to the end. In his search for finishing material, once more he drew on *Paradise Lost* and Milton, "to sum up" the adventures of Jack Presbyter, the "*Hangman* General" (195), in Section XI of the *Tale*. For example, he alludes to those with "converting

---

9   1973 *Oxford* edition: 94 (*PL* vi.26), 120 (*PL* iii.437–9), 137 (*PL* published by subscription), 140 (*PL* iv.1002–4), 154 (*PL* v.688–9), 155 (*PL* vi.605), 193 (*PL* i.500–2); 1986 *World's Classics* edition 114 (*PL* i.798).

10   "They may talk of the you know what; but, gad, if it had not been for that I should never have been able to get the access I have had." September 30, 1710. *Journal to Stella*, 1:47.

imaginations" who "reduce all Things into *Types;* who can make *Shadows* no thanks to the Sun; and then mold them into Substances . . ." (190). This reference does coincide with a passage Swift had annotated for Stella: "Or substance might be called that shadow seemed, For each seemed either" (*PL* ii 669–70).

Gleefully, Swift forces the antipapal Milton through a Dantean "trial of purgatory." The *Tale* becomes Swift's grim purgatory for Milton, Toland, the persona, and the modern world while they await the non-coming of Albion and the New Jerusalem, with Milton in the purgatory he did not believe in to wait until Doomsday for the fulfillment of his apocalyptic vision.

Toland lauded Milton's *Paradise Lost* for "being the Defence of a whole free Nation, the People of *England;* for . . . equalling the Old Romans in the purity of their own Language, and their highest Notions of Liberty" (*Life of Milton* 95). Later historians have referred as glowingly to that Grand Whig Milton (Sensabaugh) and his noble contributions to a free press, intellectual freedom, liberty of conscience, and the defense of liberty. The poet-statesman has been praised for addressing the central issue of monarchy: power from God or power conferred by the people. And his theory of the compact is acknowledged to anticipate modern European states and place him alongside Harrington in the classical republican tradition.

But notwithstanding Milton's glorious legacy of liberty, slow Time at last asks posterity to listen to the satirist's side. The period between 1697 and 1704, when Swift composed the *Tale,* produced transitional political documents and decisions in Britain that assimilated the philosophical and political reforms of the previous century in Europe and rearranged Whig and Tory alliances and purposes at home. It is only in the last two decades that historians have studied the significance of this modern transition and the importance of Toland to it, making it possible to see some of these issues more keenly with Toland's and Swift's eyes.

As recently as 1985, J.G.A. Pocock's *Virtue, Commerce, and History* independently recapitulated Swift's understanding of the attitudes, actions, and writings of Toland that inspired his anger and castigation. The Old Whig or republican canon, according to Pocock,

> moved beyond Parliament to Commonwealth, beyond the antiquity of Parliament to neo-Harringtonian ideas of Gothic liberty; it also implicitly endorsed the regicide of 1649, from which Whig historiography was a sustained attempt to deflect attention. Toland was the archivist and to some extent the myth maker of English republican theory.
>
> He appears also as a leading activist of radical deism, the promoter in England and abroad of various secret societies that look like gathered congregations of illuminist rationalism. One of the dedicatees of his [edition of] Harrington, the

city magnate Sir Robert Clayton, was a leader of the established structure of English freemasonry at a time when Toland was seeking to organize hermetic groups within it. (233)

Pocock's portrait of Toland as the epitome of republican archivist, Whig myth maker, and illuminist rationalist is, in other words, the prototypical modern on which Swift's satire is based. And what Swift treated covertly in the *Tale* in 1704, he was soon to attack overtly in political propaganda. *The Examiner,* No. 39, May 3, 1711, presents Swift's bill of particulars against his adversaries with specific charges that also apply to the victims of his satire in the *Tale.* In a passage which seems to anticipate Pocock item by item, Swift charges the Whigs

> with a design of destroying the *Established Church,* and introducing *Fanaticism* and *free-thinking* in its stead. We accuse them as *Enemies* to *Monarchy;* as endeavouring to undermine the present *Form* of *Government,* and to build a Commonwealth, or some new Scheme of their own, upon its Ruins. . . . Our accusations against them we endeavour to make good by certain Overt-Acts . . . the publick Encouragement they gave to *Tindal, Toland,* and other Atheistical Writers. . . . The Regard they bear to our Monarchy, hath appeared by their open ridiculing the *Martyrdom* of King *Charles* the First, in their *Calves-head Clubs,* their common Discourses and their pamphlets. Their denying the unnatural War raised against that Prince to have been a Rebellion. . . . Their Industry in publishing and spreading Seditious and Republican Tracts; such as *Ludlow*'s Memoirs, *Sidney* of Government, and many others. (*PW* 3:142–3)

Although mentioned only in passing, Toland bore the burden of personal leadership for *all* these schemes. According to Swift in 1712, Toland alone hosted the Calves-Head revels and alone had published the tracts and memoirs on Ludlow and Sidney alluded to in *The Examiner.* In fact, a year after the charges in *The Examiner* Swift specifically detailed the political, philosophical, and temperamental differences that placed the two forever in hostile camps. In his 1712 penny paper poem "T–l–nd's Invitation to DISMAL, to Dine with the CALVES-HEAD Club," Swift tarred all the prominent Whigs from Godolphin to his former patrons Lords Somers and Sunderland with attending Toland's secret "mystical feasts" with their "proper signs and symbols" to celebrate the regicide of Charles I as notoriously in 1712 as they allegedly had done in the early 1690s (*Poems* 1: 161–66).[11] From the *Examiner* article and the poem, it is clear that—long before Pocock and others—Swift perceived Toland as the Whigs' leading myth maker and revolutionary instigator.[12] After accusing his former Whig patrons of association with

---

[11] Dismal is the Earl of Nottingham, Tory and Churchman. Why Swift places him in company of the Whig lords is unclear.

[12] See Caroline Robbins, Margaret C. Jacob, and Blair Worden.

Toland and regicide, he relishes delivering the poem's fictitious exposé for the delight of Oxford, formerly Robert Harley, and his fellow Tories.

In 1711 and 1712, however, there is a contest for Oxford's favor between Swift and Toland with the latter recommending to the Tory leader a coalition with the Whigs. Swift's *Examiner* and his penny sheet identify Toland solely with the Whig camp for past and present evils.[13] In that contest Toland lost and registered bitterness by asking in final correspondence with Oxford in December 1711 that Swift be ousted and he be returned to favor. Then in 1714 he castigated Father Jonathan, a Jacobite lackey, for his "jobs of villainy" on Oxford's behalf in his *The Grand Mystery Laid Open* (21). If Swift had tarred Toland with Whig regicide and filled his propaganda seat, Toland would now publish an opposite extreme charge that Swift and the Tories desire to return to Stuart autocracy and Roman Catholicism.[14]

Pocock links Toland with illuminist rationalism and Swift characterizes the moderns as more mad and mysterious than rational; both propositions derive from millennial expectations generated after the Reformation. Within the context of the Christian mysteries, Milton's pretensions were in no wise limited to establishing a rational republican commonwealth in Britain. As heir and propagator of the prelapsarian dream, he cherished millennial expectations: a new dispensation from God to man to be realized in the modern world. To expose and dash such hopes, Swift concentrated much of his satire of Milton and Toland on a Milton millennial fixation, the doctrine of typology. According to John R. Mulder, this doctrine was no less than "the study of God's mode of composition" to Milton; it "informed Milton's view of history, influenced his use of biblical and classical matter, and guided him in the search for appropriate artistic design" (*Milton Encyclopedia* 8: 102). And since typology depends on a historical continuum and linear progression, it was of the utmost importance to Milton and Toland—and the *Tale* that so often dealt with them.

Assuming biblical faith, every person, event, and institution recorded in the Old Testament is a type that foreshadows a revelation—that is, its antitype— in the New Testament. In *Paradise Lost,* for example, the fall of Adam prefigures the triumph of Christ. Christ is the antitype of Adam, the type;

---

[13] In discussing this penny paper, Irvin Ehrenpreis asserts that Swift's "escape from his own severe morality" into "the free, uncontrolled" Toland forced him to hide behind Horace to excuse himself for "the disgraceful license" of his persona (3:567). While Swift may indeed have felt a hidden attraction for the irrepressible in Toland's character, the poem offers no evidence of envy or apology by a repressed moralist. On the contrary, by saddling Toland with an old charge, Swift has triumphed over him personally and politically, and relishes that triumph with his Tory benefactors.

[14] See below, p. 85.

Christ is also the antitype of Moses, Job, and Melchizedek. Only with the appearance of the antitype in the New Testament does the significance of the type emerge. The assumption is that history reveals a providential design. Hegel takes this idea of design one step further by assuming natural rather than divine forces moving inexorably from thesis-antithesis to synthesis time after time toward an ultimate, ideal *stasis* or social contract much like nature's climax forest.

But in a crucial variation for the *Tale,* typologists like Milton also moved beyond the Bible to see typological progress in all known history. For example, by a stretch of the figural imagination, pagan culture can prefigure the Judaeo-Christian experience. In the *Nativity Ode,* Milton implies that Hercules is a type prefiguring Christ (Madsen 3, 6), and elsewhere he presents the heroic death of Hercules. Typology gives Milton an opportunity to employ classical sources for Christian themes.

Like Toland's satisfaction, Swift's fury with Milton's typology centers on the figural inference that the advent of Christ and the theology of New Testament have made episcopacy and the priesthood invalid. For Milton—and St. Paul—Christ has fulfilled the law and ended the validity of the Old Testament, its Mosaic Law, and the visible church with its priesthood. Inner light, goodness, and power, all Christian virtues flowing from God to his saints, move humanity through a progressing Christocentric history toward the heavenly kingdom, alternately known as the promised land, Albion, the New Jerusalem, or the utopian commonwealth.[15] These optimistic prospects shake not only Swift's Anglican world but the classical foundations of his satire. Moreover, the extension of Milton's Protestant typology and historical world view by Toland and his generation appalls Swift, who sees the progress from Milton to Toland as part of an unbroken lineage from theocentricity to egocentricity and madness.[16] To be sure, Swift is also employing the usual Anglican case against enthusiasm which Michael Heyd and others expose.[17]

---

[15] Despite the Neoplatonic elements in this modern faith and its figuralism, Milton is less indebted to Ficino and Pico than are his contemporary Rosicrucians, the Cambridge Platonists, and the Royal Society. Pocock notes that the Anglican Samuel Parker in 1666 praises the Royal Society and Bacon as antidotes to Neoplatonism (Correspondence, April 6, 1987). But Swift deals with Neoplatonists everywhere in several parts of the *Tale.* See below, pp. 103–4, 159, 164–67, 190–95, and 205–7. References to the Scriptures, Renaissance humanism, the Puritan Revolution, and the classical republican tradition suffice to dispatch Milton.

[16] Jacob, *The Newtonians* 153. "For Toland was a deeply religious thinker, well schooled in the classics, theology and philosophy, familiar with the liberal Anglican tradition from Boyle to the Newtonians. Yet in one crucial respect Toland broke with that tradition: he was a Protestant for political reasons but he was not a Christian. He was a seeker after a new metaphysics, one that combined the new science with a naturalistic vision of the universe; in short he sought a universal religion complete with a new community and a new ritual."

[17] For Swift's relation to this tradition, see below, pp. 199–200.

In considering these influences in the *Tale*, we are fortunate that the scholarship on typology is well-documented. Paul J. Korshin's copious 1982 study, *Typologies in England 1650–1820*, finds that Milton is undoubtedly "the most important literary figure in the continuity of typological tradition in the second half of the seventeenth century" (70), and 200 pages later that Swift is "the only typological satirist of the late seventeenth century . . . who was a professional theologian" (290). He also finds Swift's typological satire far more inventive and challenging than that of Butler, Oldham or Dryden. Yet in all the array of vital evidence and insight, Korshin misses Swift's most significant typological satire—that of Milton's practice. But even though he does not draw the obvious inference that in both the *Tale*'s persona and Jack, Swift is remembering Toland, Milton, and their typology, Korshin does discover the mirror-images between the persona, "a fanatic Puritan with false pretensions to the role of scriptural exegete," (291) and brother Jack, who tends "to reduce all Things into *Types*" (301).

In *Christianity Not Mysterious* (1696), Toland announces that the Old Testament was hidden in figures and signs under the Mosaic veil that kept these mysteries secret. Toland cites Hebrews 10:1:

> For *the Law had a Shadow of good things to come;* but they were not clearly and fully revealed till the *New Testament* times, being veiled before by various typical representations, ceremonies, and figurative expressions. (93)

And he finds confirmation from Clemens Alexandrinus that

> the Christian Discipline was called Illumination, because it brought hidden things to light, the Master (CHRIST) alone removing the Cover of the Ark, that is, the Mosaick Veil. He adds in express words, that those things which were mysterious and obscure in the Old Testament are made plain in the New. (114–15)

Though this exegesis is Miltonian orthodoxy, Toland finds typology getting out of hand with the Primitive Christians, who carried their

> ridiculous Fancy at length to Numbers, Letters, Places, and what not. That which in the Old Testament therefore did, according to them, represent any thing in the New, they called the type or Mystery of it. Thus TYPE, SYMBOL, PARABLE, SHADOW, FIGURE, SIGN and MYSTERY, signify all the same thing in Justin Martyr. (115)

Swift uses this passage in the Introduction to the *Tale* to link Toland, Milton, the Royal Society, and Marsh with typology, illumination, and modern learning:

> NOW this Physico-logical Scheme of Oratorical Receptacles or Machines, contains a great Mystery, being a Type, a Sign, an Emblem, a Shadow, a Symbol,

bearing Analogy to the spacious Commonwealth of Writers, and to those Methods by which they must exalt themselves to a certain Eminency above the inferior World. (61)

As Korshin has noted, Swift makes the deliberate non-theological leap of converting typological method to all forms of learning. Typology becomes just another affirmation of the modern idea of progress.[18] In looking over the typological land mines in the *Tale,* for example, Korshin teases out one of Swift's most brilliant sexual conceits. Ancient pygmies with large male pudenda are the type for antitypes in modern learning who produce little compendiums with large indexes (*Tale* 147). The image applies to the indexes in Milton's commonplace books and also describes Swift's anticipation of our information age.

Behind Swift's clever sexual conceit stands his profoundly serious attack on the millennial dreams of the moderns. Milton, like the Neoplatonists, found foreshadowing of Christianity in pagan mysteries. The metaphysical poets Donne and Herbert thought that the New Testament foreshadows the kingdom of heaven, and the millenarians, Milton among them, believed this heavenly kingdom to be "at hand."[19] Considering these precedents, Swift pretends that all moderns, but especially Toland, Jack, and the *Tale*'s persona, that "most devoted Servant of all *Modern* Forms" (45), envision themselves as antitypes of ancient types whose performance they consider dismal.

In the Preface of the *Tale,* "the Attick Commonwealth" (51) is the conspicuous type. But how can it prefigure the Cromwellian commonwealth, "its old Antitype" (40)? There is a contradiction in terms until we realize that the persona pledges to protect the "old" antitype—old in the sense of having been attacked by the 1651 *Leviathan* of Hobbes. It may be "old" in midcentury terms, but as an antitype it must be new; it also belongs to the persona's and Toland's recent memory and future expectation. Is it any wonder that the satiric voice is concerned to save the "attick" type from the modern wits let in by the expiry of the Licensing Act?

The fortunate concatenation of Toland and Milton and of scriptural, classical, and modern typologies enables Swift to fashion one of his most devastating satiric attacks in the *Tale*'s Section III, *A Digression concerning Criticks.* It is in response to Swift's quarrel with Milton's theological contention that, thanks to the Christian dispensation, man can regain prelapsarian virtue. For Milton, at the prelapsarian beginning God gave man goodness, inner light, reason, and free choice, all of which through Christ's coming may

---

    [18] See Edgar Zilsel.
    [19] For further discussion, see Katharine R. Firth, William Lamont, C. A. Patrides, Richard C. Popkin, Hillel Schwartz, Peter Toon.

now be reclaimed. But for Swift, all expectations of virtue are, at best, problematic:

> For, as Health is but one Thing, and has been always the same, whereas Diseases are by thousands, besides new and daily Additions; So, all the Virtues that have been ever in Mankind are to be counted upon a few Fingers; but his Follies and Vices are innummerable, and Time adds hourly to the Heap. (50)

In Swift's *A Digression concerning* Criticks the satiric voice expounds the theory of the TRUE Critic as "a Hero born" (94). Swift has in mind both Milton's and Toland's use of the heroic virtue of Hercules as a type for the antitype, Christ. Swift's satiric implication is that Hercules is the type foreshadowing the heroic deeds in learning, religion, and governance of the antitypes Milton and Toland—and, by extension, all moderns. But the heroic virtue of the TRUE Critic is a mixed blessing to mankind: in pointed references to *Paradise Lost* (vii.26) and Toland's *Clito* (1700), an heroic poem in the Miltonian vein, the satiric voice notes that "Heroick Virtue it self hath not been exempt from the Obloquy of Evil Tongues" (94). Swift relishes using the last phrase as a boomerang; in a bitter personal reference in *Paradise Lost* Milton had lamented "the obloquy of evil tongues" of public hostility in "the evil days" of the Restoration (*PL* vii.26). Once again Swift plays on Milton's jeremiad despair. For Milton, Christ is the divine antitype of heroic virtue, justifying taking heroic virtue beyond Aristotle's requirement that the practitioner become superhuman and godlike and making the truly virtuous man a true image of God (*Milton Encyclopedia* 3: 180).

Toland's *Clito* had "made bold" to equate his own modern agenda with that of "antient Heroes" (5) and proclaimed that he too wished to slay monsters with a hero's rage like a modern Hercules:

> BUT what if Tyrants ne'er heard of more?
> What serves it equal Freedom to restore,
> So long as other Monsters, worse than they,
> Rule all Mankind with a despotic Sway?
> These are fit Objects of a Hero's rage;
> But where's the HERC'LES to redeem the Age? (14)

Neither Toland nor Swift had any doubt about the answer. But Swift's own "evil tongue" answers the rhetorical question in the *Tale,* posing for Toland and his tribe a mortally self-sacrifical labor. If they would truly be the antitype of Hercules, then let them commit suicide like him:

> Antient Heroes [like Hercules, Theseus, and Perseus] . . . were in their own Persons a greater Nuisance to Mankind, than any of those Monsters they subdued;

and therefore, to render their Obligations more Compleat, when all *other* Vermin were destroyed, should in Conscience have concluded with the same Justice upon themselves: as Hercules most generously did. . . . It would be very expedient for the Publick Good of Learning, that every *True Critick,* as soon as he had finished his Task assigned, should immediately deliver himself up to Ratsbane, or Hemp, or from some convenient *Altitude,* and that no Man's Pretensions to so illustrious a Character, should by any means be received, before That Operation were performed. (94–95)

Militant heroic virtue and the TRUE critic go arm in arm in the thinking of Milton and Toland—and in the voices of the *Tale.* At one time using the *begats* of the Old Testament and more than once referring to the labors of Hercules, Swift traces the "Heavenly Descent" of the TRUE CRITIC from Momus to Dennis and remarks the "close Analogy . . . to Heroick Virtue" (95). From the evidence, Swift "reasoned" that the TRUE critic is "a *Discoverer* and *Collector of Writers Faults.* . . . [which] of necessity distill into their own" (95).

Without pausing to feel any stings of the negative innuendos in the satiric discourse, the persona hastens to appropriate the satiric voice's definition of a TRUE critic as one "laid down by me" (96). He feels compelled to defend himself, not against the thrust of the satire which, as usual, does not penetrate, but against the distinction between ancient and modern, wherein as self-conscious modern he feels most vulnerable. He must prove that the wholly acceptable definition of TRUE critic has its roots in antiquity and did not derive stillborn from a modern brain. By the most convoluted logic, the persona establishes that TRUE critics indeed existed among the ancients—who, "highly sensible of their many Imperfections," were reduced to typology, satire, or "Panegyrick upon the *True Criticks,* in Imitation of their *Masters,* the *Moderns*" (97). As if to verify his credentials as a superior modern and TRUE critic, devoted to writers' faults and weaknesses, the persona prefaces this analysis with the obligatory panegyric and catechism of a modern disciple, alluding to "our Noble *Moderns;* whose most edifying Volumes I turn indefatigably over Night and Day, for the Improvement of my Mind, and the Good of my Country" (96). Read Toland as the one lauding and transcribing from Milton, Harrington, Ludlow, Fontenelle, Perrault, and Locke.

Obviously contradictions exist between the satiric voice and the persona and within the persona's rationale. Swift's TRUE critic is TRUE only to the persona. The satiric voice's exemplar, a *true,* true critic would look for excellences—the sublime and the admirable—rather than faults in authors, restoring ancient learning in the process. The persona's TRUE critic will continue to exalt his own modern kind, the fault-finders, through obsequious praise, according plaudits to those who tear down even as they fill the void with their presumed superior intellectual power and political agendas for the public good. The heroically virtuous moderns annihilate the ancients, who are both dead and typologically doomed to be superseded by the moderns.

Milton is the primary example of the TRUE critic for the satiric voice, the persona, and Toland. Toland's *Life* makes much of Milton's attacks on prelatical episcopacy in his mature years and even in his youth:

> In the second Book he [Milton] continues his Discourse of Prelatical Episcopacy, which, according to him, is opposite to Liberty: he deduces the History of it down from its remotest Original, and shews, "that in *England* particularly it is so far from being, as they commonly allege, the only Form of Church-Discipline agreable to Monarchy, that the mortallest Diseases and Convulsions of the Government did ever procede from the Craft of the Prelats, or was occasioned by their Pride." (29)

Toland also describes with pride Milton's anticlerical novitiate in college, where as a junior scholar Milton attacked young clergy then engaged in undergraduate theatricals:

> Passing over his serious and just Apology for frequenting Playhouses, I shall subjoin the Reason he gives why some Terms of the Stage might appear in his Writings without having learnt them in the Theater; "which was not needful," says he, "when in the Colleges so many of the young Divines, and those in next aptitude to Divinity, have bin seen so often on the Stage, writhing and unboning their Clergy Limbs to all the antic and dishonest Gestures of Trinculos, Buffoons, and Bauds: prostituting the shame of that Ministry, which either they had or were nigh having, to the eyes of Courtiers and Court Ladys, with their Grooms and Mademoiselles. There while they acted, and over-acted, among other young Scholars I was a Spectator; they thought themselves gallant Men, and I thought them Fools; they made sport, and I laughed; they mispronounced, and I misliked; and to make up the Atticism, they were out, and I hist." (41)

Swift uses this particular passage in Toland's *Life* to confirm Milton's animosity against the priesthood and his early election as the *Tale*'s TRUE heroic critic. Paraphrasing Milton's own priggish account of his collegiate priest-hating revels, Swift traces the progress of a TRUE modern critic. The satiric voice speaks of "*Tyros's* or *junior* Scholars," the green critics, who have learned as fledglings to search for the worst in others:

> The usual exercise of these younger Students, was to attend constantly at Theatres, and learn to Spy out the *worst Parts* of the Play, whereof they were obliged carefully to take Note and render a rational Account to their Tutors. Flesht at these smaller Sports, like young Wolves, they grew up in Time, to be nimble and strong enough for hunting down large Game. For it hath been observed both

among Antients and Moderns, that a *True Critick* hath one quality in common
with a *Whore* and an *Alderman,* never to change his Title or his Nature; that a *Grey
Critick* has been certainly a *Green* one, the Perfections and Acquirements of his
Age being only the improved Talents of his Youth. (101)

Swift concludes his portrait of the TRUE modern critic in embryo by labelling
as *Malevoli* these "young wolves" (101).

In satirizing Milton and Toland at every turn in the *Tale,* Swift asks his
readers to look behind the superficial facade of their good Old Cause to the
mad havoc they wreak in its name. The madness, says the *Tale,* is an extension
of that heroic pride in their own conscience, reason, and virtue and their
consequent republican solutions. It is important for our purposes here that the
cultural historian Pocock has concentrated on seventeenth-century English
republicanism and the subsequent realignments of Old and New Whigs during
the *Tale's* composition, mainly 1697 to 1704.[20] Harrington's and Milton's
classical republican influence in the mid-seventeenth century bulked large for
their disciple, Toland, at the end. Consequently, Pocock and Robbins have
credited Toland with articulating the republican Whig canon even as it became
a last ditch challenge to the rise of the monied Whig oligarchy from the
Williamite years to its ultimate supremacy under the Hanovers. If the canon
was last ditch, it would seem that Swift was beating a dying horse, classical
republicanism. Nevertheless Shaftesbury and Rousseau revived, curried, and
mounted the horse in the eighteenth century, with telling revolutionary effects
in America and France. The influence of intellectual on political history
depends on the multiple variables of centennial time and the relative recep-
tiveness of particular space.

Following Robbins and others, Pocock summarizes Toland's role in this
critical period—again paralleling Swift's opinion of Toland's role in fashioning "the Whig canon":

> During the years to which his edition of Harrington belongs, he [Toland] wrote a
> *Life of Milton,* he partly rewrote and then published the memoirs of Edmund
> Ludlow, and he was instrumental in producing the definitive edition of [Algernon]
> Sidney's *Discourses,* to which—as has been pointed out by Blair Worden, who
> has reestablished part of Ludlow's authentic text—we had better pay close critical
> attention. Toland was in short the main actor in creating what Caroline Robbins
> has called "the Whig canon" of seventeenth-century writers venerated by the
> eighteenth-century Commonwealthmen. (*Virtue* 232)

---

[20] Pocock *Virtue* 41. The following argument develops from Pocock's thesis on separate
discourses in modern political thought. Both Pocock and this writer recognize deep indebtedness
to Caroline Robbins, Margaret C. Jacob, Christopher Hill, Blair Worden, Robert E. Sullivan, J. H.
Plumb, H. R. Trevor-Roper, and Quentin Skinner.

Pocock, however, makes "a profound distinction" between the word *libertas* in its juristic context, or negative sense, and in its humanist context with a positive sense. Toland and Milton represent the latter usage. In the former context, freedom has been balanced by rights and sovereignty:

> What mattered about a *republica* was that its authority should be *publica*. Nevertheless, to lower the level of citizen participation in a republic could end by reconstituting it as a legal monarchy, in which every man's *libertas,* even his *bourgeoisie* [freedom of the city], was protected by law which an absolute sovereign administered. In the last moments of his life King Charles I was heard to proclaim from the scaffold that the people's liberty under law had nothing to do with their having a voice in government. The juristic presentation of liberty was therefore negative; it distinguished between *libertas* and *imperium,* freedom and authority, individuality and sovereignty, private and public. This is its greatest role in the history of political thought, and it performs this role by associating liberty with right or *ius*. (*Virtue* 40)

Milton's defense of the regicide and Toland's seconding of it dismiss the discourse of *libertas* in this Roman juristic context to raise the standard of *libertas* in the classical republican or civic humanist context of virtue. Swift's quarrel is not with Machiavelli, but with Milton and Toland and their civic humanism. Their emphasis is on private conscience and private virtue, specifically the inner voice. Whether this voice is divine or secular, religious or ethical, increasingly mattered not.

While Milton, Toland, Shaftesbury, and later Adam Smith argue for individuality or self-interest guided by an inner light or reason, divine or secular, as propelling the public good, Swift denies the sanctity, validity, and sanity of such inner pure direction, considering it insincere piety foisted on the world as inspiration:

> The first Ingredient, towards the Art of Canting, is a competent Share of *Inward Light:* that is to say, a large Memory, plentifully fraught with Theological Polysyllables, and mysterious Texts from Holy Writ, applied and digested by those Methods, and Mechanical Operations already related: The Bearers of this *Light,* resembling *Lanthorns,* compact of Leaves from old *Geneva* Bibles. (278)

For Swift, the more external the self-righteousness, the more suspect the inner corruption. All private virtues masquerading as the public good end as pride: heroic, egotistic, venal, and—above all—blind and blinding. The supposedly unifying classical republican programs to be implemented after the Civil War brought instead the proliferation of dissenting sects and conflicting public directions and the ultimate return to the oppressive juristic models of Cromwell, Charles II, and James II. With these outcomes apparent, Swift distrusted the capacity of inner light, inner reason or inner anything to nurture the public good. The conglomeration of private opinions known as modern consensus would have appeared to him to be the victory of specious but seductive arguments advanced by a demagogic few: feeble substitutes for the ancient *consensus gentium.*

Modern Swift scholarship suffers from a serious neglect of the historical sweep for his ideas. Accordingly, a comparative examination of Toland's and Milton's lasting influence on intellectual historians alongside Swift's shows a contrast of scholarly extremes. Toland's extensive twentieth-century reputation incorporates the sixteenth- and seventeenth-century European intellectual backgrounds for his thinking.[21] Milton scholarship too is vast, with literally encyclopedic documentation.[22] Miltonists have smoothly integrated classical, Renaissance, Reformation, and Puritan influences into the literary criticism.[23] For the serious study of Swift, R. F. Jones's innovative 1936 work on *Ancients and Moderns* in The Battle of the Books, Miriam K. Starkman's astute *Swift's Satire on Learning in A Tale of a Tub,* Ronald Paulson's thorough study of the *Tale*'s theme and structure, John P. Harth's interdisciplinary work on Anglican rationalism, and articles by R. S. Crane, Clarence M. Webster and R. C. Olson have contributed extensively to knowledge of the seventeenth-century background for Swift's art and thinking and to the present study. Swiftians must be grateful for these researches; but parity still needs to be sought in relation to the work done on Milton and Toland. Cultural historians without literary backgrounds have ventured into Swift territory only with extreme caution, usually by way of the interdisciplinary scholarship of R. F. Jones, Philip Harth, and J. A. Downie. Unlike Milton, Swift has not paraded wisdom and virtue; rather it lies concealed in his satiric art and his private melancholic heart. Modern disinclination to accept Swift's satiric judgments and his own inclination to disguise his special vision feed on each other. Consequently, the task of digging deeply beneath the surface is as challenging as it is necessary.

But Swift's assaults on Milton are central to understanding his values. Yet we would never know their beginnings and endings—they are not limited to his early writings—or intensities from either the annals of literary or cultural history or the satirist's bold public statements. The very conditions of suppressed truths and misinformation that Swift satirized have themselves led to purposeful misdirections that, ironically, have blunted the thrust and intention of his attacks. In other words, his satires provide the opportunities for their own suppression. On the score of muting satiric statement, coteries of

---

[21] For Toland's European background and influence, see Margaret C. Jacob, *The Radical Enlightenment Pantheists, Freemasons and Republicans.* Also see Giancarlo Carabelli.

[22] *A Milton Encyclopedia.* ed. William B. Hunter, Jr. 9 vols.

[23] See Harold Fisch, Michael Fixler, William G. Madsen.

researchers have protected their circles by agreeing to keep the iron filings in neat arrays: in this cumulatively excluding process, facts that threaten entire configurations of modern scholars are demagnetized at their source in a process that seems less deliberate than an unorganized and unwitting conspiracy of limitation based on ingrained prejudices and centuries-old conditioning of the modern mind. On the score of Swift's own secrecy, however, he himself must bear the blame. For example, he practiced a double policy with respect to Marsh, who could and did block his career. He attacked him covertly but mercilessly in his satires while sometimes placating him—even kowtowing to him—publicly.

Whatever positions against the moderns Swift articulated between 1697 and 1712, Milton was a principal symbolic adversary throughout his productive literary life. His lifelong animus against Milton is a prime instance of the long concealment in which the satirist implicated himself. When this animus is understood in the context of conflicting discourses, Milton's buoyant expectancy and Swift's resigned melancholy about modern man finally come into focus.

In this clash, Swift juxtaposes four critical code words: *wealth* and *power* are aligned against *wisdom* and *virtue*. The latter couplet, as we have seen, is a Miltonian and Tolandic byword. Wealth and power are Swift's conjoined modern enemies just as wisdom and virtue are Milton's allied republican friends. In his *An Argument against Abolishing Christianity*, Swift refers ironically to "our present Schemes of Wealth and Power" (*PW* 2:28) with the merantilist Whigs the target of the *Argument*'s indignation.[24] It may increase understanding of the context to remember that Milton, the poet of classical republicanism, had appropriated what Swift, the poet of classical satire, had always thought more rightfully his to elucidate: wisdom, virtue, the melancholy spirit, the ideal, classical and Old Testament allusions, and human nature. In his lifelong quest for restitution, Swift points to the quest for wealth and power among all republicans, belying the flaunted virtue of Milton and the vaunted wisdom of the ambitious mercantilist Whigs. As late as 1729, Swift accused Milton and his Whiggish descendants of succumbing to "the charms of wealth and power" over the rigors of conscience. *Wealth and power* epitomizes Swift's charge against Milton and the emerging mercantilist Whigs in contrast with their facades of wisdom and virtue. As he has himself lost out on venal goals, Swift feels that what they have hid behind—wisdom and virtue—are rightfully his.

---

[24] See Adams, *Mood* 92–93.

To maintain his indictment, even in 1729 Swift mines *Paradise Lost* for passages to parody. Like Dante's First Circle, Book II of Milton's *Paradise Lost* finds suitable accommodations for the virtuous classical pagans in Hades:

> Others more milde,
> Retreated in a silent valley, sing
> With notes Angelical to many a Harp
> Their own Heroic deeds and hapless fall
> By doom of Battel; and complain that Fate
> Free Vertue should enthrall to Force or Chance. (*PL* 2: 546–550)

For Harold Fisch, Milton here catches the wistful, nostalgic note of Renaissance humanism, courage and virtue inevitably defeated yet mourned by poets and singers, the author among them (134). Milton also seems to identify his own gloomy fate after the Restoration with that of the virtuous abandoned commonswealthmen.

For Swift, however, philosophical melancholy is his own preserve, with no room for Milton's mawkish self-sympathy. In 1729, Swift parodied these same lines in his Horatian *A Dialogue between an Eminent Lawyer and Dr. Swift, Dean of St. Patrick's*. The parody loses all of Milton's ambivalence about the virtuous fallen angels and his hapless association with them:

> Must I commend against my conscience
> Such stupid blasphemy and nonsense?
> To such a subject tune my lyre
> And sing like one of MILTON's choir,
> Where DEVILS to a vale retreat
> And call the laws of wisdom fate,
> Lament upon their hapless fall
> That force free virtue shou'd enthrall. (*Poems* 2: 490)[25]

Swift unequivocally identifies Milton's followers and Milton himself with devils, emerging as their sworn foe, in this instance with a halo of his own.[26] Some of this material—particularly on the freethinker Thomas Woolston—anticipates his *Verses on the Death of Dr. Swift* written in 1731–32 and published in 1739. Milton's choir of virtuous pagan angels in Hades is then transformed into Republican Whig devils in Pandemonium, with Grand Whig Milton their spiritual leader.

In the *Dialogue*, the cautious lawyer tries to advise the satirist to modify his adamantine rage as the more successful authors do to accommodate the

---

[25] The *Dialogue* was not published until 1755, a decade after his death.

[26] In correspondence relating to this parody on April 6, 1987, Pocock asked, "What is Swift up to? Isn't he turning the virtuous pagans into devils, and Limbo into Pandemonium?" Parody and animus and silence on his source allow such realignments.

factions and fashions of the time at hand. If running down priestcraft be modish, as first it was in Milton's time and continues, then join the general condemnation like a true modern critic. In his answer, Swift throws the lawyer's caution to the winds. Milton and his time-serving literary descendants stand accused where most they would be excused by three separate bodies of wise law and concepts of virtue: the Hebraic, the Christian, and the classical. Swift's wicked recension cancels all of Milton's poetic conceits: heroic deeds and free virtue among the angels (and Milton himself), blind fate, fickle chance, and bad luck in battle. The satirist also effectively cancels Milton's fusion of the four classical and Christian cardinal virtues: fortitude and patient martyrdom, temperance and humility, rectitude and conformity to divine law, and active heroism and contemplative wisdom. Swift's assembly of devils measures the theological abyss between them and God. There are no wistful notes or sorrowful recollection of a bygone age in Swift's lyre. Instead, in clarion tones, he offers a major indictment of a major poet whose baleful influence has descended among us. Milton's devils, sulky cry-babies, foolishly blame fate for the just condemnation God has ordained. In Swift's epistemology, the eternal laws of wisdom—universally manifest, practically reasoned—must prevail over idiosyncratic and egoistic infused virtue.

While 1729 may seem late for Swift to take up another attack on Milton, modern scholarship has delayed even longer in recognizing Miltonian allusions, early and late. In the 1983 *Yale* edition of Swift's *The Complete Poems*, it is speculated that "Milton's choir" may appear "in *Paradise Lost, passim*, but esp. Books I and II" (Rogers 399–400, 805). Swift's attention to Milton has completely escaped David M. Vieth's 1983 comprehensive bibliography of all studies on Swift's poetry between 1900 and 1980, and the "Dialogue" has been treated only once in this century (Vieth 19). To be sure, Irvin Ehrenpreis's three-volume biography offers nine scant allusions to Milton *en passant*. Though it analyzes this particular 1729 Horatian dialogue, it is silent on the Miltonian reference.

In 1984, after Vieth's bibliography had appeared, Mitsuo Tanaka analyzed correspondences between the original Dialogue of Horace—that is, the first satire of the second book—and Swift's imitation. Though Tanaka also passes over the direct and indirect references to Milton and *Paradise Lost*, his keen analysis helps us understand why Swift did not clearly voice his feelings about Milton and his choir—shown but not clearly in the 1704 *Tale*—until 1729. Comparison of Swift's poem with the Horatian dialogue provides opportunities to understand that Swift identifies his life and work with the tradition of satire and, by extension, satirizes Milton for defaming the classical tradition.

Both Horace and Swift use the lawyer as a foil to reinforce the writing imperatives that propel their lives. Proclaiming that "write I must," Horace follows in the steps of Lucan and of Lucilius, who boldly dared "to strip off the skin with which each all bedecked before the eyes of men, though foul within." Lucilius also "laid hold upon the leaders of the people, and upon the people in their tribes, [and was] kindly in fact only to Virtue and her friends." (Swift's 1701 *Discourse* was similarly stern.) As Tanaka records, Horace too "knows well that his proper objective is 'with bitter verse to wound' the people *high and low*" (447). Tanaka, however, sets up Horace's life, work, and time as ideals that Swift's imitation and modern satire cannot match, finding in Horace's poem "an incredible amount of directness, frankness, and candour that cannot be expected from any modern satiric work" (451). Using Horace as the standard, Tanaka condemns both modern times and Swift. Swift was haughty, "sinisterly pessimistic" (456), and self-sacrificial to the point of masochism; he laid too much stress "on the general reputation of his satirical writing" (451). Tanaka concludes correctly, as does Ehrenpreis, that Swift's dialogue lacks the Horatian comfort and "tranquil detachment" and its tone "is vastly incongruous with Horace's original poem" (456).

Swift too might not disagree. From his perspective, the differences between them is mirrored in the time. Tanaka's late twentieth-century charge against modern satiric work echoes Swift's charge against the modern world *in toto*. Horace's lawyer debates with Horace about Horace's vocation, but the lawyer of Swift's dialogue is less concerned about Swift's vocation than about keeping the modern world humming. His advice is to eliminate Horace's candor for the sake of European liberalism—a cause Tanaka condemns. But so does Swift! His time is far more out of joint than Horace's was. There is a "cursed spite" that the saturnine melancholy of Swift's satiric voice must set the modern world right. His lawyer had advised him to "live like other christian fokes. . . . Commend the times, your thoughts correct and follow the prevailing sect . . ."(2: 499):

> To WOOLSTON recommend our youth
> For learning, probity, and truth,
> That noble genius, who unbinds
> The chains which fetter free-born minds,
> Redeems us from the slavish fears
> Which lasted near two thousand years,
> He can alone the priesthood humble,
> Make gilded spires and altars tumble. (*Poems* 2: 490)

In Swift's answer to the lawyer, the singers in "Milton's choir" are not poets, but prose writers: the deist Woolston and the Whiggish historian Gilbert

Burnet. After his alteration of Milton's *Paradise Lost*, Swift adds a couplet with his two damning code words that, at one and the same time, rejects a modern, materialist route for his own poetry and implies that Milton, the poet, has traded in a classical heritage in order to serve the time:

> Or, shall the charms of wealth and power
> Make me pollute the MUSES' bower? (*Poems* 2: 490)

These lines would contrast Swift and Milton on mythological, poetic, political, and prophetic grounds. Swift's abhorrence at the idea that he would "tune my lyre and sing like one of Milton's choir" and his classical allusion to "the muses' bower" leap past his contemporary prose writers, "the choir," to anticipate the oracle of Apollo that contrasts his own poetic role with Milton's. Apollo, the god of prophecy, medicine, music, poetry, morality, law, and learning pronounces—in agreement with the lawyer and Swift himself—an immortal prophecy about Swift's literary destiny immediately and thereafter:

> [Friend] As from the tripod of Apollo
> Hear from my desk the words that follow;
> Some by philosophers misled,
> Must honour you alive and dead,
> And such as know what *Greece* has writ
> Must taste your irony and wit,
> While most that are or would be great,
> Must dread your pen, your person hate,
> And you on DRAPIER's Hill must lye,
> And there without a mitre dye. (*Poems* 2: 490–91)

This oracle reverberates with overtones of the publication of *Paradise Lost* (1666), the Calves-Head Club anthem of 1693, Toland's yoking of himself at century's end with Milton and the regicide of Charles I, Swift's satiric exploitation of this yoking in the 1704 *Tale*, and his attacks on Toland and the Calves-Head Club in 1711 and 1712.

In 1703, an anonymous author, not Swift, published *The Secret History of the Calves-Head Club: or, the Republican Unmasked* purporting to reveal the secret annual meetings of those who followed in Milton's steps to celebrate the regicide of Charles I and "the subversion of our ecclesiastical and civil establishment." "A certain active Whig" had told the anonymous author "that Milton, and some other creatures of the commonwealth, had instituted this club, as he was informed, in opposition to . . . divines of the church of England" (12: 219–20). The *Secret History* also implicated Toland in the Calves-Head Club meetings in the 1690s as Swift was to do publicly nine years later, in 1712. The exposé alluded to Toland's *Life of Milton* and accused

Toland and his fellows of "restless malice" (12: 218).[27] The anthems appended to *The Secret History* tend to legitimize the unknown author's claim that the members met and did indeed advocate "No King, no Bishop" (12: 224). The Club's 1693 Anniversary Anthem seems to anticipate Swift's parody of *Paradise Lost* and his oracular prophecy in the 1729 Horatian dialogue:

> 'Tis true, religion is the grand pretence;
> But power and wealth's the mythologick sense.
> *Chor.* Apollo's pleas'd, and all the tuneful nine
> Rejoice, and in the solemn chorus join. (12: 221)

Following Bishop Peter Browne's death at Cork on August 25, 1735, Swift wrote to Archbishop William King in his own behalf. His letter to Alexander Pope on 3 September 1735 indicates how politically—and satirically—important it had been to keep secret, even from his fellow Scriblerian, his use of Browne in the *Tale* ("I never read much of his works"). At the same time, it reveals his lifelong dilemma: how reconcile "the charms of wealth and power" and a bishopric with his war against tyrannic oppressions in Ireland and in the world:

> We have a Bishop dead Dr. Bram [Browne] of Cork, the most speculative writer of his Age, and as Scholars tell me, excellent in his way, but, I never read much of his works. I hope the D of D now the Parlmt here is to meet will find a successor for once among the Whig Divines here, and yet those they named for Candidates are the very worst they could pick up. This Kingdom is now absolutely starving; by the means of every oppression that can possibly be inflicted on mankind—shall I not visit for these things sayth the Ld. You advise me right, not to trouble about the world. But oppressions torture me, and I cannot live without meat and drink, nor yet without money; and Money is not to be had, except they will make me a Bishop. . . . (*Corr.* 4: 385)

In this letter lurks the belated suspicion that the roles of ancient satirist and modern bishop are incompatible. His resignation about preferment reinforces the oracle of the 1729 Horatian dialogue that he will in Ireland "without a mitre die" (2: 400). Swift is thus left with the satirist's allegiance to the Greek gods who have cloaked him in the mantle of righteous indignation and branded him, like Cassandra, Kronos's anointed outcast: the prophetic messenger of modern doom.

---

[27] For full discussion of *The Secret History,* see Howard William Troyer.

CHAPTER FIVE

SHAFTESBURY: VIRTUE TRAMPLED

> But Heroic Virtue it self hath not been exempt
> from the Obloquy of Evil Tongues.
>
> *Tale* 94

Though Swift abused John Toland overtly in political writing and covertly in satire from 1701 to 1711, there is only one public record of Toland's retaliation. In 1714 Toland characterized Swift as "that profligate Divine, who, prostituting his sacred function, has sold himself for hire to Iniquity, vilely turning State-Buffoon to a couple of the greatest State Mountebanks [Oxford and Bolingbroke] in the World."[1] By then, Toland was anxious over the fate of the Protestant Hanoverian succession which he had helped Oxford fashion over a decade earlier. He was also still bitter that Swift had replaced him in Oxford's favor in 1711.

In this same Whig piece, he depreciates Swift's nonsatiric and generally maligned *Proposals for Correcting, Improving and Ascertaining the English Tongue* (1712) (*PW* 4:3–21) as encouraging wits to engage in "fruitless disputes . . . endless disquisitions . . . of no advantage to themselves or the World" (21).[2] Quoting Toland on the *Proposals,* Louis A. Landa's Introduction in Swift's *Works* expands on the "Whiggish disparagement": Toland "characterized the project as a cunning job of villainy intended to divert 'the most pregnant wits from studying the Prosperity of their Country, or examining into any Mismanagement' (21)" (*PW* 4. xiv).

If Toland's 1714 hostile comment about Swift, his political enemy, registers disdain, his reaction stands in marked contrast to the severe shock and hurt shown by his friend Anthony Ashley Cooper, later the Third Earl of Shaftesbury,[3] on discovering his virtue assailed and himself a major victim in the *Tale.* Shaftesbury, in fact, found his central role in the *Tale* doubly galling. One important reason is that, exasperatingly, Swift gives pride of place to the first, pirated edition of Shaftesbury's—still Lord Ashley—monumental *An*

---

[1] [John Toland]. *The Grand Mystery Laid Open* 6.

[2] For typical reaction to the *Proposals,* see David Nokes, 97: Swift's "frequent calls for curbs on press freedom all indicate radical, authoritarian, even Utopian intentions."

[3] Anthony Ashley Cooper, Lord Ashley, referred to in the text by his later title, Shaftesbury.

Inquiry Concerning Virtue in Two Discourses brought out by Toland in 1699. Shaftesbury tried so hard to suppress the entire unauthorized edition, representing betrayal by his friend, that only five copies are extant today. But Swift ferreted out a copy and made "Book the Second. Of the *Obligations* to Virtue" of the 1699 *Inquiry* the centerpiece of *A Tale of a Tub*'s climactic Digression on Madness—essentially a point-by-point refutation of the Shaftesbury-Toland *Inquiry*. But it was still more galling that Swift eloquently exposed essential flaws in the *Inquiry*'s moral philosophy and in Shaftesbury himself—flaws that escaped the great Enlightenment figures in England and on the Continent who subsequently built moral edifices on the *Inquiry* and the man.

In 1949 A. Owen Aldridge assembled all that is known of the 1699 *Inquiry*;[4] and in 1977, David Walford prepared an edition of the *Inquiry* with an Introduction that painstakingly distinguishes, line-by-line, between the 1699 and the authorized 1714 versions. As Walford notes, the 1711 corrected version and the 1714 posthumous, definitive version of the *Inquiry* were each published, respectively, as Treatise IV in Volume II of the first (1711) and second (1714) editions of Shaftesbury's *Characterisks* (xi). On the impact of the two editions, Aldridge finds that "the influence of the 1699 edition of *An Inquiry* was negligible; the influence of the same ideas in the *Characteristics* (1711, 1714) was tremendous" (210).

The influence of the 1711 *Inquiry* crystallizing, systematizing, and elegantly presenting seventeenth-century Neoplatonic thought was indeed profound on the moral philosophy of Hutcheson, Rousseau, Hume, and Adam Smith and pervasive in contributing to the change in sensibility in the mid-eighteenth century in Europe.[5] With relation to the *Tale,* Aldridge assures readers that "since the outline and fundamental principles of the 1699 version are essentially the same as those of 1711, as far as thought is concerned the earlier version is not 'abortive,' and the revision did not consist in 'completing' the treatise" (212). It is clear that what Swift recognized about the *Inquiry,* even in its unauthorized state, was its synthesis of sixteenth- and seventeenth-century Protestant and Neoplatonic concepts; their secular, social, material, and millenarian attractiveness made the work a compelling, moral philosophy—a modern development the satirist abhorred.

In considering Shaftesbury's reaction to Toland and the 1699 edition, both Aldridge and Walford have uncovered inconsistencies. Like the *Tale,* the *Inquiry* had a long incubating period. Started in 1689, it was passed around in

---

    [4] "Two Versions of Shaftesbury's *Inquiry Concerning Virtue.*"

    [5] See Ernst Cassirer and R.S. Crane "Suggestions Toward a Genealogy of the 'Man of Feeling'."

draft form from 1691 and "somehow" came into Toland's hands "during Lord Ashley's absence in Holland":

> With characteristic unscrupulousness, and without Lord Ashley's knowledge, Toland had it published. . . . On the one hand, he [Ashley] is angered at the premature publication of the book and attempts to prevent its dissemination by buying up as much of the impression as he can. On the other hand, it is apparent from a letter, dated 21 July 1701, from Shaftesbury to Pierre Des Maizeaux, that he had actually engaged him to make a French translation of the book. (Walford ix–x)

Walford attributes Shaftesbury's anger to Toland's style that is "appallingly repetitious, cumbersome, undisciplined and wholly lacking in that polished lucidity and epigrammatic elegance for which Shaftesbury's writing is rightly famed." Nevertheless, he concurs with Aldridge that, despite changes in emphasis, "the thought remains largely unmodified" (xi).

Although it cooled after the 1699 edition, the friendship between Shaftesbury and Toland had a common ground, as F. H. Heinemann has deduced from their correspondence between 1698 and 1705. Both men belong to a tradition of European thinkers beginning in the late Renaissance who sought to convert esoteric intellectual reforms in learning and religion into exoteric political action:

> Their common aim was Protestant policy; they fought for a Protestant succession in England and for the Protestant principle that men should obey the decision of their own conscience. Both loved with equal ardour antiquity, and religious and political liberty, and tried to combine the contrary principles of Renaissance and Reformation, arriving, however, at very different results. Both are free-thinkers, belonging to the same stage in the movement of enlightenment and making the same distinction of esoteric and exoteric philosophy. Both follow the 'natural light,' but the one [Shaftesbury] interprets it as sense, especially as moral sense, the other [Toland] as reason.[6] (46–47)

Shaftesbury was more deeply troubled by Swift's abuse than by Toland's piracy for several reasons. Just as Swift realized that in undermining the *Inquiry* he had met larger quarry than Toland's works, Shaftesbury understood that—though his thought had been more easily parodied because it suffered from Toland's extravagant style and lacked the elegance of his own—beyond the style of the satirized material something more devastating was taking place. Swift's insolent invention struck home in satirizing Shaftesbury's *ideas* in the Digression on Madness.

In the Digression, Swift does not rest content with only parodying and dialectically challenging the benevolent philosopher's philosophical discourse. The satirist seems determined to make a lasting enemy of the moral

---

6 "John Toland and the Age of Reason."

philosopher by shaking Shaftesbury literally from his virtuous moorings. On all counts, he succeeds. Swift draws from the *Inquiry* what is hypothetical or abstract to its author—the definition of a vicious man—and then makes it real by giving all of the Shaftesburian concept of ugliness to the *Tale*'s satiric voice.

Shaftesbury's *Inquiry* thus lends directing scope and immense literary power to Swift's concentrated viciousness in the Digression. Shaftesbury had castigated those vicious misanthropes, inattentive to the private and public good, who take "unnatural and barbarous delight in beholding torments, and in viewing those spectacles of horror with satisfaction and joy . . . a gay and frolicsome delight in what is injurious to others; a sort of wanton mischievousness and pleasure in what is destructive" (*Inquiry* 185–86). Swift eagerly leaps at this invitation. The satiric voice in the Digression on Madness seeks to fulfill every credential required in Shaftesbury's definition of a vicious, deranged, unnatural individual. In Swift's zeal to be noxious—in fidelity to the fastidious Shaftesbury's definition of the odious—the satiric voice literally pushes aside the persona as projector until the conclusion of the Digression when he is allowed back to present the political qualifications of the inmates of Bedlam for select offices in the modern state.

How deeply the ill-bred and underground Swift had offended his aristo-cratic and moral sensibilities[7] may be seen in the Earl's letters to John Lord Somers (1705 and 1707/8) and Pierre Coste (1712), as well as in his revisions of the *Inquiry* in the *Characteristics*—revisions designed both to amend Toland's faulty diction and to answer the *Tale*'s Digression.

Swift takes special pleasure in offending Shaftesbury's delicate sensi-bilities by projecting the *Tale*'s vicious, misanthropic satiric voice; but he is equally at pains to discredit Shaftesbury's hero, the diametrically opposite man of virtue, by using arguments annoyingly developed by the vicious satiric voice to bring into question the beneficial results that Shaftesbury confidently predicts will result from the lofty public acts of the virtuous man. In positions that the Digression on Madness diametrically opposes, Shaftesbury argues that the pleasures of the mind enormously outstrip any and all pleasures of the body, that the highest pleasure of the mind is virtue, that this virtue unites the private and public good, and that only through such mental enjoyments and pleasures can humankind, singly and collectively, attain happiness. Thus the crux of the philosophical argument between the 1699 *Inquiry* and the 1704 *Tale* focuses on whether human happiness is an extension of the pleasures of

---

[7] Toland had also offended them. Aldridge correctly assesses Shaftesbury's aesthetics: "As a prose stylist Shaftesbury was, next to Addison, perhaps the most influential writer of the Augustan Age" (207).

the profoundly thoughtful, virtuous mind (Shaftesbury) or the pleasures of the profoundly deluded, wayward body (Swift).

Here is Shaftesbury's extreme thesis—puffed up with Toland's verbosity:

> THE pleasures of the Mind, being allowed, therefore, superior to those of the Body, it follows, that whatever can create to any intelligent Being a constant flowing, a series or train of mental Enjoyments, is more considerable to his Happiness, than that which can create to him the same constant course or train of sensual ones of the Body. (*Inquiry* 108)

Shaftesbury concludes the *Inquiry* with an apostrophe to virtue. Of all the mental enjoyments and pleasures—

> *Virtue,* which of all Excellences and Beauties is the chiefest and most amiable; *that* which is the Prop and Ornament of human Affairs, which upholds Societies, maintains Union, Friendship and Correspondence amongst men; that by which Countries, as well as private Families, flourish and are happy; and for want of which every thing comely, conspicuous, great, and worthy amongst Mankind, must perish and go to ruin; *that single Quality,* thus glorious in its effects, and of this good to all Society, and to Mankind *in general,* is, after this manner, equally a Happiness and a Blessing to each Creature in *particular* possessing it, and is *that* by which alone Men can be happy, and without which he can never but be miserable. (*Inquiry* 199)

On what constitutes happiness, whether its origin is mental or sensual, the Digression on Madness could not disagree more. Consequently, the satiric voice makes short shrift of Shaftesbury's primary thesis that happiness is strictly a matter of the pleasures of the mind and not those of the bodily senses. Wickedly, it concludes otherwise:

> Those Entertainments and Pleasures we most value in Life, are such as *Dupe* and play the Wag with the Senses. For, if we take an Examination of what is generally understood by *Happiness,* as it has Respect, either to the Understanding [the mind] or the Senses, we shall find all its Properties and Adjuncts will herd under this short Definition: That, *it is a perpetual Possession of being well Deceived.* (*Tale* 171)

How essential the step-by-step argument of the *Inquiry* is to Swift may be understood by analyzing the step-by-step design of the *Tale*'s climactic section. The Digression on Madness, Section IX, is a closely reasoned attack combining under the single head of madness three categories: imperial conquests immemorial (governance), new philosophic systems (learning), and new religions (religion). In Swift's view, tyrannical forces had been congealing since the Reformation and the rise of science to create a mad, modern European society in these three institutional spheres. Moribund monarchies,

Rosicrucians, the Royal Society, Neoplatonists, seventeenth-century Puritans, dissenters generally—all are of one modern piece to him. He unites them by diagnosing them all as suffering from his invented disease of madness, "my phenomenon of vapours."[8]

Shaftesbury is crucial to the central satire of the Digression on Madness on all philosophic systems, or learning, but Swift also uses him in his initial attack on absolute monarchs, or governance. In the first category, governance, in ascribing imperial conquests to his mad vapours, the satirist obliquely challenges one of Shaftesbury's basic premises—the one that guarantees virtues everywhere because rewards and punishments are meted out fairly in this life. Because Swift was highly skeptical of the validity of this guarantee, he confronted Shaftesbury about it in the *Tale* and much later in his undated sermon "On the Testimony of Conscience." In the definitive Oxford edition of Swift, Landa notes that this late sermon argues specifically with Shaftesbury's 1711 *Characteristics* including the *Inquiry*. He says that the sermon reflected

> the contemporary tendency to make the doctrine of future rewards and punishments the central doctrine in Christian ethics and to view Christianity as a system of prudential morality, a set of regulations for the well-governing of the passions. But more particularly, in this sermon Swift enters the controversy over the conception of conscience—"a Word extreamly abused by many People." Passing quickly over the dissenters' plea for liberty of conscience, he devotes himself mainly to an attack upon the heterodox view that conscience functions independently of the laws of God. This view was formulated persuasively in Swift's day by the Earl of Shaftesbury, whose *Characteristics* (1711) profoundly disturbed many readers. (*PW* 9.114)

In attacking the same ethical doctrine in the earlier *Tale*'s Digression on Madness, Swift borrows conveniently from an anonymous pamphlet ascribed to Robert Day, *Free Thoughts in Defence of a Future State* (1700). Day is the only other contemporary known to have replied to the scarce Toland edition of Shaftesbury's *Inquiry*.[9]

Shaftesbury had contended that virtue and vice would not be judged in another life, but in this one. Day, like Swift early and late, could not imagine that "every sin meets with adequate punishment or pain in this life; and every good deed with adequate reward or advantage" (30). Day's contrary illustration was Louis XIV:

---

[8] For a full analysis of this "disease" in Galenic and Paracelsian terms, see below, pp. 159–78.

[9] See A. O. Aldridge, "Shaftesbury's Earliest Critic."

> What a World of barbarous Injuries has a certain mighty Potentate caused to be committed for the enlargement of his Dominions, and the increase of his Glory? . . . With what odious Insolence has he treated not only independent States and Commonwealths, but also crowned heads, in point of due honour his equals? . . . But where's the adequate Punishment or Pain all this while? (30–31)

Swift adapts the illustration to the argument of his Digression:

> I have read somewhere, in a very antient Author [Day?], of a mighty King, who, for the space of above thirty Years, amused himself to take and lose Towns; beat Armies, and be beaten; drive Princes out of their Dominions; fright Children from their Bread and Butter; burn, lay waste, plunder, dragoon, massacre Subject and Stranger, Friend and Foe, Male and Female. (165)

Nowhere to Day's or Swift's knowledge or in real life had Louis XIV received the appropriate punishment for his behavior that Shaftesbury confidently asserted is meted out to evil men. Having rendered Shaftesbury's ethical principle nugatory, Swift raises his own psychiatric one in this sphere of governance. In keeping with his satiric view that bodily functions always control the mind—and there is constant commerce among them—Swift attributes all of the monarch's activities to the disposition of the mad vapour, or spirit, in his system:

> At last, the *Vapour* or *Spirit* which animated the Hero's Brain, being in perpetual Circulation, seized upon that Region of the Human Body, so renown'd for furnishing the *Zibeta Occidentalis* [Paracelsus's term], and gathering there into a Tumor, left the rest of the World for that Time in Peace. . . . The same Spirits which, in their superior Progress would conquer a Kingdom, descending upon the *Anus* conclude in a *Fistula*. (165–66)

These preliminaries in the Digression introduce the reader to Swift's satires on conquests, or governance, and the legacy of Paracelsian medicine; but the next five pages, at the core of the Digression on Madness, present Swift's parody, satire, and dialectic aimed at the moral philosophy of Shaftesbury's *Inquiry* and, by extension, all modern theosophic systems. The reader is thus led from the sphere of governance to the more pivotal one of learning. As philosophic illustration, the style, language, metaphors, and arguments of Shaftesbury's 1699 *Inquiry* carry the burden of Swift's larger proof.

Shaftesbury's benevolent philosophy, even as articulated in Toland's edition, derives from Plato and Plotinus interpreted by the Cambridge Platonists Whichcote and Cudworth. Just as the Cambridge Platonists had moved Anglican divines toward rationalism and benevolent latitudinarianism, they moved Shaftesbury toward a secular natural religion and nominal deism. In turn the *Inquiry,* trimmed and rephrased more elegantly in the *Characteristics*

(1711), had a profound influence on the secular benevolent tradition in literature, philosophy, and cultural life throughout eighteenth-century Europe.

For Swift, Louis XIV illustrates mad imperial conquests in governance and Shaftesbury mad philosophic systems in learning within a complex of tyrannies, old and new, traditional and reformist, impinging on the modern world. The Digression attacks Rosicrucians, Puritanism, and modern medicine with equal vigor—along with Cambridge Platonism, Epicurean atomism, Anglican rationalism, deism, and the new secular benevolent tradition. Since all of the victims are mad, modern, and coalescing what is new, their differences seem less significant to the satirist than their similarities. (In turn, the *Tale* and its unknown author were soon attacked with equal vehemence by authors of widely disparate persuasions in governance, learning, and religion.)

After his diagnosis of the political freedoms accorded diseased monarchs, Swift turns to the influential and tyrannical equals of mad monarchs—the philosophers, ancient and modern, disporting at large in the mad empire of reason:

> LET us next examine the great Introducers of new Schemes in Philosophy, and search till we can find, from what Faculty of the Soul the Disposition arises in mortal Man, of taking it into his Head, to advance new Systems with such an eager Zeal, in things agreed on all hands impossible to be known: from what Seeds this Disposition springs, and to what Quality of human Nature these Grand Innovators have been indebted for their Number of Disciples. (166)

"Of this Kind" are the moderns Paracelsus, Descartes, "and others" (166). These "others" include the juxtaposed Neoplatonic moralist Shaftesbury and the Rosicrucian empiricist John Heydon. The satirist intends to establish that all "these great Introducers" and "Grand Innovators" (166) are essentially mad, differing not one whit from Louis XIV:

> For, what Man in the natural State, or Course of Thinking, did ever conceive it in his Power, to reduce the Notions of all Mankind, exactly to the same Length, and Breadth, and Height of his own? Yet this is the first humble and civil Design of all Innovators in the Empire of Reason. (166–67)

That the philosophers and their disciples are all in agreement and all mad, Swift "proves" using two metaphors: "my *Phaenomenon* of *Vapours*" and Shaftesbury's "easy and familiar comparison" of the human passions with the strings of a musical instrument (*Inquiry* 97).

Parodying Shaftesbury, Swift conjectures that for mad philosophers to acquire disciples depends on confident tuning:

> And, I think, the Reason is easie to be assigned: For there is a peculiar *String* in the Harmony of Human Understanding, which in several individuals is exactly of

the same Tuning. This, if you can dexterously screw up to its right Key, and then strike gently upon it; Whenever you have the Good Fortune to light among those of the same Pitch, they will, by a secret necessary Sympathy, strike exactly at the same time. (*Tale* 167)

Shaftesbury argues that if the strings, "tho in ever so just proportion one to another, are strained however beyond a certain degree, it is more than the Instrument will bear; and by this the Instrument is abused, and its effect lost" (*Inquiry* 97).

Swift totally agrees with this metaphor on the human passions:

> If you chance to jar the String among those who are either above or below your own Height, instead of subscribing to your Doctrine they will tie you fast, call you Mad, and feed you with Bread and Water. (*Tale* 168)

Swift finds the rest of Shaftesbury's argument just as germane to parody:

> The same degree of strength which winds up the Cords of *one,* and fits them to a Harmony and Consort, may in *another* burst both the Cords and Instrument it self. . . . (*Inquiry* 98)

> [While each beast] is exactly well fitted for the good of their own Species; Man in the mean time, vicious and unconsonant man, lives out of all rule and proportion, contradicts his Principles, breaks the Order and Oeconomy of all his Passions, and lives at odds with his whole Species, and with Nature. . . . (*Inquiry* 99)

> Having any passion *in too high* or *too low a degree* . . . is a Vice and moral Imperfection and is prejudicial both to the private and public System. (*Inquiry* 99–100)

Heeding Shaftesbury's anathema on vicious natures that "contradict those Affections which carry them on to operate to the public Good, the Good *of their* WHOLE" (*Inquiry* 99), Swift counsels the unwary:

> It is therefore a Point of the nicest Conduct to distinguish and adapt this noble Talent, with respect to the Differences of Persons and Times. (*Tale* 168)

And having accepted the distinctions in Shaftesbury's metaphor of human passions and musical strings, Swift deduces that on such slender adjustments one could pass for a fool in one company and a philosopher in another.[10] According to the *Tale,* the modernist Wotton, for example, by some unlucky shake of his brain, has misapplied his distortion of the mind and countenance to vain philosophy instead of opting for dreams and visions.

---

[10] Swift is aware of the metaphor's common usage. This passage is also indebted to Marsh's "Doctrine of Sounds." See above, pp. 48–49. The metaphor works in context with his total dismantling of Shaftesbury's moral philosophy.

Next, Swift blends his private metaphor for madness, "my phenomenon of vapours," with Shaftesbury's vocabulary and thrust:

> Of such great Emolument, is a Tincture of this *Vapour,* which the World calls *Madness,* that without its Help, the World would not only be deprived of those two great Blessings, *Conquests* and *Systems,* but even all Mankind would unhappily be reduced to the same Belief in Things Invisible. (169)

In the last clause, Swift, like Day, is attacking Shaftesbury's emphasis on inherently good-natured humans controlling their own destinies, thus denying a divine hand in their affairs.

Swift then goes on to tie Shaftesbury's equation of strings with passions to the philosopher's larger conceit that his entire work is mathematical demonstration.[11] This is how Shaftesbury sums up, in mathematical terms, his extended and mentally taxing *Inquiry* on virtue and vice:

> Thus have we computed, in the best manner we were able, the Good and Interest of Mankind, by enumerating and casting up all those Particulars from whence, as by way of Addition or Subtraction, that Sum or general Account of Man's Interest or Happiness in Life, is either swelled or diminished: so that the method here taken may perhaps for this reason be called a sort of *Moral Arithmetic,* and be said to have an evidence as great as may be found in Numbers, and equal to Mathematical Demonstration. (*Inquiry* 196–97)

Here is grist for Swift's parody of the extreme mental labor encountered by mathematicians in solving complex and intricate problems. The cerebrations involved in Shaftesbury's strings' metaphor and in his own vapours' metaphor are mathematically relevant satiric cases. It is therefore "a very delicate Point" to know

> upon what *Species* of Brain it ascends; [and] how this numerical Difference in the Brain, can produce Effects of so vast a Difference from the same *Vapour,* as to be the sole point of Individuation between *Alexander the Great, Jack of Leyden,* and Monsieur *Des Cartes.* (169–70)

The satiric voice contends that this higher calculus on strings, vapours, human passions, and madness "strains my Faculties to their highest Stretch" (170) but that his four lines of asterisks provide "a clear Solution of the Matter" (82). He thus modulates from the metaphors of musical strings and vapours on

---

[11] Remembering Shaftesbury and Marsh, the music/mathematical satire is again developed in Book III of *Gulliver's Travels.* Swift's recurring use of *Tale* metaphors, illustrations, and comparisons, such as Browne's analogy of the blind man and the one to follow here, reinforces the evidence for the lifelong consistency of his positions and alerts the reader that the victims of the *Tale*'s satire are usually specific major contemporary figures Swift will never forget.

the vagaries of disordered human behavior to a numerical problem reducing string vibrations to "numerical Difference" and requiring the stickiest logical proof.

In each instance, after exhausting cerebrations, Shaftesbury's and Swift's closing statements on their numerical demonstrations of happiness and madness in life, respectively, are the proofs that clear the way for their opposite conclusions on the transcendence of the mental and bodily pleasures. "For," says Shaftesbury, on one side,

> it seems to us, that there has not been any degree of certainty wanting in what has been said concerning the preferableness of the mental Pleasure to sensual. (*Inquiry* 197)

Swift, on the other side, defends the priority of the senses over any aspect of the understanding:

> If we take this Definition of Happiness [being well deceived], and examine it with Reference to the Senses, it will be acknowledged wonderfully adapt. How fade and insipid do all Objects accost us that are not conveyed in the Vehicle of *Delusion?* How shrunk is every Thing, as it appears in the Glass of Nature? So, that if it were not for the Assistance of Artificial *Mediums,* false Lights, refracted Angles, Varnish, and Tinsel; there would be a mighty Level in the Felicity and Enjoyments of Mortal Men. (172)

Swift's subsequent attack on the benevolent mind is directed against Shaftesbury's confident, reiterated premise:

> Whatever can create to any intelligent Being a constant flowing, a series or train of mental Enjoyments, is more considerable to his Happiness, than that which can create to him the same constant course or train of sensual ones of the Body. (*Inquiry* 108)

Swift turns the equation around. What follows next in the Digression on Madness are probably its most remembered, analyzed, and oft-quoted passages, looked at more closely below: credulity and surfaces versus curiosity and the depth of things, the woman flayed and altered for the worse, the carcass of the beau laid open by degrees only to find "the Defects increase upon us in Number and Bulk" (173–174), the mock ironic plea for a philosopher to patch up the imperfections of nature, and the final restatement of Swift's definition of happiness:

> This is the sublime and refined Point of Felicity, called *the Possession of being well deceived;* The Serene Peaceful State of being a Fool among Knaves. (174)

Let us all live happily in the ideal, insulated world of Shaftesbury, since the real world is a painful, vicious mistake.[12]

In the full text of the above paragraph Swift parodies and refutes, in great detail and profound subtlety, the benevolent philosopher's intricate comparisons and contrasts of the outside and the inside of both the mind and the body. The entire *Tale* concentrates on the differences between inner and outer, mind and body, soul and mind, microcosm and macrocosm, inner light and God's omnipotence, the astral psyche and divine nature. Inner-outer differences form the major jest in the coats allegory, the history of religious fanaticism, the conceit of all the dissenting Jacks, and the underpinnings of Paracelsian medicine and Neoplatonism.

Like a physical anatomist—his 1711 revision actually appropriates Swift's simile of anatomy—Shaftesbury had penetrated to the inward parts of the mind to establish that the outward benevolent mind is more to be cherished than the outward sensual body. In opposition, Swift meant to establish that the outward sensual body dominates the outward benevolent mind and that any experiments inside the body reinforce the need for sensual man to concern himself only with the surfaces of things. Since Swift's position contradicts Shaftesbury's at every point, his anatomical demonstration looks at the outside and the inside of the body, mimicking the same work the philosopher did for the outside and inside of the mind in the *Inquiry*.

In it Shaftesbury sets off the inner and outer mind:

> TO HAVE THE NATURAL AFFECTIONS [such as are founded in Love, Complacency, Goodwill, and in a sympathy with the Kind or Species], IS TO HAVE THE CHIEFEST SATISFACTION AND HAPPINESS OF LIFE [his outer mind] (139). On the other hand, there are those inward parts of the mind or Temper, any one of which may receive abuse, injury, impairment, maiming, or offense.
>
> The parts and proportions of the Mind, their relation to, and dependency on one another, the connexion and frame of those Passions which constitute the Soul or Temper; in short, the whole Order or Symmetry of this *inward Part* being no less real and exact than that of the Body, yet by not being obvious to sense as that other is, it comes not into consideration. (*Inquiry* 104)

Since the inward parts hold commerce with the outward mind or integrated whole, Shaftesbury devotes a portion of his discourse to them. "Temper or Mind, that being wounded or hurt in any one particular [inward] part, the whole should be the worse for it" (*Inquiry* 105).

For Swift, Shaftesbury has expounded "that pretended Philosophy which enters into the Depth of Things, and then comes gravely back with the

---

[12] Shaftesbury and Temple were friends who Swift believed lived in the same insulated world. For understanding of Temple's ideal world, see below, pp. 137–57.

Informations and Discoveries that in the inside they are good for nothing" (173). Swift makes a quick transition from his critique of Shaftesbury's inward parts of the mind to his satiric thesis on the virtues of outer bodies and the ascendancy of sense experience over Shaftesbury's treasured natural affections. Since credulity is a more peaceful possession [of the mind] than curiosity, Swift advocates that "Wisdom which converses about the Surface":

> The two Senses, to which all Objects first address themselves, are the Sight and the Touch; These never examine further than the Colour, the Shape, the Size, and whatever other Qualities dwell, or are drawn by Art, upon the Outward of Bodies; and then comes Reason officiously [read Shaftesbury], with Tools for cutting, and opening, and mangling, and piercing, offering to demonstrate that they are not of the same consistence quite thro'. Now, I take all this to be the last Degree of perverting Nature: one of whose Eternal Laws it is, to put her best Furniture forward. (*Tale* 173)

Here Swift calls Shaftesbury's natural affections a perversion of nature—reversing Shaftesbury's meaning by making it self-evident that the senses, programmed for delusion, give no quarter to private virtue and public good.

Finally, in a brilliant parody of Shaftesbury's psychological probing of the anatomy of the inward parts of the mind—parts that determine its outer integrity—Swift undertakes an anatomy of the inner parts of the body. Stay at the surface, says the satiric voice, whether it is mind or body. Swift also presents himself as the vicious character Shaftesbury later accused him of being by seeming to be identical with the *Inquiry*'s worst case: possessed of a deranged, vicious inward mind. The satiric voice becomes a mind bent on wanton mischievousness and revelling in a "an unnatural and barbarous delight in beholding torments and in viewing [even worse in the *Tale:* in creating] those spectacles of horror with satisfaction and joy" (*Inquiry* 185–86). What could possibly incense an aesthete like Shaftesbury—or any aesthete—more than the public display, in a work of art, of this vicious mind with seeming inward derangement conducting rational, scientific experiments?

Of course, more is going on than the offending of Shaftesbury's refined sensibilities. Swift is himself sickened by the barbarities undertaken in the experimental cause of modern scientific inquiry. What he is doing is making a "spectacle of horror" of what presumably could go on in a virtuoso's closet in order to expose the insensitivity of the modern experimenter and at the same time to offend the sensitivity of the modern aesthete—demonstrating not only the barbarity of the modern virtuoso but the vulgar mischief of the satirist. Swift again hits several targets at once. What Shaftesbury finally abhors in the *Tale* is not Swift's satire of experimental science, but his viciousness in using

Shaftesbury's own anatomical premises to contradict his major pious theses of mind over matter and of the benevolent, outer mien as reflecting a pacific, inner makeup. Here is the much remarked offending passage from the Digression on Madness:

> And therefore, in order to save the Charges of all such expensive Anatomy for the Time to come; I do here think fit to inform the Reader that in such Conclusions as these, Reason is certainly in the Right; and that in most Corporeal Beings, which have fallen under my Cognizance, the *Outside* hath been infinitely preferable to the *In:* Whereof I have been further convinced from some late Experiments. Last Week I saw a Woman *flay'd,* and you will hardly believe how much it altered her Person for the worse. Yesterday I ordered the Carcass of a *Beau* to be stript in my Presence; when we were all amazed to find so many unsuspected Faults under one Suit of Cloaths: Then I laid open his *Brain,* his *Heart,* and his *Spleen;* But, I plainly perceived at every Operation, that the farther we proceeded, we found the Defects encrease upon us in Number and Bulk. (*Tale* 173–74)

The terms *universal, Mankind, the public good* and *improvement of virtue* appear throughout the *Inquiry* and are strategically placed in over 70 different places throughout the *Tale,* whose full title is *Written for the Universal Improvement of Mankind.* Swift thus mocks Shaftesbury's notions of universal benevolence, inherent human goodness, and social decorum. Then, by exposing Shaftesbury's arguments concerning the vicious, unnatural, and disordered inward parts of some minds, he makes them seem Hobbesian, a label the moral philosopher would surely detest; it was specifically to counter Hobbes that the Cambridge Platonists, the latitudinarians, and Shaftesbury developed the concept of a more natural, humane nature. Not only does Swift provide Shaftesbury's theory with his own worst case, but he offers the antic and wanton behavior of the satiric voice in the *Tale* as part of the argument. Further, by highlighting the predictable proclivities of seduced human nature, he subverts Shaftesbury's main argument that vicious elements in human nature lead to self-misery but our more instinctive inclinations are to synchronize the private and public good. Paradoxically, Swift's *Tale* achieves its ultimate success by forcing the benevolent Shaftesbury in 1712 to declare Swift his worst example of human depravity: applying the satirist's aesthetic and philosophical standards, the Digression on Madness afforded Swift pure joy, as it offers readers who understand its implications.

When Swift is confident that he has undercut the fundamentals of Shaftesbury's discourse and established his own, he mock piously asks relief from the philosopher's tortured reasoning and pleads for recognizing the omnipotence of self-deluding, sensual human nature:

> That whatever Philosopher or Projector can find out an Art to solder and patch up the Flaws and Imperfections of Nature, will deserve much better of Mankind, and

teach us a more useful Science, than that so much in present Esteem, of widening and exposing them. (174)

Swift delivers the *coup de grace* to the aristocratic nobleman, the Third Earl, and his philosophy by recommending that his physically delicate adversary retire to his estate to dabble with the superficialty of sensuous things:

> And he, whose Fortunes and Dispositions have placed him in a convenient Station to enjoy the Fruits of this noble Art; He that can with *Epicurus* content his Ideas with the *Films* and *Images* that fly off upon his Senses from the *Superficies* of Things; Such a Man truly wise, creams off Nature, leaving the Sour and the Dregs, for Philosophy and Reason to lap up. This is the sublime and refined Point of Felicity, called, *the Possession of being well deceived;* the Serene Peaceful State of being a Fool among Knaves. (174)

If there is a shred of consolation for Shaftesbury, it is that Swift acknowledges Shaftesbury's philosophy of private and public good; he believed it to be highly eccentric and open only to philanthropic men of position, wealth, and leisure, but considered it merely foolish, not knavish behavior. What Swift challenges is Shaftesbury's putative role and the pervasive corruption of the philosopher's cherished modern environment. For differing reasons, retirement from commerce with official knaves to perform good works alone in a library was ultimately Shaftesbury's and Temple's solution; and ironically, it was to be Swift's as well—first at Moor Park and later in his cathedral close.

Shaftesbury's incensed responses to the 1704 *Tale* show that he felt it necessary to juxtapose his virtuous world to Swift's vicious one. From 1705 until 1712, he was obsessed with the contrast between the trashy texture of the *Tale* and the integrity of his own writing, between the vicious world of this unknown low-life and the exquisite camaraderie he shared with Lord Somers and other articulate men of taste, wealth, and power.

Shaftesbury entrusted his unpublished works and often confided his intimate thoughts to Lord Somers. On 20 October 1705 he sent him a letter, along with the treatise later known as "Moralists":

> My Lord,—Enclosed is an odd book, without date, preface, or dedication. It might have been dedicated to you, perhaps, if it had been to be published. But the author has more kindness for you and himself than to call either name in question for meddling with such subjects. You have had a "Tale of a Tub" dedicated to you before now, but a "Tale of Philosophy" [his own manuscript] would be a coarser present to come publicly upon you as that did. (*Letters* 336)

In his letter Shaftesbury sets his own virtuous philosophy, discrete manners, use of extravagant praise, and aristocratic intimacy against the satiric

fashion—the crude insolence, scornful encomiums, and coarse intrusiveness
of Swift. He speaks of "we moderns" who may

> lend a hand upon occasion to a discerning man, help him, perhaps, out of the
> vapours and give him a good night's rest when he may want it. Is it not just that
> you, who lose so much of your rest for the public, should enjoy all the tranquillity
> or happiness that philosophy, the muses, or human wit can present you with?
> (*Letters* 339)

He is seriously concerned for and solicitous of his heroic patron. In contrast
with Swift's publicly mocking dedication of the *Tale* to Somers, Shaftesbury
sends a private dedicatory letter of commiseration suggesting that Somers, as
public figure, must needs be put upon by the disgraceful likes of the still
unknown author.

It is also apparent that Shaftesbury sets off Swift's intrusive rudeness
against his own restrained brahminism. May we surmise from this letter that
Swift's satiric dedication forestalled Shaftesbury's genuine dedication of
"The Moralist" to Somers? The letter insists on this contrast, strongly
suggesting that contemporary men of sense and influence found the dedication
of the *Tale* to Somers by a venal bookseller more demeaning and *méchant* than
satiric. Adams reached the same conclusion in 1972:

> What he [Swift] has written sounds more like a burlesque of dedications than a
> real one; when we find the dedicator touching rather heavy-handedly on such
> delicate matters as Lord Somers's physical prowess (he was short and sickly) and
> his noble lineage (he was the son of a country lawyer), and find Jonathan Swift
> voicing in *The Examiner* a ferocious personal attack on Somers for these very
> qualities,[13] we may suspect the complete and simple sincerity of Swift's attach-
> ment to Somers in 1704. (Adams, *Mood,* 84)

Seventeen months later when Shaftesbury again announces in a letter to
Somers that a new publication, *A Letter Concerning Enthusiasm,* is in hand,
his obsession with the *Tale* again intrudes. Hugh Ormsby-Lennon has discovered and commented on this unpublished March 1707/8 letter:

> When Shaftesbury wrote to Somers about his own *Letter* [*Concerning Enthusi-
> asm*] and its relationship to Swift's *Tub* [*Tale*], he apologized for the "borrowd
> hand & seeming reserved way"; a note at the top of the letter indicates that it was
> "Written in Jack's hand."[14] With its rigmarole about elusive manuscripts and "a
> certain Club of Authors"—"of worthy Character and good Estate, great Reading
> and wonderfull Curiosity in search of Books and Authors"—the letter represents

---

[13] *Examiner,* no. 27 (25 January 1710/1).
[14] "March 1707/8," Shaftesbury Papers, Sec.5, no 4, Bundle 22, *Letters 1703 & 1704* [sic],
PRO 30/24/22/4, pp. 67–68.

a necessary exercise in studied obliquity. What emerges is that "the Author of *ye Tale of a Tub*" was grouped by "Divines & University-men," willy-nilly, with "*Toland, Tindal, C——, Asgil,*" yet was, nonetheless, deemed remarkable for choosing to mock religion not "barefac'dly . . . but in so Burlesque a manner as overthrew it more effectually."[15] (Ormsby-Lennon 67)

In distinguishing Swift from Toland and the other freethinkers here, Shaftesbury is again concerned primarily with Swift's rude, underhanded treatment of serious, even sacred subjects. This letter shows the same tendency to juxtapose for Somers' supposedly discerning eye the unknown author's mean composition with his own. He again uses the Dedication to Somers as Exhibit A. As Ormsby-Lennon notes, Shaftesbury describes Swift to Somers as "your [pretended] good friend" (67).

Shaftesbury's letter to Pierre Coste, 25 July 1712, offers fewer circumlocutions against his vicious enemy, no longer veiled as "the unknown author" of the *Tale*. The fine-grained intellect now speaks assuredly of the "mixed satirical ways of raillery and irony, so fashionable in our nation":

> Witness the prevalency and first success of that detestable writing of that most detestable author of the *Tale of a Tub,* whose manner, life, and prostitute pen and tongue are indeed exactly answerable to the irregularity, obscenity, profaneness, and fulsomeness of his false wit and scurrilous style and humour. Yet you know how this extraordinary work pleased even our great philosophers themselves, and how few of those who disliked it dared declare against it.[16] (*Letters* 504)

In all three letters, written over the last seven years of his life, what a humorless stream of vituperation the benevolent philosopher visited on his sniper, Swift! It is remarkable that Shaftesbury discerns no distinction between the contrived, vicious satiric voice that contradicts the *Inquiry* in the Digression on Madness and the character of Swift himself.

If Swift read Shaftesbury's 1711 revision of the *Inquiry,* then he found in Section 138, for the first time, specific references to *anatomy* reminiscent of his own use of the word in the *Tale*'s Digression on Madness. This direct borrowing reveals a private bravura performance that went into the public writings of both men. That is, each delivers private messages and ripostes to the other that are usually over the heads of their readers. For example, in order simultaneously to link himself with and distance himself from Shaftesbury, Swift insists in his 1710 Apology for the *Tale* that he is *not* the author of

---

15 "March 1707/8," p. 68. Swift is described as "your [Somers's pretended] good Friend the Author of *the Tale of a Tub*" (p. 69).

16 Who these "great philosophers" are, Shaftesbury doesn't say. Perhaps he is being ironic. Obviously, the currency of the book—five editions—has not been matched by the storm of forthright criticism Shaftesbury believes overdue.

Shaftesbury's *A Letter concerning Enthusiasm to My Lord * * * * * [Somers]* (1708).[17] In this highly visible reference, he provokes Shaftesbury's ire by claiming that the public has noticed in his parody "a *Similitude of Style or way of thinking*" (*Tale* 6) between the two works. Of course, Swift knows, as perhaps only Shaftesbury also knew, that any similarities are simply the result of parody and satire. It is a secret shared by the adversaries only.

Adams gives us an important perspective on Swift's reference to Shaftesbury here:

> Among the varied atmospheres in which the *Tale* grew to maturity was the rather *désabusé* and worldly tone that men like Somers, Shaftesbury, and Shrewsbury (a close-knit club intimately acquainted, until his death, with Sir William Temple) carried through the world. They were tough, worldly, secular-minded men; and Swift clearly plumed himself on managing their dry, sophisticated wit as well inside the church as they did outside it. (Adams, *Mood,* 90–91)

In employing Swift's notion of "anatomy" in the revised *Inquiry* (1714), Shaftesbury intends to demonstrate—at least to the abominable Swift—that he understood and rejected Swift's satire with its philosophical point. Moreover he means to reiterate, by boldly dipping into Swiftian terminology, the fundamental thesis of correspondences between the inward and outward mind. Thus in 1714, the *Inquiry* refers to the parts and proportions of the mind: their relations, dependencies, connections, and passions "which constitute the soul or temper, may easily be understood by anyone who thinks it worth his while to study this inward Anatomy" (52).[18] Put differently, the word *anatomy* was absent from the 1699 edition, but contextually both Swift, immediately, and Shaftesbury, belatedly, realized it was the most appropriate term:

> We never trouble ourselves to consider thoroughly by what means or methods our *inward Constitution* comes at any time to be impaired or injured. The *Solutio Continui,* which bodily Surgeons talk of, is never applied in this case, by Surgeons of another sort. The notion of *a Whole and Parts* is not apprehended in this Science. We know not what the effect is, of straining any Affection, indulging any wrong Passion, or relaxing any proper and natural Habit or Inclination. (1714 *Inquiry* 52)

At a distance from the mean tactical exchanges, Swift and Shaftesbury seem to share excellences that separate them from their contemporaries. Swift

---

[17] *"Yet several have gone a farther Step, and pronounced another Book to have been the Work of the same Hand with this; which the Author directly affirms to be a thorough mistake; he having yet never so much as read that Discourse, a plain Instance how little Truth, there often is in general Surmises, or in Conjectures drawn from a Similitude of Style, or way of thinking"* (*Tale* 6).

[18] 1714 *Inquiry,* ed. Walford.

may have been more prepared to acknowledge their mutuality—if only grudgingly. Although these philosophical and aesthetic brahmins assumed diametrically opposed positions on the enduring sanctity or inevitable corruption of human nature, the force of their works derives from the fact that each marshalled the very best arguments of the ancient humors and the modern benevolent traditions to support with elegance of style.

The *Inquiry*, like the *Tale*, "seems calculated to live at least as long as our Language, and our Tast admit no great Alterations" (3). And in political and social philosophy, if not in aesthetics, Shaftesbury can number Hutcheson, Rousseau, Hume, and Adam Smith among his disciples. As for the *Tale*, acknowledgement in its Apology of a "Similitude of Style, or way of thinking" between the two writers may be mischevious on one count, but it also expresses Swift's increasingly confident assessment of the worth of the satire by 1709. After all, it is a devastating attack on Shaftesbury, Toland, Milton, and Newton. "And do they think such a Building [the Product of the Study, the Observation, and the Invention of several Years] is to be battered with Dirt-Pellets?" (10). One of the eloquent readings of human nature provided by the writers considered here—Shaftesbury's—has prevailed in the modern world. In retrospect, it is instructive to see the traditions that Swift and Shaftesbury represent—the humors and the benevolent—played out on the three-century battleground of the European novel by Fielding, Richardson, Sterne, and Smollett, as well as by Pushkin, Gogol, Dostoevski, Tolstoy, and Solzhenitsyn.

Yet evidence of the early dispute between Swift and Shaftesbury only partly illuminates the core five pages in the crucial Digression on Madness. Two other figures, the empiricists John Heydon and Paracelsus, and one group, the Puritans, must be reckoned with there. Taken together with Shaftesbury they encompass Swift's many-faceted attack on Neoplatonism— which, like all aspects of the modern consciousness, embraces disparate elements, some in opposition, that for Swift deserve equal censure for co-sponsoring the doomed condition of the present world. The passages already examined in this chapter on one plane of Neoplatonism can be considered just as fruitfully on another.

One of the difficulties in reading Swift's satire is that he aims at several discrete targets simultaneously. Thus he casts the empiricist Heydon, in addition to the satiric voice, against the idealist Shaftesbury. To be sure, he opposes them both: Heydon, the disciple of the Neoplatonic Rosicrucians— later to become the European Masonic movement—and of their spiritual father, the Neoplatonist Paracelsus, and Shaftesbury, the disciple of Whichcote and the Cambridge Platonists. Both intellectual movements, Rosicrucianism and Cambridge Platonism, descend from the fifteenth-century

Florentine school of Ficino and have remained potent intellectual forces under other guises—e.g., holistic medicine, Jungian psychology, and belief in kind and gentle human dominance over constantly replenishing nature.[19] Since the rise of the public ecological conscience in the 1960s, holistic medicine has increased its hold but nature has reasserted its dominance by exacting irreversible penalties from humans who would exploit its ecology.

It may be profitable to look again at the Digression on Madness to understand some of Swift's reasons for opposing the diverse strands of Neoplatonism. Shaftesbury demeaned the pleasures of the senses in order to exalt the pleasures of the mind; but in Heydon's slightly earlier writing Swift discovered an equally extreme, equally reasoned, equally modern, position that recognizes the priority of the senses. His argument in no sense depends on Swift's make-believe phenomenon of vapours or on his satiric definition of delusive happiness, yet, oddly and felicitously, it serves to support both. Heydon's alchemical-mystical-scientific Rosicrucian discourse is simply thrown into the breach, presumably on Swift's side. His treatise, *A New Method of Rosie Crucian physick: Wherein is shewed the Cause; and therewith their experienced Medicines for the Cure of all Diseases, Freely given to the inspired Christians* (London, 1658), "demonstrated" the empirical Rosicrucian way to happiness through the outward body, opposing Shaftesbury's "demonstrated" arithmetical way to happiness through the outward mind. Their opposite positions serve Swift's cause of demonstrating the general madness of modern philosophies.

The deception of the senses is Heydon's scientifically valid theme:

> As in vision, so also in Conceptions that arise from other senses, the subject of their inherence is not in the object, but in the Sentient; And from hence also it followeth that whatsoever accidents or qualities our senses make us think there be in the world, they be not there, but are seeming and apparitions only; the things that really are in the world without us, are those motions by which these seemings are caused; and this is the great deception of sense, which also is to be by sense corrected. (*A New Method* 17–18)

Of course, Swift is not interested in possible empirical corrections but instead builds his satiric edifice upon Heydon's concepts of the priority of sense experience and the accompanying deception lurking in all sense perceptions that the conscientious empiricist would need to record. In modulating the tone of the *Tale* to accommodate Heydon's discourse, the satiric voice warns readers that no modern philosophers would have tried to change the world if they had rested their brains in the common forms and observed

---

[19] For an analysis of the saturnine melancholy of Ficino and Swift, see below, pp. 214–20.

due humility in acknowledging their private infirmities and widespread, stubborn ignorance:

> But when a Man's Fancy gets *astride* on his Reason, when Imagination is at Cuffs with the Senses, and common Understanding, as well as common Sense, is Kickt out of Doors; the first Proselyte he makes, is Himself, and when that is once compass'd, the Difficulty is not so great in bringing over others; A strong Delusion always operating from *without* [Heydon's main contention] as vigorously as from *within.* (171)

At this point, Swift manipulates Heydon's argument on the senses:

> For, Cant and Vision are to the Ear and the Eye, the same that Tickling is to the Touch. Those Entertainments and Pleasures we most value in Life, are such as *Dupe* and play the Wag with the Senses. (171)

Then, ignoring Heydon's limitation of delusion or apparition to sense experience, Swift expands the definition to encroach on Shaftesbury's territory; delusions of the mind prevail equally with those of the senses:

> And first, with Relation to the Mind or Understanding; 'tis manifest, what mighty Advantages Fiction has over Truth; and the Reason is just at our Elbow; because Imagination can build nobler Scenes, and produce more wonderful Revolutions than Fortune or Nature will be at Expense to furnish. (171–72)

Expatiating on deceptions in the mind, Swift "advocates" concentrating on the delusive modern imagination as the womb of things instead of on the fading memory as the grave of things.

Having efficiently included the mind as delusive and thus rendered Shaftesbury's concepts of mind and happiness null and void, the *Tale* returns to Heydon's opposing arguments on the senses:

> Again, if we take this Definition of Happiness [delusion of the senses], and examine it with Reference to the Senses, it will be acknowledged wonderfully adapt. How fade and insipid do all Objects accost us that are not conveyed in the Vehicle of *Delusion?* How shrunk is every Thing, as it appears in the Glass of Nature? So that if it were not for the Assistance of Artificial *Mediums,* false Lights, refracted Angles, Varnish, and Tinsel; there would be a mighty Level in the Felicity and Enjoyments of Mortal Man. (172)

In this passage, Swift relies on several of Heydon's illustrations of apparitions to further his discourse on happiness. To quote Heydon on the glass of nature, "Every man hath so much experience as to have seen the Sun, and other visible objects by reflexion in the water and glasses" (15); on false lights, "There appeareth before the Eyes, a certain light, which light is nothing without, but an apparition only. . . . That apparition of light is really nothing but motion within" (15–16); on refracted angles, "The exterior part of the eye presseth the interiour, (the Laws of refraction still observed)" (16). And further, "I have seen them [stones with geometrical accuracy] there [Arabia], or ordinarily quinquangular, or have the sides but parallels, though the Angles be unequal" (20). As for raising the level of felicity by duping the senses through the imagination:

> *Pulchritude* is conveyed indeed by the outward senses unto the soul, but a more intellectual faculty is that which relishes it [Heydon encroaching on Shaftesbury]; as an *Astrologicall,* or better, a *Geometricall Scheam* is let in by the eyes, but the *Demonstration* is discerned by *Reason:* And therefore it is more rational to affirm, that some intellectual principle was the Author of this *Pulchritude* of things, then that they should be thus fashioned without the help of that principle: and to say there is no such thing as *Pulchritude,* and some say, there is *no way to felicity;* The first, I answer, is because some mens souls are so dull and stupid. And the second is that they never knew *The* [Rosicrucian] *way to bliss.* The first cannot relish all objects alike in that respect; the second knows not *Happiness,* nor the way to *long life,* nor the *means to Health,* nor how to *return from Age to Youth, etc,* which is as absurd and groundless as to conclude there is no such thing as *Reason* and *Demonstration,* because a natural fool cannot reach unto it. But there is such a thing as *The way to Bliss, Long life,* and certain way to *Health,* not as yet known in *England,* I will demonstrate in a Treatise by it self. (*A New Method* 19)

Since Swift denies both opposing modern reasoners—the benevolent philosopher, idealist and the Rosicrucian empiricist, dreamer—his next move in the Digression on Madness is to recommend that all reasoning philosophers, his two exemplars and other modern ones, converse with the surface of things instead of exposing weak sides, publishing infirmities, probing the depth of things and discovering "that in the inside they are good for nothing" (173). To argue for credulity over curiosity, the deluded bodily senses over the rational mind, and the surface over the inside, Swift again paraphrases Heydon:

> The two Senses, to which all Objects first address themselves, are the Sight and the Touch; These never examine further than the Colour, the Shape, the Size, and whatever other Qualities dwell, or are drawn by Art, upon the Outward of Bodies. (173)

On the sight's examining only the outer qualities of shape and colour, Heydon explains:

> Because the Image in vision consisting of colour and shape, is the knowledge we have of the qualities of the object of that Sense, it is no hard matter for a man to fall into this opinion, That the same colour and shape are the very qualities themselves. . . . (*A New Method* 6)

His argument as to the deceptiveness of surface evaluations of the senses is preamble to his examination of the physical anatomy of objects and of the eye itself.

> But that from all lucid, shining, and illuminate bodies, there is a motion pro-
> duced to the eye, and thorow the eye, to the *Optick Nerve* and so into the Brain, by
> which the apparition of light or colour is effected, is not hard to prove. (*A New
> Method* 16)

Swift's reaction to Heydon's attempt to distinguish between the apparitions of surface sense experience and the inner reality of objects and subjects, like his reaction to Shaftesbury's dissection of the mind's inward anatomy to find the sources of outward vice and private and public virtue, leads him to castigate them both as exemplars of modern reason who probe too deeply and imagine too extremely to prove too little.

While Swift's genius delighted in provoking adversaries by acting out the vicious part expected of him, that same genius simultaneously manhandled multiple targets in the *Tale* while still maintaining the focus of his satiric theme. The single sentence commenting on the "woman-flayed" offers Swift's most telling satire against those moderns from all quarters bent on reforming the European world. The tension is between modern reformation and human restoration, with restoration for Swift meaning some modicum of sanity and balance about the realities of existence and recourse to those rigorous virtues practiced by Sir Thomas More and extolled by the classical satirists in ancient times.

Having imaginatively conducted his own modern experiments, Swift reports them in a seemingly scientific treatise. He "demonstrates" the asinity of the modern way to come at useful, optimistic "truth" through probing deeply, measuring mathematically, and hinting at imaginative, new mysteries. He "proves" that the outside is preferable to the inside of things and observes that the deluded sense in human nature takes precedence over the virtuous mind, but that in such mischievous wantonness, seeming hatred of mankind, and malicious, sadistic pleasure there lies a happiness more profoundly virtuous and more acutely conscious of the public weal than Shaftesbury's and Toland's pretentious concern for the public good of mankind. His "finding" is that the mass of people in any age are so much putty in the grasp of pontificating innovators and controlling improvers. The gruesome passage on inhuman butchery justified as undertaken in the carefully reasoned interests of the public good of mankind not only anticipates *The Modest Proposal* but prophesies the distribution of social benefits vouchsafed by virtuous innova-tors in science and governance to the victims of mass consumption in the twentieth century and beyond. The passage also means to lift the embroidered veil from Shaftesbury's seductive moral philosophy that lulls the modern world into believing that wayward humans, their heroic leaders, their computing information systems, and their planned societies are somehow gaining on the vicious natures that give resonance to the *Tale*'s nasty satiric voice.

CHAPTER SIX

HARRINGTON: MANY AGAINST THE BALANCE

> A Modest Defence of the Proceedings of the
> Rabble in all Ages.
>
> *Tale* 54

The newly understood internal evidence of Swift's analysis of John Toland's publications between 1696 and 1700 indicates clearly that his satire of all modern learning, religion, and governance drew from a very wide selection of occasional publishing sources over many years. But despite the completion of all of the *The Battle of the Books* and Section II of the *Mechanical Operation of the Spirit* by 1697, Swift's main satire was still inchoate in 1701 when he published *A Discourse of the Contests and Dissentions between the Nobles and Commons in Athens and Rome,* to be referred to as *Discourse,* a calculated piece of Whig propaganda.[1] The 1701 *Discourse* allows us to observe Swift as his thinking germinated for important parts of 1704 *Tale.*

We begin with the fact that "With the expiration of the Licensing Act in 1695, the number of printers and presses both in London and the provinces expanded rapidly" (Belanger 8). This publishing proliferation reflected new struggles for power and public opinion in the wake of the Glorious Revolution of 1688. In a reversal of party roles, the battle was joined in the so-called Paper War of 1697–1702 between Court Whigs and Country Tories,[2] and just as surely between Swift and Toland over the balance of power among monarch, parliament, and people—that is, among the one, the few, and the many. Swift remained loyal to the beleaguered John Lord Somers and the Whig Junta around William III—though little good it did him—against the violent thrusts at the royal prerogative managed by Robert Harley and the Tory Commons. After the Dublin debacle, Toland, like his new patron, Harley, switched party allegiances, though not political convictions. Toland's extensive publications over these stressful years struck at Harley's immediate political targets but also supported his own long range republican, philosophical, and religious goals.

---

[1] Frank H. Ellis's 1967 edition, with an Introduction and Notes, remains an elegant landmark and reliable source in Swift studies.

[2] For discussion of the Paper War, see Ellis 1–14, 66–73.

Toland now revealed even more zeal for dismantling the Whig Junta and the King's prerogative to establish a republican commonwealth with a titular ruler than he had shown earlier for dismantling priestcraft and implicit faith to establish a rational religion without priests. Between 1697 and 1702 Toland increasingly identified himself with the reformations of the Socinians and the classical republicans in Britain and on the Continent; and during this period he published in London and journeyed abroad, arguing simultaneously for the Protestant Succession and the republican ideal.[3]

Just as Swift had scrutinized the roles of the principals in the controversy over religion in Dublin, he scrutinized anew the impact of his former Whig rival Toland, now propagandizing for the Tories in the uncompromising clash for political control in London. If he believed that his epistemological adversary had shaken the foundations in religion in 1696, now, as the Paper War progressed, Swift became equally alarmed about Toland's widening encroachments on learning and governance. But, as he had in the Dublin Controversy, he bided his time while he attended to Sir William Temple's literary affairs.

Despite intellectual, temperamental, and social differences,[4] both Temple and Swift felt themselves sufficiently allied, morally and rhetorically, to be on firm ground to challenge the smug prejudices of those who spoke for the moderns: they reiterated the corrupt nature of humans and the inefficacy of linear progress, information gathering, and modern syntheses. As a public defense of Temple and a mockery of modern learning, *The Battle of the Books* served as an obbligato to Swift's personal battles with his antagonists Toland and Browne for political patronage, ecclesiastical preferment, literary recognition, and epistemological space. But in Dublin Marsh continued to ignore Swift and reward Browne while Browne, like his adversary, Toland, took the publishing route to recognition and success. Swift installed himself in Temple's library in Moor Park, set aside the religious narrative of the *Tale,* and alertly served his political apprenticeship by editing Temple's papers and reading intensively. Following Temple's death in 1699, Swift edited Temple's final volume of miscellanea and accepted minor posts in church and state in Ireland.

It was not until 1701, a date midway between Swift's initial work on the *Tale* in 1696 and 1697 and its publication in 1704, that the 1701 *Discourse,* his first acclaimed literary work, appeared.[5] He had entered the fray at last with

---

[3] See Ellis 36–42 and Robert E. Sullivan 12–16.

[4] For full analysis of the Swift-Temple relationship, see below, pp. 137–57.

[5] For another discussion of Swift's interrupted progress in writing the *Tale,* see the 1973 *Oxford* edition xliii–xlvii.

his late mentor's flags flying. At the outset, however, we must grant the scholarly consensus that analogies and propaganda, not allegories and satire, dominate this work on governance and that it pales beside the fully realized satire of the *Tale*, which discourses on learning and religion as well.[6] Still, in the course of a limited controversy over genre, literary critics and historians in literature, politics, and culture have shrouded critical revelations in two major areas of that *Discourse*. First, the *Discourse* provides an unparalleled opportunity to observe Swift trying to extricate himself from the interlocking private and public relations circumscribing his actions with those of Temple and Toland. Establishing his independence from radical Whig positions becomes a task that was to threaten much of Swift's career and consumed his writing until the 1709 Apology to the *Tale*. Second, although it is not satire, the *Discourse*—written at the mid-point in the seven-year gestation of the *Tale*—provides an equally unparalleled glimpse into the satirist's craftshop for articulating and refining the universal issues and artistic designs that would determine the tasks that his personae would need to assume in the *Tale*.

The *Discourse* concentrates on the theory and practice of governance, ancient and modern; but it also sharpens and consolidates Swift's satire on all modern thought. While work on the *Tale* remains in abeyance, the *Discourse* advances its development. Three years later, in 1704, Swift can transfer vital metaphors, satiric clues, absurd devices used by and against demagogues, and the Galenic humoral pathology from the *Discourse* to the *Tale*. The Toland who appears overtly as an inflaming orator in the patently propagandistic *Discourse* reappears in the mock epic *Tale* covertly as parodic and satiric victim. By relating what may be projected as Swift's private reactions to the Dublin Controversy with his public commentary on the Paper War, modern readers may follow the genesis of the coordinate design of the *Tale* and begin to understand his linking of religion, governance, and learning under the rubric of modern mysteries.

To bind his political allegory with the Galenic humors tradition on a cosmic scale in the *Discourse*, Swift juxtaposes the writings and temperaments of two incompatible Whigs, Temple and Toland. On one hand, Swift aligns his political mean with the moral philosophy and sanguinity of Temple: elder statesman, deceased patron, a Davenant target, and in Frank H. Ellis's persuasive view the *Discourse*'s calm persona who had cautioned about a "further reformation." (149). On the other, Swift finds his unbalanced humoral case in Toland, the "unquiet spirit" (123) and enthusiast of change.

---

6 See Ellis's 1967 edition, Edward Rosenheim, "The Text and Context of Swift's *Contests and Dissentions*," and J. A. Downie, "Swift's *Discourse:* Allegorical Satire or Parallel History?"

Again, the *Discourse* reflects faithfully on the memory of Temple and the humoral tradition of the golden mean; but it also reflects alarm at the ambition, modernity, humoral imbalance, and notoriety of the activist Toland. The essential counterpoint in the *Discourse,* between Temple and Toland, represents at once oligarchic stability and populist tyranny; public principles and extreme humoral imbalance; sanguinity and ill humors; continuity and change.

Temple becomes the gentlemanly persona—without the genius and learned scope of Swift, yet well-informed and astute in contrast with the *Discourse*'s intended audience. This persona propagandizes against popular governments to serve as Swift's boomerang to Toland's enthusiastic recommendation—in his 1697 Preface to James Harrington's *The Oceana* (x)—that ancients be studied to affirm the superiority of a popular commonwealth. In obedience to Toland, and Swift, the *Discourse*'s persona diligently scours classical sources only to find populist tyrannies rampant.

The ideas, premises, and sources common to Swift, Temple, and Toland become as difficult to sort out as the meaning of party labels after the Glorious Revolution of 1688. On the latter score, both Edward Rosenheim and J. A. Downie acknowledge some rule-of-thumb assumptions common to both Whigs and Tories in the Paper War in progress during composition of the *Discourse.* All concurred in the balance of power theory, with the efficacy of a mixed government resting on a balance among the one, the few, and the many. Acceptance of the principles of the Revolution and deflection of attacks from William III allowed the factions to concentrate on destroying one another: either impeaching the Whig Court Junta as venal and corrupt or branding the Tory Popular Commons as demagogic and tyrannical. On this latter score, the propaganda thrust of the *Discourse* is to establish that the Tory Commons led by Robert Harley has broken the tripart balance of power among the many, the few, and the one. The Tory intention to impeach the Whig Junta accelerates the tyranny of the many, prefiguring a tyranny of the one.

As Ellis amply documents, the premises and conclusions of the *Discourse* often reflect Temple's thoughts that Swift had recently organized for publishing as executor of the late statesman's papers. Swift finds the main adversarial positions against Temple and himself in the propaganda of Richard Davenant and Toland. And though Ellis and Rosenheim see Davenant as the prime target for Swift's retaliatory attacks, both also treat Swift's critical use of Toland's contemporary works. But Swift's real target is their sponsor, Harley. Swift asserts that Harley, the former Country Whig now leader of the Tory Commons, has allowed the two inflaming orators Davenant and Toland to stand on his shoulders like Clodius and Curio.[7] He is appalled that two men holding such diverse positions—Jacobite and republican populist, respectively—should be jointly engaged in the ruination of their country.

It might seem from the above that Swift succeeds in separating himself and Temple from Toland. Not so. Toland does not refrain from praising Temple publicly and fulsomely, first in his *Life of Milton* (1699), and, as Rosenheim notes (65), again in *The Art of Governing by Parties* (1701). Rosenheim also pinpoints areas of tacit agreement between Swift and Toland on commonly accepted classical republican principles that Temple and Harrington had articulated earlier. So many crosscurrents of agreement and respect must surely have upset Swift, who had not yet achieved the public visibility of Toland but sought a modicum of recognition in publishing Temple's letters and miscellany.[8] Toland continued to embrace Temple and the original Whigs as his ideological base despite his current service to Harley's Tories. Much as Peter Browne had earlier occupied career space that Swift coveted and in 1710 was to snatch a bishopric in the Church of Ireland from him, the ubiquitous Toland now complicated Swift's political positions and allegiances. Toland had already succeeded in gaining favors that Swift vainly hoped for from the Whig Sunderland—favors that Swift had to wait to receive from the Tory Harley, who became the Earl of Oxford, a decade later.

Swift's quandary concerns his epistemological links with Temple and, by association, with his patron's deism and Toland. His attention to this problem in 1701 was fully justified by the initial reactions to the *Tale* three years later. In earlier chapters we have shown the centrality to the *Tale* of Toland's *Christianity Not Mysterious* and his *Life of Milton*. Yet to his peril, Swift could not resist identifying himself with Toland's ideas against priestcraft at the same time that he was taking on William Wotton and Richard Bentley in the cause of Temple, pinning the label of religious fanaticism on the Anglican rationalists Marsh and Browne, and parodying, too closely for readers to separate artist from victim, the writings of Toland.

It is an irony of his artistic design that Swift became tarred with the fictitious roles he assigned Toland in the *Tale*. Toland the "unquiet spirit"

---

[7] Ellis's candidate for Clodius is Sir Edward Seymour (151–52).

[8] Newport J.D. White, *An Account of Archbishop Marsh's Library, Dublin.* "In 1703 Swift brought out Sir W. Temple's *Letters to the King*, etc. with his own name on the title-page as publisher. The presentation copy that he sent to Marsh, preserved in the library with the Primate's other printed books, bears on the fly-leaf the following inscription:—*To His Grace / Narcissus, Lord Primate of all Ireland By His Graces / most obedient and most humble servant / The Publisher.* . . . Marsh was translated from Dublin to Armagh [Primate of Ireland] in February, 1703, and to that year almost certainly the inscription belongs" (20).

(123) quoted directly in the political *Discourse,* becomes the "unquiet spirit" (41) quoted covertly in the satiric *Tale*. From Swift's point of view, the ubiquitous zealot demanded scope to purvey his modern wares; the *Tale* is his freethinking vehicle. Ellis has quoted Toland to confirm that he was then "Harley's creature," but Rosenheim believes that Toland was never anyone's creature but his own—and so Swift thought at the time (Ellis 36; Rosenheim 65).

The contrast in Swift's approach to Toland in the two works we are considering reinforces the scholarly consensus that the *Discourse* is propaganda that pales beside the *Tale*. Here is the visible, vital counterweight to the *Tale;* the latter is a work of art veiled both by its aesthetic design to purvey newfangled mysteries and by Swift's private intent to conceal his agreement with Toland on priestcraft and camouflage his savage satire of Marsh and Browne in the *Mechanical Operation*. In contrast, for the very reason that the *Discourse* is such patent propaganda that Downie can easily expose Swift's historical distortions, this work serves as an unusually open book to elucidate Swift's thought processes—and his workshop—as he begins to transform his political attacks on Toland's works to the satire of Toland himself as the quintessential modern in the *Tale*.

Ironically, it was the complex of Swift's attacks, parodies, and satires on Toland, his support of Temple's positions against his foes, especially in the *Battle of the Books,* and his unrelenting parody and satire of the works and characters of Browne and Marsh that forced the then unknown author of the *Tale* into contortions, between 1704 and 1710, to extricate himself from his presumed affinities with Toland, Temple, deism, and atheism. In this cause, the *Tritical Essay upon the Faculties of the Mind* (1707) (*PW* 1: 246–51) defines most precisely the satirist's innermost convictions expressed covertly by the satiric voice in the *Tale*. Unlike this 1707 *Essay,* the 1709 Apology appended to the Fifth Edition of the *Tale* must be read as politic cover of satiric traces following the critical and career-threatening storm after 1704. If we wish to know Swift's design and epistemology, it is the 1701 *Discourse* and the 1707 *Tritical Essay,* discussed fully in chapter ten, that provide the only two royal roads in contrast with the myriad blind alleys of the 1704 *Tale*. Parenthetically, in 1710, in a new edition of the *Discourse,* Swift removed the last paragraph wherein he had obliquely attacked Harley for the political damage wrought by Davenant and Toland.

Under the parlous circumstances at the turn of the century in which Swift shifted for career and publishing space, it is natural that the *Discourse* concentrates on two areas of his agreement with Temple: one that Toland politically opposed and the other in which he was not knowledgeable. In governance, Temple is a libertarian oligarch, Toland, a libertarian populist.[9] In psychiatric medicine, with its analogies to the body politic, Temple and Swift are strict Galenists; but medicine is beyond Toland's purview. Swift so immersed himself in medicine[10] that his deep knowledge of the alliance of Galenic medicine with the equally waning humors tradition in literature offers him analogies quite beyond Temple's and Toland's ken. These analogies, first offered in the *Discourse,* receive profound development in the Digression on Madness in a Commonwealth, Section IX of the *Tale.*

On the political front, clearly both Temple and Swift abhorred populist government. In 1700, coincident with Swift's publication of Temple's works, Toland, nudged by Harley, had published *The Oceana* (1656), *The Rota* (1659), and other works of the political theorist James Harrington.[11] He hoped thereby to strengthen Harley's hand in the Commons against William III's prerogative and the Court Whigs and at the same time to promote his own republican cause (Sullivan 12–15). In his Preface, Toland sought to align Harrington's theory of a mixed government directly with the populist cause. But in the *Discourse,* Swift accuses Toland of offering his own thinking as the exalted voice of the many. Challenging Toland's interpetation of *"Vox Populi, Vox Dei"* in *Anglia Libera* (1701), Swift counters that the term

> ought to be understood of the Univeral Bent and Current of a People, not of the *bare majority* of a few Representatives; which is often procured by *little Arts,* and great Industry and Application, wherein those who engage in the Pursuits of Malice and Revenge, are much more Sedulous than such as would prevent them. (114, 146)

Instead of Harrington's tyranny of the one, the *Discourse* finds Toland's encroaching tyranny of the many. With the king's prerogative restricted, the virtuous few immobilized, and popular encroachments becoming the Tory order of the day, Swift sees Britain in 1701 as a *Dominatio Plebis.* In a metaphor borrowed from the *Oceana,* he suggests that Toland threatens to outreach his master Harrington:

---

[9] Temple's Whig associates and his Dutch connections, both before and after his retirement, were oligarchs. As long as Swift propagandized for the Court Whigs in the *Discourse,* he defended their role as the rule of the few. But even in the *Discourse* he found them suffering from a lethargy that created opportunities for Tory demagogues. From his later close political affiliation with Harley, who became Oxford, and Bolingbroke, it would seem that Swift was most comfortable with an alert and sophisticated coterie.

[10] Ch. 8 discusses the extensive medical corpus in his library, the depth of Swift's medical knowledge, and his understanding of the still lingering clashes between Galenic and Paracelsian medicine in the modern world.

[11] For a comprehensive study of Harrington's *Oceana,* see James Holstun 166–245.

> But to fix one Foot of their Compass wherever they think fit, and extend the other to such terrible Lengths, without describing any Circumference at all, is to leave us and themselves in a very uncertain State, and in a sort of *Rotation,* that the Author of the *Oceana* never dreamt on. (120)

In a more oblique, but loaded, reference, Swift yokes Harrington's *Oceana* with Toland's writing. He also yokes the Old Testament wrath of God and Kronos-Saturn's tumultous sea with his own saturnine indignation against Toland:

> The *Raging of the Sea*, and the *Madness of the People* are put together in Holy Writ; and 'tis God alone who can say to either, *Hitherto shalt thou pass, and no further.* (120)

Ellis points out that Toland's propagandistic Preface to the *Oceana* provides a source for one of Swift's attacks in the *Discourse;* yet another reference in the same Preface provides Swift with his substantive design and the central oppositions that he sets up in the opening paragraphs of chapter one and the closing ones of chapter five.

In his Preface to Harrington's works, Toland extravagantly praised Harrington's theoretical ideal of a commonwealth as "the most perfect Form of Popular Government that ever was. . . ." (ix). In *The Rota,* Harrington had claimed that "the Government of one against the Balance, is Tyranny" (621). But Swift differs with Toland's praise of popular commonwealths and Harrington's oblique attack on absolute monarchy. While he subscribes to Harrington's cardinal principle of the need for political balance among the many, the few, and the one, Swift believes that tilting the balance in favor of the many ultimately leads to the unthinkable tyranny of one.

To undermine Toland's populist positions, Swift devises a jest in answer to Toland's Preface that forms the dialectical basis for the *Discourse.* In his Preface, Toland had patronizingly recommended that his readers "delighted with reading" Harrington should also study other good Books:

> Especially a careful perusal of the Greec and Roman Historians, will make 'em in reality deserve the Title and Respect of Gentlemen, help 'em to make an advantageous Figure in their own time, and perpetuat[e] their illustrious Fame and solid Worth to be admired by future Generations. (x)

Downie has suggested that the target audience for Toland's and Swift's propaganda were gentlemen of the middling sort, occasional readers with only modest educations. Hence Toland's intentions are clear. History will convince these middling gentlemen of the need to support a popular commonwealth, and this action will serve to keep them abreast of the wave of the future.

To dampen Toland's enthusiasm and question his populist interpretations, Swift accepts the propagandistic assignment of the Preface to win over gentlemen of limited learning who would be *au courant*—largely the same audience that he addressed. If Toland ordered "a careful perusal of the Greec and Roman Historians," Swift will dutifully comply. The scholarly, gentlemanly persona of the *Discourse* quotes all the recognized Greek and Roman historians "carefully"—that is, to impress the same superficial readers—to demonstrate ironically that the weight of classical evidence does not support but rather undermines the premises and conclusions of Toland's political Preface. Unintentionally, Toland has again come to Swift's rescue. As the possibilities for parody and satire in Toland's *Christianity Not Mysterious* (1696) called into being the religious sections of the *Tale,* so his Preface to the 1700 edition of Harrington's *The Oceana* gives historical substance a contemporary point and provides propagandistic openings to the *Discourse.* And since truth, if it interferes with persuasion, has never been a criterion for propaganda, it is hardly surprising to discover invalidities and specious distortions in Swift's historical analogies. With Toland and Swift addressing the same unthinking audience, overturning a public adversary's position is the day's work, rather than creating a studiously valid logical exercise.

To refute Toland's and the Tories' view that tyranny is solely the province of a single person, Swift marshals "historians of those ages" (113), "the best authors" (105), "exact and diligent writer[s]" (104) including Thucydides, Herodotus, Plutarch, Polybius, Dionysius, Diodorus Siculus, Appian, Caesar, and Cicero:

> This gives the truest account of what is understood in the most ancient and approved *Greek* authors by the Word *Tyranny,* which was not meant for the seizing of the uncontrouled or absolute Power in the Hands of a single Person (as many superficial Men [Toland?] have grosly mistaken) but the breaking of the Balance by whatever Hand, and leaving the Power wholly in one Scale. For *Tyranny* and *Usurpation* in a State, are by no means confined to any Number, as might easily appear from Examples enough, and because the Point is material, I shall cite a few to prove it. (85)

> In the time of the second *Punick* War, the Balance of Power in *Carthage* was got on the side of the People, and that to a Degree, that some Authors reckon the Government to have been then among them a *Dominatio Plebis,* or *Tyranny of the Commons.* (86–87)

This and other classical instances, Swift's persona declares, "make appear the Error of those who conceive, that Power is safer lodged in many Hands than in one" (88). The persona warns the Nobles and Commons, the few and the many, not to overreach themselves after power, lest they "be sure to run upon the very Rock they mean to avoid, which I suppose they would have us think is the Tyranny of a single Person" (91).

Swift does not limit his argument to the rise of popular tyrannies in classical times. Toland had suggested elsewhere that since the Norman Conquest power had gradually tilted toward the Commons in Britain—in his opinion, a good tendency. Swift had earlier attempted his own schematic history, noting the same tendencies since the Conquest. But he and Temple had seen the popular movement toward contract, compact, and consensus as threats to hierarchical and patriarchical power and finally to stability in state and church.

That the Reformation had signaled modern political change in favor of the many, Temple and Swift had no doubt. To emphasize the political damage to England of this "further reformation," Swift retells English history with borrowings from Toland and Davenant. What they had recorded with pride, however, he rephrases with alarm as he places the rise of popular government within the contexts of English history. The power of the Commons had been gaining slowly since the Norman Conquest. It accelerated in Henry VII's reign, coincident with the Reformation; Henry VIII's "Dissolution of the Abbies . . . turned the *Clergy* wholly out of the Scale, who had so long filled it; and placed the *Commons* in their stead" (119). The Commons careened toward revolutionary change with the appearance of the Puritan Faction toward the end of Elizabeth's reign. The epitome of change, the Puritans grew "Popular, by molding up their new Schemes of Religion with Republican Principles in Government" (119) and at last, "according to the usual course of such Revolutions, did introduce a Tyranny, first of the People, and then of a single Person" (119).

Toland's *Anglia Libera* (1701) also had concluded that power had fallen "into the Scale of the Commons" (19). They are tripping over the same terms, concepts, and results, but what appalled Swift seemed an unmitigated boon to Toland. Swift's *Discourse* defines "commonwealth" as popular government; Toland, on the other hand, would willingly apply the term to the existing mixed government without quibbling over form:

> I mean by the word *Commonwealth* not a pure Democracy, nor any particular Form of Government; but an independent Community, where the Common Weal or Good of all indifferently is designed and pursued, let the Form be what it will. (92)

Whatever the form of government, Toland was filled with certainty that it would ultimately be popular:

> Our Historys are full of the Contests between the King, the Clergy, the Nobility and Commons, about their several Powers and Privileges. . . . But the Overbalance

of Property (and consequently of Power) fell into the Scale of the Commons, where it seems to be now wholly fixt. (18–19)

Thus both Swift and Toland would have understood the Hegelian dialectic that all power inexorably devolves to the people: for the pre-Hegelian Toland, as the dynamism of natural law and the millennial direction of human destiny; for the Juvenalian Swift, as guaranteed corruption, anarchy, and madness.

Swift cherished a single-minded schematic view of English and British history from Henry VIII to William III that remains consistent from the 1701 *Discourse* to his 1725/6 *Sermon upon the Martyrdom of K. Charles I* (*PW* 9: 219–31). He outlines this schematic history in heads for Sections after XI that never materialized in the 1704 published edition of the *Tale*. His consistency may be seen by aligning the condensed histories in his 1701 *Discourse,* the actual 1704 *Tale,* the proposed "Additions to *A Tale of a Tub*" (to be referred to as *Additions*), first published piratically in 1711, and his 1725/6 *Sermon.*[12] These condensed histories uniformly describe an inexorable movement away from balanced government toward populism in Britain; it begins with the Norman Conquest, accelerates from the Reformation through the Puritan Rebellion, and has since insinuated itself in modern European comity and polity. An alignment of his diverse references to British history demonstrates the historical underpinnings of the *Tale,* Swift's ideological consistency over his lifetime, and his psychological convictions of the profound impact of origins on future reality.

Since the Norman Conquest, the Commons by slow progress had been gaining on the balance of power in England. Henry VIII's dissolution of the abbeys "turned the Clergy wholly out of the Scale . . . and placed the Commons in their stead" (*Discourse* 119). Power "grew to lean to the side of the people" (*Sermon* 9: 220). "*Harry Huff* [Henry VIII] after a deal of blustering, wenching, & bullying, died" (*Additions* 143). Under Queen Mary's "cruel persecution," Protestants in great numbers fled to Geneva, "a commonwealth governed without king and . . . without the order of bishops." Under Queen Elizabeth, the Protestants returned home, but had grown "fond of the government and religion" of Geneva (*Sermon* 9: 220). This Puritan Faction "began to grow Popular, by molding up their new Schemes of Religion with Republican Principles in Government" (*Discourse* 119). "*Martin*'s friends left the Country, & traveling up & down in foreign parts, grew

---

12 "Additions to *A Tale of a Tub*" in *A Tale of a Tub and Other Works: The World's Classics* 1986 edition. 142–148. In the *Introduction* (xvii) the editors say that they "have raised all three [Additions] to the text of the present [1986] edition in consideration of Swift's well-documented practice as an author of writing down his preliminary ideas in the form of notes, which he called 'hints', terse but grammatically complete sentences. . . ."

acquainted with many of *Jack*'s followers, & took a liking to many of their notions & ways, which they afterwards brought back into Albion, now under another Landlady [Elizabeth I] more moderate & more cunning than the former" *(Additions* 143). Lady Bess, unable to reconcile Peter, Martin and Jack, set up her own "Dispensatory" with "Physicians & Apothecarys of her own creating" *(Additions* 143). After her death, a North Country Farmer [James I] and his successor [Charles I] "occasioned great disorders" and "miscarried, because *Jack*'s pouders, pills, salves, & plaisters, were there in great vogue" *(Additions* 144). In "the space of about sixty years," the Puritans "did introduce a Tyranny, first of the People, and then of a single Person" *(Discourse* 119). These Puritans "were the founders of our dissenters." By degrees, they quarreled with "the kingly government" because their fathers had earlier taken refuge in Geneva, "a commonwealth, or government of the people" *(Sermon* 9: 221).

"The House of Commons grew so insolent and uneasy to the King [Charles I]" that, "Having the reins in their own hand, [the Commons] drove on furiously":

> In a few years after, they ["that odious parliament"] murdered their King; then immediately abolished the whole House of Lords; and so, at last, obtained their wishes, of having a government of the people, and a new religion, both after the manner of Geneva, without a king, a bishop, or a nobleman; and this they blasphemously called the kingdom of Christ and his saints. *(Sermon* 9: 222–23)

After "mighty quarrels & squabbles between *Jack & Martin,* . . . at last both sides concur to hang up the Landlord [Charles I], who pretended to die a Martyr for *Martin,* tho he had been true to neither side, & was suspected by many to have a great affection for *Peter*" *(Additions* 144). Then

> That murderous Puritan-parliament, when they had all in their own power, could not agree upon any one method of settling a form either of religion or civil government, but changed every day from schism to schism, from heresy to heresy, and from one faction to another. From whence arose that wild confusion still continuing in our several ways of serving God, and those absurd notions of civil power, which have so often torn us with factions more than any other nation in Europe. *(Sermon* 9: 223)

"Jack's friends fell out among themselves, split into a thousand partys, turned all things topsy turvy, till every body grew weary of them, & at last the blustering Landlord [Cromwell] dying *Jack* was kicked out of door, a new Landlord [Charles II] brought in, & *Martin* re-established" *(Additions* 145).But

> Those very Puritans, of whom ours are followers, found by experience, that, after they had overturned the church and state, murdered their King, and were

projecting the power and possessions they only panted after, by an upstart sect of religion [Fifth Monarchists] that grew out of their own bowels, who subjected them to one tyrant, while they were endeavoring to set up a thousand. (*Sermon* 9: 226)

"The old Government was revived . . . for almost thirty years under the reigns of two weak Princes [Charles II and James II]" until the Glorious Revolution of 1688. "However, as it is the Talent of human Nature to run from one Extream to another; so, in a very few years we have made mighty Leaps from Prerogative Heights into the Depths of Popularity" (*Discourse* 119–20):

> Between these two extremes [tyrannic kings and anarchic populism], it is easy, from what hath been said, to chuse a middle; to be good and loyal subjects, yet, according to your power, faithful assertors of your religion and liberties. To avoid all broachers and preachers of new-fangled doctrines in the church; to be strict observers of the laws, which cannot be justly taken from you without your own consent. In short, *to obey God and the King, and meddle not with those who are given to change.* (*Sermon* 9: 230–31)

> The new Landord [William III after 1688] secured *Martin* in the full possession of his former rights, but would not allow him to destroy *Jack* who had always been his friend. How *Jack* got up his head in the North & put himself in possession of a whole Canton [Scotland], to the great discontent of *Martin*, who finding also that some of *Jack*'s friends were allowed to live & get their bread in the south of the country, grew highly discontent of the new Landlord he had called in to his assistance. (*Additions* 146)

In summary, aside from departures in the 1725/6 *Sermon* when Charles I and the Anglicans receive infinitely more reverence, Swift's publicly offered schema of two hundred years of English and British history remains essentially consistent during the thirty years of his satires and homilies.

But let us return to the contemporary issues in the *Discourse*. Swift indeed yokes the Jacobite Davenant and the republican Toland as "opposite Parties, who can agree in nothing else, yet firmly united in such Measures as must certainly ruin their Country . . ." (117, 147). Swift finds that the public zeal of these contemporaries differs from their practices; they "are not such mighty Patriots, or so much in the true Interest of their Country, as they would affect to be thought, but seem to be employed like a Man who pulls down with his right Hand what he has been Building with his left" (88). Davenant had paraded his patriotism in his propaganda as had Toland, with characteristic self-praise and universal-topical references in the Preface to the *Oceana*: "I constantly aimed . . . at the benefit of Mankind, and especially of my fellow Citizens . . ." (ix).

Swift refers to both Tory propagandists as ruinous, but he was harsher on Toland. Ellis has uncovered seven disparaging allusions to him in the

Discourse, extracted from four of Toland's works published in 1700 and 1701 (268).[13] Swift attacked specifically Toland's advocacy of change and his contribution to a purportedly unified movement toward popular government in Britain.

In the Preface to the *The Oceana,* Toland had announced

> that every day I can discern in it [the Constitution] many things deficient, some things redundant, and others that require emendation or change. And of this the supreme Legislative Powers are so sensible, that we see nothing more frequent with them than the enacting, abrogating, explaining, and altering of Laws, with regard to the very Form of the Administration. (viii).

Swift answers Toland's enthusiasm for reform by asserting, in the *Discourse,* that power follows property in "slow marches":

> To pretend that great Changes and Alienations of Property have created new and great dependances, and consequently, new additions of Power, as some Reasoners have done, is a most dangerous Tenet. . . . (89)

Ellis points to the cant phrase "the united Wisdom of the Nation" in the works of Toland and other Tory propagandists (122, 151). Swift refutes the comforting notion it carries by referring to a different kind of change than the one Toland had in mind. He argues for the humoral tendency toward instability and inconsistency. He could see no

> Reason why the Genius of a Nation should be more fixed in the Point of Government, than in their Morals, their Learning, their Religion, their common Humour and Conversation, their Diet, and their Complexion; which do all notoriously vary almost in every Age, and may every one of them have great Effects upon Men's Notions of Government. (118)

Swift uses topical party strife to draw public opinion to awareness of the menace superintending it, boding ominous political and social change. He places modern trends toward populism within the larger social context of the Reformation and its unending legacy. Specifically, in examining the universal meaning of modern change with what Ellis recognizes as "the Galenical balance of humors" (168), the *Discourse* equates the body politic with the body natural. Diseases in the one reflected diseases in the other. Thus Swift and Temple's two areas of agreement may be bridged into one psychopolitical discourse. Both men reject populist governments because demagogues always arise whose emotional stability may be seriously questioned.

---

[13] *The Art of Governing by Parties, The Oceana of James Harrington and his other Works, Limitations for the Next Foreign Successor, Anglia Libera.*

It is the operation of pathological Galenic humors, in the body politic as in the body natural, that constitutes the other area of large agreement between Temple and Swift. Using this concept, Swift challenges Toland's populist persuasions but moves beyond his adversary's purview, bringing the discourse to another plane—one to be central to the *Tale*. Ellis has recognized Swift's critical use of Galen. "The basic metaphor is the body politic, which keeps its health so long as there is a Galenical balance of humours." He traces this metaphor to Temple, asserting that "Like so much of the *Discourse,* the outside-inside contrast has a counterpart in Sir William Temple: 'The Decay and Dissolution of Civil, as well as Natural Bodies, proceeding usually from outward Blows and Accidents, as well as inward Distempers or Infirmities' " (168).

Ellis also notes the use of the wind image to account for discipleship in the *Discourse*. It becomes the central image of the Aeolist sect suffering from the phenomenon of vapours, as it will become the prime distinction of Galenic and Paracelsian medicine in the *Tale*. Swift has recognized that the decline of the Galenic tradition at the hands of Paracelsian empiricism matches the decline of the classical humors tradition in literature because of the rise of Shaftesbury's benevolent tradition in philosophy, religion, and literature. At mid-eighteenth century, Henry Fielding and Laurence Sterne would illustrate this change of sensibility by invoking both traditions in the novel, a new genre. On the score of benevolence, Toland's augmented pirated edition of Shaftesbury's *An Inquiry Concerning Virtue, or Merit* (1699) adds grist to the *Discourse* and, like Toland's *Christianity Not Mysterious* and *Life of Milton,* receives pride of satiric place in the *Tale.*[14]

If we look both back from the 1704 *Tale* to Swift's 1701 *Discourse* and ahead to his 1707 *A Tritical Essay,* first published in 1711, we find further corroboration of the consistency of his psychopolitical discourse. Each of these works begins by advancing the psychological premise that informs the *Tale:* examining either the body politic or the body natural is an identical diagnostic exercise:

> *Discourse:* "Tis agreed that in all Government there is an absolute unlimited Power, which naturally and originally seems to be placed in the whole Body, wherever the Executive Part of it lies. This holds in the Body natural. (83)

> *Tritical Essay:* Philosophers say, that Man is a Microcosm or little World, resembling in Miniature every Part of the great: And in my Opinion, the Body Natural may be compared to the Body Politick. (*PW* 1: 246)

---

14 See above, pp. 85–108.

What shift of emphasis there is among the three works under review may be seen in the fact that the influence of Temple on Swift's psychopolitical discourse in the 1701 *Discourse* (and the 1704 *Battle of the Books*) has lessened in the 1704 *Tale*. However, the *Tritical Essay* and the *Tale*, with their utter disdain for philosophy, the *Tale*'s critics, and the modern world, find Swift's method fully wedded to satire. In the *Essay* he purposely misreads the Neoplatonic correspondences as between man and his political society rather than man and the universe.[15] As Temple's influence gradually recedes between 1695 and 1707, Swift's own satiric voice emerges with authority.

Swift makes clear in the opening sentences of the *Discourse* that the body politic is an extension of the body natural and that there is an executive part to the whole body politic. But let us suppose that the executive part of the body politic has become diseased because it is led by someone psychically deranged or, worse, by a coterie of such madmen. Both the *Discourse* and the *Tale* assume that the executive part of the body politic, like the negative potential in the mind of the body natural, has indeed become deranged. The key term in both works for mad modern leaders, *unquiet spirits* desiring change, appears first in the *Discourse* (123) and subsequently in the *Tale* (41). Once in the saddle, these unquiet spirits—sometimes treated as popular orators—easily stir up the "inconstant humor of the People" (*Discourse,* 97); and the *Tritical Essay* repeats the charge that in republics "Orators flourish . . . [and] inflame the People, whose Anger is really but a short Fit of Madness" (*PW* 1: 250). Thus the modern leader for Swift parades the worst aspect of human nature: the destruction of continuity and the encouragement of change as a vehicle for the most depraved *libido dominando:*

> So endless and exorbitant are the desires of Men, whether considered in their Persons or their States [the bodies natural-politic premise recapitulated], that they will grasp at all, and can form no Scheme of perfect Happiness with less. Ever since Men have been united into Governments, the Hopes and Endeavours after universal Monarchy have been bandied among them, from the reign of *Ninus* to this of the *Most Christian King*; in which pursuits Commonwealths have had their share as well as Monarchs . . . (*Discourse* 90)

Ellis has illuminated this passage with a quotation from Temple's *Miscellanea, The Third Part* (1701), a work Swift published simultaneously with the *Discourse,* almost as a gloss. It illustrates how completely Swift borrowed his definition of modern unquiet spirits directly from Temple, who accepts as a given the wayward nature of mankind:

---

[15] For a full analysis of the *Tritical Essay,* see below, pp. 203–11.

No civil or politick Constitutions, can be perfect or secure, whilst they are composed of Men, that are for the most part Passionate, Interessed [sic], Unjust, or Unthinking, but generally and naturally, Restless, and Unquiet; Discontented with the Present, and what they have, Raving after the Future, or something they want, and thereby ever disposed and desirous of change.[16]

Temple and Swift were not alone in defining moderns as unquiet spirits, nor was Swift alone in identifying Toland as a prime example. In 1700 George Stepney, Whig propagandist and diplomat, also used the term to describe Toland and his classical republican tendencies. He wrote to reassure Sophia, the Electress of Hanover, that "le génie des Anglois . . . n'est nullement porté aux principes républicains . . . Le souvenir de l'an 1648 nous fait encore horreur." He may have prepared the Electress for Toland's visits to her court in 1701 and 1702:

Les esprits inquiets dont notre pays est très fertile s'amusement plus que jamais à feuilleter des libres dangereux qui traittent cette matière, scilicet Sidney *Of Government,* Harrington *Oceana,* dont le dernier est fameux pour avoir esté escrit par un habile homme du temps de la rébellion, et pour être publié d'une belle impression depuis peu par un libertin nommé Tolon [Toland] comme si la conjoncture présente favorisoit des sentiments semblables.[17]

The corollary passages of Swift and Temple on the governments of men, particularly the passionate agitators in them, present the reader with an area of substantial agreement between the retired privy councillor and the maturing classical satirist. They agree especially on the potential for corruption high and low in human nature. As W. A. Speck put it succinctly, "There are indications throughout Swift's works that he subscribed to Hobbes's view of human nature rather than to Locke's" (*World* 76). Further, Speck's discussion suggests that Temple's judgment above echoes Hobbes:

Hobbes had reasoned that in that state [of nature] men were governed by their passions, and each sought his own selfish advantage, so that life had been poor, solitary, nasty, brutish and short. Locke, on the other hand, had argued that in the state of nature men were governed by reason, and life had been tolerable. (76)

The Hobbesian given adapts itself to Temple's Chinese utopia, with its need for a learned elite, as well as to the view that men, governed by their passions, require the scourge of classical satire, and to the doctrine of original sin requiring the episcopacy of orthodox Christianity. Swift's *Tale* single-

---

[16] *Discourse* 133n l. 284. Temple. *Miscellanea, The Third Part.* [October] 1701. 13–14.

[17] *Correspondance de Leibniz avec l'électrice Sophie de Brunswick-Lunebourg.* Hanover n.d., 2.209. Quoted by Venturi 51.

mindedly uses the pessimistic view of the human condition to overthrow the epistemology of Locke's three leading contemporary disciples: Toland, Browne, and Shaftesbury. But Temple's cast of mind falls between two stools—ancient and modern. He is as anxious as the classical republicans Harrington and Milton, and Toland later, to create a new utopian European society based on reason and sound political theory. The original republican model is the learned Rome of Tacitus; Temple's is the learned China of Confucius. What sets him apart from his contemporary republican allies is the lack of populist elements in his thinking.

Temple was not alone among Charles II's closest ministers in hoping to implement a model utopian oligarchy with subservient underclasses. Shaftesbury's grandfather, Anthony Ashley Cooper, like Temple wanted to create reality from the visionary abstractions of Bacon, Andreae, and Harrington. According to M. Eugene Sirmans, the Fundamental Constitutions of Carolina, promulgated in 1669 by Lord Proprietor Ashley, later to become the First Earl of Shaftesbury, with the aid of his secretary, John Locke, was Ashley's "version of the perfect society, one in which power and property preserved 'the Balance of Government' between aristocracy and democracy." This first Shaftesbury sought to avoid "the dangers [to the future South Carolina] of 'erecting a numerous democracy'" (Sirmans 10).[18] Like Temple, he recognized Harrington's dictum that power follows landed property. And his Constitution provides for toleration of all religions, just as Temple's secular Eastern government admits religion as necessary for the "mob." But no matter how enlightened Temple's and the first Shaftesbury's statecraft seemed alongside the absolute, repressive tyrannies they argued against, their utopias—ideally and in practice—represented throwbacks to medieval manorial systems dependent on the jurisdiction and uncertain bounties of lords proprietors. While the "perfect" world Shaftesbury's and Locke's Constitution created still determines the immense political and propertied baronial power in the hands of an inheriting few in South Carolina, the modern myths of enlightened, representative statecraft belong to the heirs of Locke.

But Swift differs from them all—Temple, Locke, the two Shaftesburys and Toland—in one fundamental respect. They would fashion utopias, feudal and modern, for Prince Posterity. Swift warns the Prince of what will occur once a consortium of enlightened oligarchies becomes fixed permanently in the modern seats of power.

If he is not a subscriber to utopias—feudal or modern—where does Swift stand? Later we will explore satire's Golden Age of Astraea and the dualism

---

18 For a full discussion of the Fundamental Constitutions of Carolina, see Sirmans 6–16.

of Kronos-Saturn.[19] In the actual world, as Speck argues cogently, Swift is guided by more realistic principles. Because he and Temple belong to the pessimistic school of human nature, they are authoritarian in insisting on the power of the State. But when it comes to moral and spiritual enforcement, they part company. As an ideal, Temple would place the most learned moral philosophers in power over emperor, the other nobility, and the mass; Swift advocates a state Church with episcopacy supreme over all. Speck further convinces us that Swift believed in the contract theory of government over the divine hereditary right of kings, citing Swift's pencilled assent to a passage by Gilbert Burnet in his *History of His Own Time:* "The kings were bound to defend their people, and to govern them according to law, in return for which the people were bound to obey and serve the king" (76; Burnet 5:291). Speck concludes that "Swift's ideas on Church and State coincided. Between them the Anglican Church and contractual government were the best guarantees of 'order and purity'" (79).

Lockeans and latitudinarians and eighteenth-century Whigs left Temple's enlightened and rational plans for a utopian society to gather dust. Ultimately, Swift too abandoned Temple's precincts of secular moral philosophy and oligarchic statecraft to perfect the art of classical satire, continue the humors traditions in medicine and literature, and follow the policies of High Church Tories. At the time of the 1701 *Discourse,* however, he had unfinished business with Temple and Somers's Court Whigs.

James Holstun's *A Rational Millennium* emphasizes the modern loss of the body politic as a political metaphor. To Holstun and his subject, Puritan utopians, the body of man is not an analogy for the entire state, but raw material susceptible to control by larger corporate bodies (91–93). That is, the mass can be manipulated politically by a rational elite corps. To the satirist, in contrast, the bodies of man and of his extension, the state, are all psycho-somatic animals self-manipulated by instincts, appetites, emotions, prejudices, corruptions, vicissitudes, eccentricities, follies, and vices. Thus Holstun correctly assesses the satiric dystopia of Bishop Joseph Hall, an adversary of Milton and an early seventeenth-century influence on Swift: "For the dys-topian imagination, the New World is a space for the socially therapeutic purgation of the body politic" (106). Since it disparages the motives of heroic, rational leaders, satire is a pejorative that Holstun sets off against the Puritan utopia.

Since Holstun's analysis of satire is limited to its political as apart from its aesthetic and psychological aspects, this position challenges the rhetoric of the *Tale*'s discourse. On one hand, Swift in the *Tale* sees that "the Ship in danger"

---

[19] See below, pp. 203–24.

is the modern commonwealth and the threat proceeds from emotionally disturbed "unquiet Spirits." (39–41). On the other, Holstun invokes Sigmund Freud's term, *the repetition-compulsion,* ignoring its deleterious pathological implications and equating it instead with what he believes is the Puritan utopists' laudable "impulse to mastery through rationalizing repetition" (273). Freud postulated this principle in 1924 as "instinctual" and asociated with "the daemonic character, and still very clearly expressed in the tendencies of small children." His follower Ernest Jones defined it in 1938 as "The blind impulse to repeat earlier experiences and situations quite irrespective of any advantage . . . from a pleasure-pain point of view."[20] Nonetheless, Holstun advocates the utopist who reacts to "irrational practices of enclosure, warfare, and customary domination" (273). Assuming incorrectly that repetition compulsion explains a Freudian "theory of psychological adjustment" (272), Holstun contrasts the Puritan utopia with the satiric comedy of humors:

> This genre proposes restoring a balance of humors according to some essentially conservative social vision. . . . The dystopist satirizes the utopist and his positive proposals, judging them according to a preexistent standard of individual moderation and social order. But since Puritan utopia offers a mechanism for the creation of new kinds of individuality and social order, it seems unfair to fault it for its lack of self-conscious and reflexive humor. (274)

Since the repetition compulsion defines neurotic imbalance in psychoanalytic practice, it contrasts with the golden mean of the judicious humors tradition. In fact, Holstun's supporting description of Puritan utopist behavior is heavily loaded with the typical abnormalities the practicing analyst listens to daily from his dysfunctioning patients: threatening particulars, behaviors carefully staged, illusions of control, urgent proposals that demand rigors of discipline, strategies against authority, fixations, over-organization, ritualized rationalities, and the tedium of over-disciplined repetition. All these running-in-place neurotic games are supposedly endured for "the promise of an irreversible progress in the imminent future" (Holstun 272–275 *passim*). The utopian patient's litany of presenting problems in Holstun's rational millennium exhibits all the telltale schemes of the *Tale's* unquiet persona. Like the postmodern world, Holstun's is the modern one revisited in its run-down deconstructed state, with some of the inmates loose with *libido dominando.*

One turns from Holstun, as from Toland and other world-changers, to recognize Swift's familiarity with ancient and modern medicine. Modern

---

[20] See Leland E. Hinsie and Robert Jean Campbell, Ed., *Psychiatric Dictionary: Fourth Edition* (1973). Above quotes from *Repetition-compulsion* entry (659) ascribed to Freud's *Collected Papers,* vol. 4 and Jones's *Papers on Psycho-Analysis.*

medical scholars acknowledge Galen's voluminous, vital, and profound contributions to medicine and psychology.[21] Active in the second century A.D. Galen served as the bridge from Hippocrates, Plato, Aristotle, Epicurus, and Erasistratus to William Harvey, Robert Boyle, A. von Haller, and other modern medical theorists. Galen's concerns that Swift exploits liberally in the *Tale* include the Pneumatic School, air and blood flow, the experimental method, anatomy and vivisection, Stoic logic, and, above all, the physiology and psychology of the four primary humors and glands. In contrast, the modern Paracelsus and his medical heirs—key satiric victims in the *Tale*—reject Galen's thinking.[22]

From Galen's medical cosmology by way of Temple, Swift developed a psychoanalytic notion in the *Discourse* that has only recently, in the 1980s, begun to interest psychoanalysts and political scientists. Neither of the latter discrete disciplines, talking past each other, has yet matched Swift's combined achievement here. He has taken the principles of modern psychoanalysis one natural, clinical step beyond individual diagnosis. A pioneer political psychologist, he has asked readers of the *Discourse* who would comprehend the present state in human affairs to look at historical origins in government in the same manner that psychoanalysts scrutinize the pathological history of an individual from birth. The *Discourse,* in fact, posits the interaction between the political imbalance inherent in the many, ending in public anarchy, and the chronic humoral imbalance inherent in their corrupt leaders, ending in madness or private anarchy.

The *Discourse* claims not only instability in individuals and their governments, but comparable mortality in both. Here again Swift fashions a boomerang from one of Toland's overstatements in his Preface to Harrington: the Commonwealth of *Oceana* is "an immortal government" (xxxix). Swift's introduction of Galenic humoral medicine in the *Discourse* mirrors Temple's views and rejects Toland's idea of immortality anywhere. He attacks Toland's claim and influence simultaneously by asserting that governments "instituted by men, must be mortal like their Authors" (117). He cites the present state of Britain as a case in point. Though only a few "turn their Thoughts to examine how those Diseases in a State are bred, that hasten its End" (117), yet those responsible few had best confront the deepening national crisis:

> For tho' we cannot prolong the Period of a Commonwealth beyond the Decree of Heaven, . . . Yet we may . . . purge away an ill Humour that is lurking within: And by these, and other such Methods, render a State long-lived, tho' not immortal. (117)

---

21 For discussion of Galen, see Owsei Temkin and David J. Furley and J. S. Wilkie.
22 For a full treatment of Galenic and Paracelsian medicine, see below, pp. 159–78.

By appeal to the Galenic humors, Swift deflates Toland's claim of immortality for a commonwealth and levels a charge against him: diseases in a state are bred in a private brain. Having diagnosed a public menace, Swift next accounts for the success of populists: they bring virtuous leaders to a lethargy while they spread contagion among the populace. When the sting of demagogues has reduced good men to torpor, they fall into a drowsiness rather than "engage with a usurping People and a Set of *pragmatical ambitious Orators*" (114). The political allegory is designed to awaken these virtuous men, "a Set of sanguine tempers" (118), to the dangers of a "Concurrence of many Circumstances . . . working their Destruction" (117). The body politic must be purged somehow from within, lest it become prey to the "vulture" Louis XIV—just another madman in the *Tale*—the spectre who hovers without. By observing the first signs of popular encroachments, those responsible for the balance may, "by early Remedies and Application, put a Stop to the fatal Consequences that would otherwise ensue" (115).

Ellis identifies passages in the final chapter of the *Discourse* that are similar to those in the *Tale*, the Galenic humors tradition providing the bridge. Diagnostically, the *Discourse* contrasts men like Temple, who act "*upon Public Principles, and for Public Ends*," with unquiet spirits and inflamers like Toland, who "*procure Majorities for their private Opinions*" (121). Ellis (150) notes that the *Tale* has set up the same dichotomy between disease and "the Brain in its natural Position and State of Serenity, [that] disposeth its Owner to pass his Life in the common Forms, without any Thought of subduing Multitudes to his own *Power,* his *Reasons,* or his *Visions*" (171). This passage in the *Tale* calls for "human learning" so that one would be less "inclined to form Parties after his particular Notions; because that [human learning] instructs him in his private Infirmities, as well as in the stubborn Ignorance of the People" (171).

The spawning of disciples also appears in both works. Since "the species of Folly and Vice are infinite" (*Discourse* 121, 150), leaders with humoral infirmities never lack for followers. Swift echoes this idea in the *Tale* (275). In the *Discourse,* such "Parties are bred in an Assembly" (121); at the same time, Swift casts about for ingenious remedies to purge away their ill humors. The seminal development of these two major satiric inventions in the *Discourse*— the contagion of discipleship and the humoral cure—affords insight into the way the inventions will be fully combined satirically in the *Tale*.

In anticipation of the *Tale,* the *Discourse* looks for an appropriate humoral cure to treat the private emotional disturbances of "unquiet spirits" like Toland who threaten political stability. Having diagnosed ill humors in his adversaries, Swift would prescribe remedies to put "it out of the Power of

Men fond of their own Notions, to disturb the Constitution at their Pleasure by advancing private Schemes. . . ." (*Discourse* 123). To remove hot, unquiet spirits who promote political change necessitates a public purging. Swift recalls how the Sybarites inhibited such venturesome innovators. If a private scheme or alteration did not receive general approval, the proposer would be hanged immediately:

> I am deceived, if a more effectual one could ever be found for *taking off* (as the present Phrase is) those hot, unquiet Spirits, who disturb Assemblies and obstruct Publick Affairs, by gratifying their Pride, their Malice, their Ambition, or their Avarice. (123, 152)[23]

Though Swift was delighted with the Sybaritic solution, he needed a modern public remedy "to take off," or, remove from the public scene, modern unquiet spirits. To restrict the influence of private brains, the *Discourse*, as we have seen, verbally attacked the opinions of Davenant and Toland. Yet what might a humoral physician do to thwart the private notions of these modern unquiet spirits? These seductive proponents of change, these inflamers of popular opinion, had already banded together in coffee-houses, secret clubs, sects, and assemblies. Should one silence them? Disperse them? Hardly. In the *Tale*, Swift's satiric invention treated Toland and his fellow moderns more profoundly. He had found his cure to "take off" the emotionally disturbed.

If the Reformation had brought about changes in learning, religion, and governance, with printing sowing the seeds, and if with the expiry of the Licensing Act in 1695 Toland and other moderns had literally rung the changes on all phases of this north European publishing upheaval, then the satiric purging needed to fit the particulars. To preserve the psychic and political balance in society, the humoral physician committed Toland to a modern publishing Bedlam, out of harm's way, in the *Tale*. There he could insanely spin out his new myths and mysteries—his modern republican discourse—on "the use and improvement of madness in a commonwealth" (*Tale*, 162) for the edification of his Aeolist sect.

Neurotic utopists and world changers, then and now, have been saddled with vast encyclopedic learning and information systems. The humoral

---

23 See Ellis 152n252. "*l.* 252. Cf. Burnet (i. 268, 382): 'The chief men that promoted this [a parliamentary committee appointed December 1668 for examining the accounts of funds voted for the 2nd Dutch War], were taken off, (as the word then was for corrupting members)'; 'They had taken off the great and leading men'; *A Tale of a Tub:* 'there has been much Thought employ'd of late upon certain Projects for taking off the Force and Edge of those formidable Enquirers. . . . This is the sole Design in publishing the following Treatise, which I hope will serve for an Interim of some Months to employ those unquiet Spirits' (*TT.* pp. 39–41)." Gilbert Burnet. *History of My Own Time.* 2 vols. 1723, 1734.

remedy that gave license and range to Swift's wit and parodic talent, making it possible for both the persona's and the satirist's discourses to take place simultaneously, enables the perceptive reader to interpret the relative soundness of the premises and conclusions of each. Swift hopes to help the reader understand the modern world that he or she will some day need to cope with. Sections VIII and IX of the *Tale,* on the Aeolists, fully exploit humoral medicine to dismantle the Reformation, the new learning, republican politics, modern utopian myths—and all modern discourse.

The novel idea for the malady of the Aeolist sect, too much wind in the digestive tract—"my phenomenon of vapours"—appears at the end of the *Discourse* before it becomes the central metaphor for communal chaos in the *Tale* (154). Swift playfully explores it in the *Discourse.* Sects are bred when the modern leader conveys his private opinions to his followers "as Wind is thro' an Organ. . . . The nourishment he receives has been not only *chewed,* but *digested* before it comes into his Mouth" (124).

In the *Tale,* Swift mocks Toland, Harrington, Milton, and Marsh, among others, as exemplars of theosophic and political change—and therefore, of the Aeolist madness and vapours. Wind and human chaos have replaced the *Logos,* the divine order of Genesis; *pneuma* propelled by psychosomatic disorders in the alimentary canal have led to chemical imbalances in the Galenic bloodstream, then risen to contaminate the brain and insure unbalanced behavior. The ideals of linear progress and the dream of a secular, materialist utopia have cancelled out the sane notions of cyclical human behavior, follies and vices, the dependable social norms, the golden mean, the necessity of a stable social order, and the roles of the exalted human spirit and the infinite in human affairs.

Coming to a terminus of Swift's use of Toland overtly and covertly, we had best sum up. Domestic injury and universal issues confounded both men's careers. Toland's expectant return to his homeland in 1697 turned ugly, as verified by Molyneux's letters to Locke and the *Tale*'s oblique references to actions of the ill-natured Browne. Swift may well have felt about Toland that there, but for more fortunate accidents of birth, go I—for he and Toland were more alike than either cared to admit.

Swift certainly parodied Toland as a twin might. Both men had to make their lonely ways by their ingenuity, wits, and pen. One illegitimate, the other fatherless from birth, the paternities of both at times were subjects of scandal.[24] From the 1690s until 1710, both competed for political tasks at first for Somers' Whig ministry and later for Robert Harley's Tories; and because

---

[24] For questions on Swift's paternity, see Frank H. Ellis's review of A.C. Elias, Jr. *Swift at Moor Park: Problems in Biography and Criticism,* 76.

both were exasperatingly beholden to vain and powerful oligarchs who usually withheld what they could freely give, they competed for similar posts in Ireland through the Whig patronage dispenser, Lord Sunderland. Between 1701 and 1714, they were often pitted as fighting cocks even as they changed parties: Swift as Whig-Tory, Toland as Whig-Tory-Whig. Toland sooner than Swift switched allegiance to Harley, the erstwhile Country Whig become politic Tory, and both continued to languish or flourish at his bidding when Harley, later Earl of Oxford, headed Anne's government during the first decade of the eighteenth century. With Harley's blessing at the turn of the century, Toland helped unfold the diplomatic carpet for the Protestant Hanoverian succession in Germany. It is one of the ironies of their relationship that in 1711 Oxford dropped Toland in favor of Swift to the former's bitter chagrin. On 7 December 1711, Toland pens a fruitless appeal to Oxford, concerning the Electoral Highness Sophia's Memorial:

> Don't you now find by experience that what I wrote to you about that [Hanoverian] Court near a twelve month since is exactly true. Instead then of your [Matthew] Priors and your [Jonathan] Swifts you ought to dispatch me privately this minute to Hanover.[25]

Both post-seekers skilfully exploited contemporary issues in print and viewed their world within the frameworks of rational millennial movements, both believing that profound changes were occurring in the European order of things. Within these broad historical frameworks both assumed challenging intellectual positions that drew more adversaries than friends. And both men had high opinions of their own intellectual powers and ability strategically to influence events and sources of power. Toland meant to propel linear progress, Swift to warn of the emotional instability and consequent rational distortion of self-anointed world changers like Toland.

For public and private reasons, Toland is the linchpin that connects much of Swift's discourse; yet they shared many of the same Country Whig principles. Both upheld the cause of liberty against all forms of tyranny. "Depart, wayfarer, and imitate if you can a man who to his utmost strenuously championed liberty," Swift wrote for his epitaph. "He was an assertor of liberty," Toland wrote for his.[26] Both supported the compromise of William III's constitution and government, believed power followed property, opposed standing armies, and advocated the Protestant succession and a civil theology. According to Sullivan, "He [Toland] had turned it [Scripture] into a tool for

---

[25] Letter from J. Toland to [the Earl of Oxford], 7 December 1711, 5:126–27.

[26] For Swift's epitaph, see 1986 *The World's Classics* edition of the *Tale*, 694. For Toland's, see British Museum, Add. MSS, 4285, f. 76.

fashioning his civil theology" (132). Swift similarly asserted, "As I take it, the two principal Branches of Preaching are first to tell the People what is their Duty, and then to convince them that it is so" (*PW* 9:70). And both saw history as a continuum. With more retrospection and prophecy and less of a power base in the present than their contemporaries, they concentrated on a panoramic, long-term historical view and used classical, European, and English history as commentaries on the politics of their time.

Each man had what the other lacked: Toland, zeal for precipitate action and populist causes, Swift a temperament for reasoned restraint within a circumspect private life. Toland fearlessly challenged absolute power and current orthodoxies in liberty's cause, but Swift saw tyranny as a more pervasive given of the human condition. Swift the High Churchman and Toland the deist clashed more over moral philosophy than religion. They agreed on priestcraft and disagreed on implicit faith because they remained poles apart about the human condition.[27] As political writer or satirist, Swift had an unshakeable belief in the proclivity of human nature to repeat its infirmities, corruptions, follies, and vices from generation to generation. And as extensions of human nature, he understood that governments displayed the same aggravating frailties with predictable consistency from age to age.

What may be less apparent is that Swift also championed triumphs of the human spirit, not necessarily Christian. His moral philosophy reflected the influence of Temple's ideas, Juvenal's satire, Sir Thomas More's virtue and satire, and the all-embracing humors traditions in medicine and satire.

We have seen that Toland preferred promising expectations to present discouragement. While Swift concentrated on the limitless failures in deed and perception, in body and soul, embedded in human history, Toland discounted human limitations optimistically to project the modern possibilities accompanying the republican tradition. To resuscitate the classical republicanism of the English Revolution at the end of the century, he published the mid-century works of James Harrington, John Milton, and Algeron Sidney as well as the memoirs of Edmund Ludlow and Denzil, Lord Holles. Swift thought that Toland's exaggerated classical republican stance discounted human nature and fostered political imbalances in favor of popular government—a result both believed inevitable.

This outcome Toland awaited optimistically, Swift with foreboding; yet despite these polar expectations, both acted to transfer their compelling visions to political life. If we accept their epitaphs in their entirety, Toland would still be restlessly propagating universal truth—as independent thinker

---

[27] For Swift, Toland, and implicit faith, see Landa, "Swift, the Mysteries, and Deism," and above, pp. 21–23.

retracing the cross-channel pilgrimages of Bruno, Dee, Fludd, Andreae, Comenius, and Milton—but Swift is finally at rest, rooted in classical learning, the Established Church, and Ireland.

A wealth of new scholarship has accorded Toland his rightful place in the republican pantheon at the same time that related scholarly insight now reveals the contemporary and historical bases of Swift's opposition to Toland's cosmic view. Swift's minority opinion on the modern tradition ran against the tide then as it does now. The *Tale* recognizes a long line of propagators of the modern faith, sharing the sense of a new European communal destiny: an approaching rational millennium. Fortunate in their generational and geographical overlap, these modern prophets traveled the Continent and England undermining static European political systems and spreading advances in modern learning and new theosophies. Twentieth-century historians like Franco Venturi, Hugh Trevor-Roper, Frances Yates, and Margaret Jacob have by now drawn attention to their affinities and their profound impact on the modern worlds of learning and governance. Swift sounded the alarm bell on what he considered "dark authors" in the *Tale*. If he and Toland found urgent and profound political uses for history in their time, modern readers may surely follow. The light now cast on seventeenth-century intellectual and political history, complemented by an acute examination of the revelant epistemological encounters, extends the late twentieth century's understanding of its modern origins. Swift studies can now be integrated with Toland studies to contribute to largely uncharted directions in political discourse.

Partly because Swift was gifted with the satiric urge, he vouchsafed to careful readers a disquieting revelation about the modern European world as an unexamined new tyranny; he also possessed an ironic bent for hiding its fate from fools and knaves—still protected behind widely sanctioned modern mysteries. Toland, an object of opprobrium and an outcast throughout his public career, served Swift's satiric purposes as the quintessential modern in quotable word, eccentric deed, and insatiable enthusiasm for change. Their historical-biographical counterpoint furnishes the *Tale* with a design and portent still germane. Ironically, following the 1704 *Tale,* it was the public identifying of Toland with Swift through Temple that the satirist struggled for six years to correct.

CHAPTER SEVEN

TEMPLE AND THE SENTINELS OF EDEN

> From this Heavenly Descent of *Criticism,* and
> the close Analogy it bears to *Heroick Virtue,*
> 'tis easie to Assign the proper Employment of
> a *True Ancient Genuine Critick.*
>
> *Tale* 95

By an acute Swiftian irony keepers of the modern faith in his own time tarred Swift with being unduly influenced by Sir William Temple as the true deist-atheist, but a keeper of the modern faith in ours tars him with Temple as presumed High Churchman. A left- or right-wing intellectual affiliation with Temple—take your pick—has continued to be charged against Swift by supporters of the modern myth even to the end of the twentieth century, partly because it has taken as long to isolate the important strands in an extremely complex relationship between employer and assistant. Were they master and disciple, surrogate father and son, alternately friend and foe? The permutations resulting from meticulous inquiry with conflicting conclusions can help us define Swift's character.

Shaftesbury denounced the *Tale* and its unknown author immediately. Within a year, the Boyle lecturer, Samuel Clarke, and other publicly certified myth makers damned it as a fiction of the deist Toland or the atheist Temple. Needless to say, the seemingly fatal linking of these suspect heretics with the *Tale* plagued Swift, who was then fighting for career space. Because Temple and Swift shared many philosophical positions, the task of extricating the *Tale* from that yoking occupied the still unknown satirist from the date of its publication in 1704 until the Fifth edition in 1710.

Clearly linkages between Temple and the *Tale* must be addressed since the Ancients-Moderns Controversy revolving around Temple not only cast long shadows over *The Battle of the Books* but produced residual reflections on its companion piece, the *Tale.* It is useful to recount the facts. Except for a two-year interval in Ireland from 1694 to 1696, Swift served as secretary to Temple at Moor Park from 1689 to 1690, from 1691 to 1694, and from the summer of 1696 until Temple's death in January 1699 (*Tale* xlvi–xlvii). In 1690 Temple published *An Essay upon the Ancient and Modern Learning* and *Of Heroic*

Virtue, two writings that led to William Wotton's bitter attack *Reflections upon Ancient and Modern Learning* (1694) and ultimately to his *A Defense of the Reflections upon Ancient and Modern Learning* (1705). Wotton offered his assistance in blurring both the authorship and the intention of the *Tale:* in the 1705 *Defense,* he was sure that Temple had written the *Tale,* probably in 1697, and taken the title from his fellow deist Toland.[1] For him, the *Tale* was of a piece with Temple's 1690 essays with their sinophilism, religious skepticism, secular moral system, and challenge to revealed religion. Wotton judged the *Tale* irreligious, profane, and crude—"a banter upon all that is esteemed as sacred among all sects and religions. . . . In one word, God and religion, truth and moral honesty, learning and industry are made a May-Game, and the most serious things in the world are described as so many several scenes in a *Tale of a Tub*" (*Tale* Appendix B 316–17). In 1694 and again in 1705, with allusions to the *Tale,* Wotton concentrated on the fundamental religious issue of the Ancients-Moderns Controversy: Temple's deism and atheism—an issue that scholarship has only recently addressed. Thus he misguessed in believing that the author still unknown in 1705 was the deist Temple or some other modern belonging to an anticlerical conspiracy. In Wotton's eyes, the controversy— like the *Tale*—was a major threat, not to learning but to orthodox Christianity.

Professionally, Swift paid dearly for throwing contemporary critics off the scent. By parodying Toland as consummate modern throughout the *Tale* and by adding the *Battle of the Books,* an ostensibly partisan and highly visible advocacy of his late patron Temple in the Ancients-Moderns Controversy, Swift compounded the problems of his career among latitudinarians and High Churchmen and among Whigs and Tories. With publication of the *Tale,* the critics found Temple and Toland compatible bedfellows. But alas for Swift, he himself seemed compatible with them! Temple and Toland were both Country Whigs, classical republicans, deists, and actual fellow travelers with the Dutch rationalists who had published heterodox positions. In 1698, Toland lauded Temple fulsomely in his *Life of Milton.* A year later, Swift was preparing Temple's collected writings for publication. And just as Swift had borrowed ruthlessly from Temple's essays for ridicule in the *Tale,* as we have seen, he did the same from Toland's tracts.

During the six years from its anonymous launching in 1704 until the 1710 Fifth Edition with its crafted Apology, the *Tale*'s still unknown author had to endure charges that he was a shameful priest, a deist, a heterodox freethinker,

---

[1] William Wotton, charges in his *Defense,* appended to the 1973 *Oxford* edition of *A Tale of a Tub.* 312–328, that "The Author, one would think, copies from Mr. *Toland,* who always raises a Laugh at the Word *Mystery,* the Word and Thing whereof he is known to believe to be no more than a *Tale of a Tub.*" 319.

or an atheist and to hear speculation that he was, in fact, either his late patron, Temple; the *Tale*'s major satiric victim, Toland; or Jonathan's despised "little Parson-cousin" and sometime collaborator, Thomas Swift. (It was especially galling that, through the good offices of Temple and Somers, Thomas had gained the comfortable English living denied Jonathan.)

But these were not all the ironies. Temple was another modern enthusiast for the light of reason with a very specific, secular position advocating the virtues of the learned government of ancient China. To quote Frank T. Boyle, "His message was that the people of this remote land were living healthier, happier, more prosperous, more peaceful lives than Europeans, and that they were doing so without the superfluous interference of 'temples, idols, or Priests' " (206). Temple was proud of his former functions as king maker, pivotal diplomat, and world-changer and hoped in his retirement to exert a comparable political, not religious, influence on a changing Europe. In this cosmic endeavor, the European Christian religion was a superstitious impediment with inadequate Scriptural information, suitable only for the mob, that need not stand in the way of oligarchs who would place secular learned elites—men like Confucius and Socrates—at the source of political power. All this modern enthusiasm, faith in reason, natural law, deism, and oligarchal benevolence with their utopian agendas made Temple fair game for Swift's *Tale*, which we have seen had a comprehensive agenda of its own that made use of both Temple and his enemies.

Emphasis on Temple the deist-atheist calls for reassessment of scholarly received opinion of him as apologist for the Ancients and foot-dragger impeding the realization of the Newtonian synthesis and Whig supremacy. It is only since 1989 that we have had an analysis of the controversy over Temple's ideas, supported by readings of his essays, that digs below the surface. Boyle's Trinity College, Dublin dissertation clears the scholarly underbrush that had stunted interpretations of the love-hate Temple-Swift relationship so integral to the *Tale*. No longer can we define the Temple-Wotton encounter as simplistically reduced to learning, nor can we accept the more sophisticated scholarly view that Temple the Modern was "pounced on" by his fellows merely for the egregious scholarly blunder of believing Phalaris to be a true Ancient.

Boyle modestly presents copious evidence that Temple learned the positions he espoused in the two orthodox offending essays at the feet of the sinophile and skeptic Isaac Vossius. Vossius advocated Chinese moral philosophy and the rule of all society by secular, learned priesthoods to whose decisions even the emperor would bow; he contrasted his ideal society with the corruption of European Christian orthodoxy and the inadequacy of its priest systems. It is true that Temple's essays sought to humble the learned men of modern Europe—Fontenelle, for example—for believing that they had reached new heights. But his argument runs that Western knowledge, both ancient and modern, is fragmentary because it has left out our learned forebears, the *Eastern* Ancients, for whom his praise is extravagant: "The kingdom of China seems to be framed and policed with the utmost force and reach of human wisdom, reason, and contrivance; and in practice to excel the very speculations of other men, and all those imaginary schemes of the European wits, the institutions of Xenophon, the republic of Plato, the Utopias, or Oceanus, of our writers" (III 342).

What makes Temple stand apart from other modern rationalists is his unwillingness to admit revealed religion to the modern world. Newton, Locke, and the latitudinarians saw no conflict between reason and Christian revelation: they were designedly orthodox and zealously protective of the powerful oligarchical establishment. They preached modern *reform* of existing institutions with time on their side; but Temple, Toland, and a host of freethinkers wanted revolutionary change in Europe to begin with religion. It is not surprising that Wotton, the Royal Society, and the Boyle lecturers believed that Temple and whoever had released the deceased Temple's *Tale* were part of a well-organized freethinking, deist conspiracy against revealed religion that had gained momentum after expiration of the Licensing Act in 1695 and was in full operation by the time the *Tale* appeared in 1704.

If Swift became one of the freethinkers' major critics from the 1704 *Tale* forward, where then did he stand in relation to Temple's ideas and influence? For an accurate answer, Boyle pleads against the tendency of scholars to approach the Swift-Temple relationship with inflexible notions (13). It is unfortunate that choosing sides has been an occcupational tendency of Swiftian scholarship, evidenced in the post-war "hard" and "soft" schools and in longstanding British and American chauvinistic biases about Swift; and by allowing all opinions free rein, the new historicism compounds the difficulties. The goal in this study is to direct attention away from shrewd guessing games and ingenious private readings to incontrovertible evidence. With A. C. Elias's findings in *Swift at Moor Park* and Boyle's on the centrality of Temple's rational sinophilism—a theme developed in *Gulliver's Travels*— the case for Swift as admiring disciple of Temple dramatically recedes.

Several of Temple's positions did receive approval in the *Tale*. Swift agreed wholeheartedly with most of Temple's moral philosophy, and with his positions on veneration of the ancients, the cyclical theory of history, the intellectual pride of the moderns, the cause of liberty, psychiatry, the rule of a mixed government with Protestant Succession, and the abomination of Roman

Catholicism specifically and priestcraft generally. Still, he combed through Temple's essays for his satire, which agreed or disagreed with Temple's ideas without fear or favor. Temple would have registered satisfaction with the surfaces of the *Tale* at which Swift might have expected him to pause. But if the *Battle of the Books* reflects directly and the *Tale* indirectly Swift's championship of some of Temple's ends, the *Tale* far more crucially and more directly championed the satirist's own epistemological cause. Like Newton's an outpouring of genius, that cause was infinitely more learned, more cosmic, and more profound than Temple's.

It is far easier to yoke Temple's deistic-oriented modernism with Toland than his Chinese-oriented ancient positions with those of Swift. Boyle identifies Temple's central concerns with those of the Freethinkers and deists who came after him: "Prominent in Temple's essays and attacked directly in Wotton's *Reflections*, Temple's challenge to scriptural chronology with his claims for antiquity, and his challenge to Christian moral superiority with his successful search for heroic virtue in remote and heathen nations, presage the attacks by the Freethinkers and deists which would dominate the religious controversy of the next generation" (212). Conjectures remain as to whether at any time during the 1690s with him, Swift embraced Temple's deistic and classical republican positions—and if he did, whether he subsequently foreswore them.[2]

A.C. Elias's 1980 *Swift at Moor Park* examines the limits of Swift's admiration for his renowned employer by exploring minutely a natural, but hitherto neglected source. He has carefully recreated nuances of the round of life at Moor Park, the setting where Swift and Temple forged their intellectual kinship and Swift independently forged and furnished his mind between 1689 and 1699, as well as where the *Tale* and the *Battle of the Books* germinated. His examination of the profuse twentieth-century literary scholarship on Temple's role in the *Tale* and the *Battle of the Books* can thus add a salutary coda to these studies. Elias devotes a quarter of his book to the Temple elements in the complementary works, most of it to Temple's "muddled" and contradictory Epicureanism as it is treated in the Digression on Madness.

To be sure, Elias's results confirm Swift's "remarkable intimacy with Temple and Temple's works" (199). But he also arrays a wealth of internal evidence that convincingly illustrates Swift's simultaneous support of some of Temple's most cherished positions and his attack on others. Some "ambivalent passages" (155) reflect ironies often private to Swift himself that would not be detected by readers "less familiar than Swift with Temple's character

---

[2] For background on the British classical republicans of the mid-century who had another political agenda than the Puritans, see Blair Worden.

and writings" (189). In this vein, Elias reasonably conjectures that Temple may have been treated to passages of the *Tale* and the *Battle of the Books* which he would have simultaneously enjoyed for positions shared and felt "uncomfortable" about because of shafts aimed at him that his wit and learning would never fully fathom.

Swift's specific ironies usually engage multiple targets, reflecting profundities when seen from the different perspectives of each; under the rubric of self-deceived moderns they effectively join as satiric victims Temple, Shaftesbury, Locke and his disciples, the natural philosophers in learning, Somers and the Whigs in the state, the Anglican latitudinarians in the church, and the Dutch and English mercantilists in commerce. These rising alliances of groups and individuals ostensibly work for the benefit of mankind while insuring their own tranquility and material well-being, Temple not excluded. We have seen that in the Digression on Madness Swift finds Shaftesbury's ideas of virtue and happiness a foolish delusion and sends him to an appropriate retreat where he can spin out his philosophical musings. For Elias, the same passage applies equally to Temple. Swift apparently concluded that both men should be parodied and satirized for pat associations of happiness with virtue: the former for his dedicated Platonism, the latter for his muddled Epicureanism.

Still scholars have had difficulty resolving Swift's conflicting uses of Temple in the *Tale*. Although some have thought of Swift as the admiring disciple of Temple, the privy councillor to kings, elegant essayist, and moral philosopher, the famous passage we have seen on fools and surfaces, quoted again below, parodies and satirizes jointly the writings and philosophic persuasions on happiness and virtue of both Temple and Shaftesbury:

> He that can with *Epicurus* content his Ideas with the *Films* and *Images* that fly off upon his Senses from the *Superficies* of Things; Such a Man truly wise, creams off Nature, leaving the Sower and the Dregs, for Philosophy and Reason to lap up. This is the sublime and refined Point of Felicity, called, *the Possession of being well deceived;* The Serene Peaceful State of being a Fool among Knaves. (*Tale* 174)

When the twentieth-century reader arrives at the passage that defines happiness in the Epicurean sense of preferring surface over substance, senses over reason, serene self-deception over penetrating the depth of things, the scholar must decide whether Swift actively champions Temple in the *Tale*, as he most certainly does in the *Battle of the Books*, or whether he has made his employer a prime satiric victim. Elias's evidence challenges the "admiring discipleship" school of Irvin Ehrenpreis, David P. French, and Richard Olson. He believes that Temple's gardening essay, justifying the joy of the quiet life, is Swift's "immediate inspiration" (159). Finding the essay "meandering," "fuzzy-minded," and "self-indulgent" (160), Elias asks if Swift and other learned readers might not have reached similar conclusions. After tracing the essay's convoluted reasoning, he concludes that

> Temple unwittingly rejects the need for moral or rational standards in happiness, whether internally or externally applied. By implication, then, a man may achieve true happiness by indulging himself, deluding himself, or stultifying himself. So long as he feels at peace with himself, he has achieved the highest good. 162

If it seems "harsh in Swift to base his satire on so faulty a passage in Temple . . . unfortunately the great man's muddle about Epicurean tranquility was all too typical" (163).

Elias accumulates the evidence in Temple's works that allowed Swift to offer "a travesty of Temple's ideas about happiness" (164). Temple "is accused out of his own mouth—all too appropriately accused, as it turns out. If Swift speaks of the man, 'truly wise,' who achieves happiness by living as a fool among knaves, so had Temple in speaking of himself" (164). Elias's conclusion here is that the multi-pronged satire of the fools and knaves passage would have gained Temple's approval on several levels of their agreement, but in also holding up "a kind of satiric mirror for Temple . . . [Swift] makes sure that he would discover in it every face but his own" (171).

One cannot read further in Elias's study of the Moor Park period and the *Tale* without appreciating how effectively Swift learned to distance himself and his satires from Temple's "genteel generalizing essays" (177) even as he perforce edited and ultimately published them. He would have found grating their fuzziness and lack of learning, particularly in areas like natural philosophy where his modern adversaries were most accomplished but he himself had far more than a working knowledge. Further, Temple's desire to contribute to the public good and his worship of heroic virtue with martial overtones opens him to Swift's satire in company with the bravura performances of Hercules, Milton, Toland, and other contemporaries.

The main fact of Swift's independence of mind does not obliterate his borrowing blatantly from Temple in attacking moderns such as Wotton and Bentley, whose writings are limited to the exposure of others' faults; he also copied Temple in attributing madness to diet, education, temper, and climate and in ironically defending the ancients like Homer (Elias 173–84 *passim*). As described in the previous chapter, Swift's greatest indebtedness to Temple may be for his psychological insights on the correspondences between mind and body and between the body natural and the body politic. Diplomacy has always been practiced as a delicate psychological art on behalf of the body politic, and Sir William had been an extremely astute diplomat at The Hague.

It is true that Elias feels an animus toward Temple that may or may not echo what he attributes to Swift; but he balances this animus by the detailed examination and acute reading of primary sources. Certainly one can agree with Elias's conjecture that Temple would have relished Swift's satire against the Wottonian modern if Swift read it to him. However, since Temple's philosophizing "did not descend to evidence" (185) and he did not realize his own "contradictory attitudes" (184) or his proneness to vanities and follies, he would have missed many of the satiric arrows aimed at him. It seems that Swift's satiric canvas was large enough to accommodate his agreements and disagreements with Temple. Certainly his compelling satiric purposes and deep commitment to learning transcended any immediate career or emotional needs dutifully to align his own positions with the renowned authority and privy councillor to kings.

If Wotton identified the *Tale* with Temple, Toland, and deism, his thinking was not an isolated case. Among his contemporaries, only Samuel Clarke, the rational philosopher and divine, in 1705 had the intellectual reach to understand and misunderstand the *Tale* simultaneously.[3] In 1705 Clarke defended rational theology, but not deists; like Sir William Petty earlier, he maintained that ethical law is as constant as mathematical law. Within Neoplatonic, latitudinarian, and modern frameworks, Clarke considered the still unknown author of the *Tale* one of the "prophane and debauched Deists" (100). (Unlike Wotton, he did not speculate that it was specifically either Temple or Toland.) In his 1705 Boyle Lecture, Clarke presented deists as atheists and finds in the author of the *Tale* one of his prime illustrations:

> They [alluding to the *Tale*'s author specifically] discover clearly that they have no sense at all of the dignity of human nature, nor of the superiority and excellency of their reason above even the meanest of the brutes.[4] (100–101)

His argument sees precisely *how* Swift proceeds in the *Tale;* but having accepted and combined all the optimistic tenets of seventeenth-century European philosophy and theology—the ingredients of Swift's modern myth—Clarke has no capacity for understanding *why* Swift is up to these antics. Ironically, Clarke is as blind to Swift's motives as Shaftesbury, the nominal deist, in the same year. Their views correspond.[5] "They seem,"

---

[3] This study is indebted to Frank T. Boyle for uncovering Clarke's extended critique of deism and the then unknown author of the *Tale.* For a full background on Clarke's and other contemporary responses to the *Tale,* see Boyle's "Profane and Debauched Deist."

[4] Clarke's 1705 Boyle lectures consisted of eight sermons published as a collection in 1706. The published lectures-sermons were reviewed and extensively quoted in the annual journal *The History of the Works of the Learned,* from which we have drawn the Clarke excerpts.

[5] See above, pp. 85–108.

Clarke claimed, meaning deists-atheists in general and Swift as his particular illustration—

> not to have any esteem or value for those distinguishing powers and faculties; by induing them wherewith, God has taught them more than the beasts of the field, and made them wiser than the fowls of the heaven. In a word, whatsoever things are true, whatsoever things are honest, whatsoever things are just, whatsoever things are of good report, if there be any virtue, if there be any praise; these things they make the subject of their constant drollery and abuse, ridicule and raillery. On the contrary; whatsoever things are prophane, impure, filthy, dishonourable and absurd; these things they make it their business to represent as harmless and indifferent, and to laugh men out of their natural shame and abhorrence of them, nay, even to recommend them with their utmost wit. Such men as these—continues our Author [Clarke]—are not to be argued with, till they can be persuaded to use arguments instead of drollery. For banter is not capable of being answered by reason; not because it has any strength in it; but because it runs out of all the bounds of reason and good sense, by extravagantly joining together such images, as have not in themselves any similitude or connection; by which means all things are alike easy to be rendered ridiculous, by being represented only in an absurd dress. These men therefore are first to be convinced of the true principles of reason, before they can be disputed with; and then they must of necessity either retreat into downright Atheism or be lead by undeniable reasoning to acknowledge and submit to the obligations of morality, and make open recantation of their prophane abuse of God and religion. (101)

Swift's discourse challenging *animal rationale* succeeded in frustrating Clarke and, then as now, its satire was powerless to pierce the modern's mind set. Clarke, like Shaftesbury and Rousseau later, asserts man's essential goodness, rationality, divine sponsorship, and communal readiness. In attacking Swift as supposed deist-atheist, he upholds human reason and virtue: he does not wish humanity's reputation sullied. Salvation is imminent in our modern world of decency, moral obligations, good manners, civil laws, and accomplishments. Beasts are in the zoo. His contemporary defense system against satire is a model of its kind, correlating with the rise of parliamentary government to power *in perpetuo* during a transitional decade. Swift's later *Modest Proposal* correlates with Clarke's expectations of the satirist and the satirist's expectations of rational mercantilists in parliament:

> They [In this context, he means the author of the *Tale* specifically] despise also the wisdom of all human constitutions made for the order and benefit of mankind, and are as much condemners of common decency as they are of religion. They endeavour to ridicule and banter all human as well as divine accomplishments; all virtue and government of a man's self, all learning and knowledge, all wisdom and honour, and every thing for which a man can justly be commended or esteemed more excellent than a beast. They pretend commonly in their discourse and writings to expose the abuses and corruptions of religion; but (as 'tis too

manifest in some of their modern books as well as in their talk) they aim really against all virtue in general, and all good manners, and against whatsoever is truly valuable and commendable in men. Of which a late author has given us a very impious and prophane* instance.[6] (100)

Ironically, in asking his enlightened readers to look at their mortal natures, Swift brought down on himself the charge of being the infectious serpent in the Anglican parliamentary garden. Clarke's complete assimilation of the religious, philosophical, and scientific elements in modern optimism required suppression of Swift's meaning: his satire has been reduced and misapplied to serve as an instrument against its own discourse. Twentieth-century defensiveness against him would attempt to echo Clarke's dismissal of Swift for his "negative" nature; but attacks today lack the imperious assurance, classical elegance, and rhetorical flourish with which an established contemporary could then relegate spoilers to perdition.

In attacking the deist Toland through covert parody and satire, Swift complicated his life from its artistic beginning and from that beginning was identified with Toland—by Clarke, Wotton, and doubtless other early readers of the *Tale*. We have seen that much of the reason is that Swift saw Toland, with his more profound assimilation of modern optimism and his iconoclastic attacks on the old and new establishments, as having a more lasting impact on modern European society than figures like Marsh and Wotton, still saddled with moribund institutional commitments. And, like Toland, Swift increased the difficulties attending his original exclusion from established power by unrelenting challenges to its basic assumptions. Toland envisioned a new polity and comity of equality beyond monarchy and oligarchy. Against modern Anglican liberalism and Toland's radical positions, Swift asked for a return to an evangelical humanism in which rigorous ethical, intellectual, and political disciplines cultivated virtue, liberty, and peace and tried and trusted stewards of established institutions served these humane ends.

Wotton's thrust against the *Tale*'s author as destabilizing the modern myth in religion and Clarke's similar thrust against the author for destabilizing the modern myth in learning and governance have their twentieth-century counterparts. Swift would have enjoyed responding to one critical model readily at hand. Seldom has a major historian of science ventured into the Swiftian world as deeply and intrepidly as Richard Olson in his 1983 analysis of "Tory-High Church Opposition to Science." Remarkably, no Swiftian has stated more cogently the implications of the Newtonian synthesis that Swift recognized as inevitable. Olson concludes that Swift's insights

---

[6] In the original, the asterisk is identified as "(*Tale of a Tub)."

saw science as being more dangerous the more its techniques are extended to political and religious concerns, because he saw excessive pride as endemic, rather than accidental, to scientific speculation, and because like Pascal and Rousseau (in *The Discourse on Arts and Sciences*), he saw religion and morality as simply part of a different order of existence, one that is forever untouchable by the reason of natural science. (191)

But alas, in a paragraph preceding this precise summation of Swift's trenchant criticism of the entire modern European polity he saw evolving, Olson felt duty-bound to load Swift with all the *ad hominem* clichés and musty received opinions that have obscured the uncomfortable warning that Olson detects so accurately. Olson finds that

> in some ways Jonathan Swift comes dangerously close to being Margaret Jacob's typical High Churchman, with an "ignorant and obscurantist opposition to everything new and modern." (191)

Thus Olson alerts us to a "dangerous" warning for our world from a super-annuated watchman, "dangerously close" to being an ignorant obscurantist.

Again ironies multiply. Jacob's identical charge, the one Olson accepts, was hurled at Swift three centuries ago by Toland, who referred to Father Jonathan who does all the Tories' "jobs of villainy."[7] In other words, a circle of villification begins with Swift's prime modern victim in the *Tale,* who happens to be the major figure Jacob finds most responsible, according to her exhaustive researches, for furthering the Radical Enlightenment in Britain and exporting it to the Continent. The reductive Ancients-Moderns division—read "reactionary-radical"—can thus be perpetuated down the centuries and used again for choosing sides, and allegiances can be followed by political propaganda with simplistic labels in an historical arena where objective analysis should most prevail. To further the ironies, Olson is caught between honoring his trenchant conclusion on the fundamental thrust of Swift's satires and reinforcing Jacob's conclusion that throws suspicion on the man, thus rendering his satiric discourse nugatory. It is unfortunate that he chooses the latter task—an irony forcing him to abandon the evidentiary and objective requirements of the scientific epistemology to embrace unsubstantiated assertions and populist emotional propaganda.

Olson scrupulously avoids dealing with Swift as satirist, making him instead the "opposition." In his view, Swift's entire intellectual outlook establishes that he is primarily Temple's creature:

> Temple's religion was High Church Anglicanism of a particularly shrewd anti-philosophical and antidissenter variety. . . . From the first of his youthful poems

---

[7] Toland, *The Grand Mystery Laid Open,* 21.

written in Temple's household to the last of his polemical tracts, Temple's protégé
Swift held to this basic attitude toward religious belief and behavior, which linked
an absolutely nonromantic but transcendent faith with a rigid civic conformity.
(183)

It is difficult to find in Robert C. Steensma, Frank H. Ellis, Elias, or Boyle
any focus on Temple's High Church beliefs.[8] If anything, Temple's irreligious
positions encouraged Toland and other freethinkers, deists, and classical
republicans to praise him as one of their own. Swift did not learn High Church
Anglicanism at Temple's feet; he had already had a surfeit of priestcraft at the
hands of Archbishop Marsh in that proud modern's Anglo-Irish barony. But it
should be noted that Olson correctly assesses Temple's advocacy of the public
over the spiritual value of religion as a necessary means of state control.

Olson insists that Temple persuaded Swift to scorn natural philosophy:

> Just as Swift followed Temple in focusing on the externalities of religion because
> belief and true piety seemed to be beyond the reach of force and argument, so he
> followed Temple in criticizing modern learning, especially scientific learning,
> because he felt that the most important issues—those of true piety and virtue—
> were certainly beyond the range of human investigations of nature. . . . The impact
> on Swift's ideas of Temple's attitudes toward scientific learning seems to have
> been immediate, intense, and lasting. (184)

Olson is, of course, correct—and ironically self-implicating—in recognizing
that both Temple and Swift agreed on the intellectual pride endemic in modern
learning:

> For Temple, as for Arbuthnot, modern scientific knowledge, while incapable of
> providing important moral and religious guidance, was both capable and demon-
> stratively effective in producing a vain, presumptive, and destructive sense of
> pride in intellectual accomplishment. (184)

Having selected areas of general agreement between Swift and Temple,
Olson unscientifically overstates Temple's isolating, reactionary, elitist influence without recourse to the full evidence and more balanced appraisals.
Olson also turns to emotionally loaded vocabulary to denigrate the satirist
further, for example referring to Swift's "parroting" (184) of Temple and
expressing "conservative anti-scientific sentiment" (185).

---

[8] For the most convincing analysis of Swift's High Church positions in the *Tale,* see Robert
M. Adams, "The Mood of the Church and the *Tale of a Tub.*" Adams presents Swift as a High
Churchman set off against the worldly Temple. He refers to "Somers, Shaftesbury, and Shrews-
bury (a close-knit club intimately acquainted with Sir William Temple). . . . They were tough,
worldly, secular-minded men; and Swift clearly plumed himself on managing their dry, sophisticated wit as well inside the church as they did outside it" (91).

Careful evidence on the extent and character of Swift's discipleship to Temple explodes Olson's effort at dismissal. Like some of the cultural historians, Olson unintentionally makes Swift's case by summarily dismissing him. He attempts to prove that Swift's intellectual attitudes are of whole cloth and solely an extension of Temple's world, reflecting an uninformed, visceral reaction against science: "In some sense Swift's lifelong concern with science was only occasional and incidental and his scientific knowledge superficial" (185). He would thus discredit Swift's scientific knowledge out of hand, despite the evidence of respected twentieth-century sources that he has acknowledged.

His reduction of Swift to feckless, know-nothing proportions by binding him to Temple's uninformed approach to natural philosophy also fails. His "in spite of Nicolson and Mohler and Colin Kiernan," recognized authorities on Swift's considerable medical and scientific knowledge, merely suppresses critical evidence and leads to another sweeping dictum that when challenged falls to the ground:

> There seems to me no reason to believe that the distinctions between Newtonian, Cartesian, Paracelsian, and Epicurean science, which were central to the latitudinarians as well as to both Temple and Arbuthnot, penetrated Swift's awareness at all. (185)

Yet Swift's medical knowledge alone—of the theoretical and clinical discriminations in the Paracelsian-Galenic clash—opens the way for long overdue interdisciplinary medical and literary reassessments of Swift's work.[9]

Colin Kiernan's net, even wider on Swift's science than his medicine, does not deserve Olson's summary dismissal. If Swift believed intellectually that Newton's achievement was irrelevant to man's moral purpose, "this was not because his [Swift's] own mathematics were inadequate. What is not recognized," Kiernan asserts "is that Swift's criticism of Newton was far more sophisticated and fundamental" (711). What Kiernan wants to emphasize is that Swift, concerned with renaming human priorities and employing appropriate epistemologies to go with them, did not need to lash out blindly at a scientific epistemology he could not comprehend. The latter charge represents fraudulent tarring by offended systemizers. As the present study will argue, Swift was deeply cognizant of the issues, intricacies, methodologies, and scientific principles in the struggle for predominance that developed between the Paracelsian iatrochemists and the Cartesian mechanical physicists in the seventeenth century. Kiernan offers this solid confirmation:

---

[9] See below, pp. 159–78.

> Swift's assault on the Newtonian orthodoxy of his day has not passed unnoticed. What needs to be recognized is that this was only one side of a double satire aimed at two scientific extremes, namely, the mechanical science of Newton and Descartes, on the one hand, and the life [chemical] science tradition of Paracelsus and of Van Helmont, on the other. The importance of recognizing this two-pronged assault is that it then becomes possible to see Swift's science as an attempt at compromise, to steer a middle course between what he rightly regarded as two diametrically opposite points of view in science. (713)

Kiernan has recognized that satire of the Aeolists—read *mad projectors*—in the *Tale* reflects direct reading and assimilation of Paracelsian medicine:

> Theorists like Paracelsus tended to identify God with the Third Person of the Trinity, the Holy Spirit, and to identify the Holy Spirit with the breath of life, with the soul and with the wind or atmosphere. Swift drew attention to this. (714)

More intent on discovering Swift than dwarfing him, Kiernan praises "the magnitude of the scientific synthesis achieved by Swift which, while it has not been fully appreciated by his interpreters, stands as a further example of the brilliance of his genius" (722).

Olson, however, claims that the *Tale* and *Gulliver's Travels* "contain classic statements of conservative antiscientific sentiment" (185), and asks that these works be defined as "opposition" to science, not as satire. Fortunately for Swift's satiric cause, once Olson examines the text of the Digression on Madness microscopically, internal evidence leads him inexorably to discovery of Swift's fundamental premise: the ascendancy of, and overdependence on, scientific epistemology has dangerous consequences for all social, political, and religious institutions in the modern world.

If Swift has encountered a universal misunderstanding and negative reaction to his 1704 *Tale* within and outside the established elite in his own time and by historians of science now, his fate in the hands of other twentieth-century historical and literary critics is much the same. The most comprehensive review of this historical scholarship and its consistent tendency to classify Swift as Anglican High Churchman can be found in Michael Heyd's "The Reaction to Enthusiasm in the Seventeenth Century: Towards an Integrative Approach."

Heyd's title recognizes fundamental flaws in twentieth-century historical scholarship. It has been piecemeal rather than integrative, dealing separately with the theological, philosophical, medical, literary, social, cultural, and political bases of enthusiasm. Further, he correctly sees "enthusiasm" as a conveniently vague, derogatory label, useful in the polemics of the elite in reacting against Puritans, millenarian sects, heretics, atheists, and Paracelsians. Heyd tries to integrate these discrete elements and define *enthusiasm*

more precisely in an effort to refocus scholarly attention away from the nature
of the enthusiasts attacked to the reactions of their critics within a profoundly
threatened European establishment. For Heyd, the attacks on enthusiasm by
an ensconced elite reflect disruption of the religious, moral, social, and
political order, the crisis of authority. This study agrees generally, but with an
important reservation: Swift, not himself a member of the ensconced elite
(though he had to be concerned with advancement, as the Apology makes
clear), was not so simply determined or reactive as Heyd's formulation
suggests all opponents of enthusiasm were. But in that this study attempts to
reorient the focus of attention to the *Tale* from eighteenth-century English
literature and to integrate it with seventeenth-century European intellectual
and cultural history, it shares Heyd's desire for a more integrative approach
that reflects the change of ideological foundations, recognizes flexibility and
accommodations within European elites, and notices the subtle psychological
and medical connotations in the attacks on enthusiasts.

To be sure, Swift's satire on enthusiasts or zealots in the *Tale* uses an
omnibus approach to enthusiasm in religion, learning, and governance; and
he borrows the Anglican latitudinarian stance of regarding sectarians,
millenarians, Paracelsians, Socinians, and atheists as psychically disturbed.
Questions remain, however, as to where Heyd and his roll call of scholars on
enthusiasm have hit the mark and where Swift offers a more sophisticated and
subtle commentary on the period. Who can be dismissed as *passé,* Swift or his
current commentators? Their commentaries are distinct, but complementary,
in dealing with tyrannies, old and new; but Swift's saturnine discourse may be
more profound.

Heyd, like the *Tale*'s Martin, is particularly fine in separating the strands of
seventeenth-century enthusiasm. Theologically, the opposition of law, Scripture, the church, tradition, doctrine, and organized confession is arrayed
against the workings of the Holy Spirit within as demonstrated in sects,
individual faith, zeal, and divinations. The theological dialectic also included
separate attacks by the established Anglicans against deists, atheists, and the
worldly. Earlier in the century Robert Burton, Henry More, and Meric
Casaubon provided the most convenient weapon for the power elite by tying
enthusiasm to medical theory on melancholy in its negative sense of black bile
leading to madness. Heyd alludes to the slow diffusion of these early
psychological and medical explanations and, as a case in point, he refers to
John Phillip Harth's study tracing their influences directly to the modern
Aeolists in the *Tale,* concluding that Harth has correctly placed Swift in a
well-defined tradition of Anglican rationalism (267). What Heyd and Harth
both miss, however, is that Swift attacks moderns in, as well as outside, the
Anglican establishment.

Heyd, who is not concerned with literary art, criticizes the failure of literary studies to contribute to historical understanding. He exempts Harth, but complains of

> the main limitations of literary studies on seventeenth-century reaction to enthusiasm. While contributing to our understanding of a tradition of anti-enthusiastic polemics and pointing to its continuity, these studies usually fail to put each of the individual phases of that tradition in its proper historical context. (268–69)

By joining Heyd's and Swift's independent interpretations of the crisis of authority in the seventeenth century, we may understand more completely the crisis of the individual in twentieth-century Europe. As succinctly put by Heyd,

> By the second half of the seventeenth century it was becoming increasingly clear that Aristotelian scholasticism, traditional humanism, scripture, and the strict orthodoxy of an authoritarian Church no longer provided a firm enough basis for the social and cultural order. And these were precisely the traditions attacked by the so-called "enthusiasts." (279)

Among the old bulwarks, Swift's undying allegiance was to the traditional humanism of Thomas More and the classical satirists Horace and Juvenal. He supported established institutions, as he did proverbial wisdom, so long as they served as repositories of truths and sources of social stability. He recognized them equally as privileged sanctuaries of ancient learning and bastions of tyranny. His arguments for liberty and individualism are strictly within the classical frame of the *furor poeticus* of the melancholy temper. As for the Scriptures, he concentrated on the poetry, myths, divine justice and mercy of the Old Testament; the New Testament Christ, Pauline doctrine, and the covenant of grace—the foundations of the Protestant Reformation— scarcely appear in his literary works or sermons. As for the New Testament in the *Tale,* the satiric voice claims that "it consisted wholly in certain plain, easy Directions." Jack, on the other hand, "became the fondest Creature of it imaginable" (190). The *Tale* bristles against the arbitrary authority operating within the institutionalized protection of the church. As his contemporaries recognized and this study has shown, the *Tale*'s profane author joined Toland in attacking institutionalized priestcraft.

Swift's satiric eye was on reforms in learning that prefigured changes in religion and governance. One modern conceit, faith in the efficacy of human reason, appalled him. Toland, Shaftesbury, and Browne claimed discipleship to Locke. Anglican rationalists and the Royal Society made common cause defending reason. For Swift, illuminist reason is the tool of modern dexterity and delusion even as false mysteries serve priestcraft. Modern rationalists are thus enthusiasts in Swift's satiric cosmos.

Equally scourged at the other end of the modern spectrum in learning are the Hermeticists, Paracelsians, millenarian sects, and empiricists. Henry More, the defender of Descartes and reason, and his enthusiastic foil, Thomas Vaughan, the Hermeticist and mystic, and John Heydon, the Rosicrucian empiricist, are all as much Swift's mad Aeolists as Toland and Browne. Rationalists and empiricists, the elite, and the iconoclasts reflect a uniform desire for reform either from without or within established institutions. Their modern myth is fashioned of reason, empiricism, and apocalyptic expectation. Where Swift saw a commonality among these moderns, Heyd, the typical modern historian, sees conflict followed by flexible accommodation, an Hegelian dialectic: thesis-antithesis-synthesis. In Heyd's view, the critique of enthusiasm is the reaction of the elite to popular culture and charismatic "anti-structure" critics; it is a response to a more secular basis of the social order. Swift recorded the same modern tendencies. But his reaction against the old and new orders and modern ideological positions implied in Heyd's integrative approach was uniformly negative. Swift could agree with Heyd that the reformers would become a team ultimately working together within and outside the establishment. But they are not Swift's team to liberate us from tyrants: they have become the new tyranny.

Consider Swift's attack on the lapsing of the Licensing Act in 1695. Every Stuart monarch had upheld that Act. Milton's, Toland's, and modern democracy's cries for liberty of conscience and freedom of the press related to what Heyd has characterized as individual regeneration fighting an ossified church—and one might add—a moribund monarchy. Swift's critique of this liberty and freedom in the *Tale* seems to place him among the old guard of Stuart absolutism and to align him with the compromise defense system of Anglican rationalism. But his unique concepts of liberty, authority, and enthusiasm set all sides against him. For him, the modern advocacy of freedom of information was at least as subversive as the private absolutism of the French monarchs damned in the *Tale*. It was not a cry for pluralism. It stemmed from the same motivation as the monarchs, self-interest, presented in a much cleverer guise as benefits for mankind. This freedom pretended to achieve what absolute tyrants saw as wasted effort. For Swift, Milton and his ideological descendants promised the tyranny of the many ending in a more virulent tyranny of the one. Demagogic tyranny had elements even worse than absolute tyranny since it was more seductive ideologically, more infused with madness, more likely to originate with charismatic, private visions, and more pervasive through its extravagant promises—myths—to the popular culture.

The resulting inundation of information with the same ideological basis wreaked for Swift a kind of violence against the wisdom of the past and guaranteed a clash of theosophical sects and systems holding out the same promises to humanity. The satiric voice in the *Tale* sees a profound qualitative information loss as a result of the information explosion. Standards and *regula* to judge "the sublime and the admirable" in the productions of the learned have been abandoned and "restorers of ancient learning" occupy no modern place (92–93). Thus modern capitalist and socialist societies stemming from the same European watershed may engage in violent public polemic and even military conflict against one another, blocking out all other information, other values, and other information-delivery systems in their overarching competitive effort to secure one and the same European franchise—monopoly—of secular materialism. Each proclaims louder than the other that only its theosophy can realize universal social and economic benefit. Yet even now as these brittle economic ideologies coalesce, image and facade, that is, appearance and illusion, become increasingly dominant. The main attempt of oratorical mountebanks in the *Tale* is to engage in the same frenetic competition to erect *the* superior mechanical information-delivery system above the heads of the crowd. Content is subordinate to fixing the attention and sustaining an image.

In contrast to the complexity of Swift's pessimism, Heyd hopes that an integrated study may "show that the established elites are by no means as monolithic and conservative as they are sometimes taken to be" (280). His notions of progress, amelioration, dialectic, accommodation, scholarly cooperation, pluralism, and liberalism reflect the modern assumptions that Swift satirizes. Swift's charge against old established elites and new elites forming is that they do indeed reflect a common cause. They all seek to be monolithic and conservative, but the new ones have found more mythologically seductive and efficient information delivery to reach their ends.

For Swift, the abuses in learning lead to inevitable consequences in governance. There is a pertinent context. Recent historiography on republicanism has come to recognize a fundamental separation between the civic humanism or classical model and the juristic entity or Roman law model. While both stress liberty, the classical republican model, as we have seen with Milton, emphasizes virtue, while the Roman juristic model emphasizes rights. J. G. A. Pocock has argued cogently that the organizing presuppositions in the modern history of political thought have not sufficiently recognized that this distinction reflects two discontinuous discourses with unique vocabularies. For example Hobbes argued juridically and Harrington as a humanist. They therefore premise different values, encounter different problems, and employ different speech and argument. "The two men were talking past one another."[10]

To correct the historiographic imbalance, Pocock would set the "civic humanist mode of discoursing about politics alongside the philosophical and juristic, since it is here that recent historiography has been most interestingly problematic" (39). Pocock defines the word *virtue* in the classical or humanist republican vocabulary:

> Since citizenship was above all a mode of action and of practicing the active life, it [virtue] could signify that active ruling quality—practiced in republics by citizens equal with one another and devoted to the public good—which confronted *fortuna* and was known to Renaissance Italians as *virtù*, but which, as Machiavelli was to show, entailed practice of a code of values not necessarily identical with the virtues of a Christian. (41–42)

But the historiographer's perception of the two discourses of republicanism has yet to be an interest of literary history. Nor has Swift's own seventeenth-century discourse been examined sufficiently within the two republican contexts either by historians or by literary critics. These neglects have tended to diminish Swift's third or satiric discourse, even to deny that there is one or that Swift perceived the need for one applicable to the political context. His disturbing satiric discourse presents certain harsh realities of the human condition that are ameliorated by the healing voice of the medico-satiric man of humor. To the irony of ignoring his discourse may be added the modern tendency to fend off Swift's logic.

From the mid-seventeenth century forward, the civic humanist *libertas* of Harrington and Milton and the Cambridge Platonism of Henry More and Ralph Cudworth opposed the Hobbesian *ius* view of human nature and the Hobbesian solution of authoritarian government. Hobbes and the juristic discourse are concerned with political controls over wayward nature, but Swift's satiric discourse to a similar end is more personally directed.

If Swift's satiric discourse needs to be distinguished from the ideas of Hobbes, it also needs comparison with and separation from the thinking of Harrington and Toland. Both Swift and Toland accepted the classical republican ideal of *virtue*, although Swift thought it required infinitely more private rigor, prudence, self-restraint, and judgment than Toland's egoism, optimism, and activism encouraged. In his political writings between 1697 and 1709 Swift wrestled with the ideal and with the practicalities of governance. By

---

10 Pocock 41. The following argument develops from Pocock's thesis on separate discourses in modern political thought. Both he and this writer recognize indebtedness to Caroline Robbins, Margaret C. Jacob, Christopher Hill, Blair Worden, Robert E. Sullivan, J. H. Plumb, H. R. Trevor-Roper, and Quentin Skinner.

way of Temple and along with Toland, he accepted Harrington's concept of the needed balance in a mixed government, with power distributed judiciously among the one, the few, and the many; but he feared Toland's and the Tory Commons' Neo-Harringtonian interpretation favoring the many over one—as did Milton (Holstun 246–65) who also favored the few. Swift also feared the machinations of a corrupt few: the oligarchs. Over this same period, Toland identified his own classical republicanism with Milton's radical Christian virtue and Harrington's ideal civic virtue. Therefore, despite Swift's philosophical overlap with the other two republican discourses, his two voices in the *Tale,* the persona—deranged civic humanist—and the satiric—Kronos's priest—talk past each other.

Pocock asks that the humanistic republican discourse be recognized alongside the Roman juristic one. The argument of this study is to ask recognition for Swift's satiric discourse challenging the other two. With Juvenalian vigor, Swift challenges the modern world to engage in an encompassing epistemological dialogue. What is the end of human life? Assuming the limitations of mortality, physical nature, follies, corruptions, and vice, how may an individual life best be lived? What political institutions serve these limitations best? The *Tale* offers the authority of two allied humor traditions: the rational, medical Galenic and the ancient literary wisdom of the Aristotelian golden mean.

Let us imagine Swift looking now at Prince Posterity. Using this metaphor, Swift would accept the inevitability that Milton's and Toland's shining expectations have received modern currency, esoterically and exoterically, and that the utopian populist branch of classical republicanism represents conjoined modern European forces in learning, religion, and governance. But in Swift's discourse, beastly man, ancient and modern, type and antitype, uses reason pridefully to delude himself with new mysteries. Among the utopian mysteries that hold moderns enthralled, the satirist would include the unproved assumptions of basic goodness in man, the unflagging heroism of virtuous great men, the idea of progress, and the happy return to a material paradise. Swift's concept of liberty accepts neither these mysterious virtues *nor* the rationed rights vouchsafed by proponents of the other discourse. He would not be surprised to find that sovereign oligarchies (the juristic rights model) operating behind the diversionary facade of the modern mysteries (the civic virtue model) have merely used the facade to tighten the Machiavellian noose. Temple and other modern utopians with brahmin proclivities, scornful of the mass and single-minded in their republican idealism, could easily manipulate both models simultaneouly. The privileged practitioners of this modern republican blending are a self-perpetuating elite of powerful propertied families still ensconced in Western, as in Middle and Far Eastern, dynasties. The result is that in the twentieth-century European state, modern republicanism and feudalism uneasily co-exist. As their incompatibility dawns on the many, anarchy, terror, and futility result. This way lies the improvement of madness in a commonwealth. The modern ship in danger, boarded by the many and the few, the fools among knaves, will founder unless it becomes reconciled to the mortal truths embedded in Swift's satiric discourse.

CHAPTER EIGHT

PARACELSUS: ASTRAL CHEMISTRY

> Then has this *Madness* been the Parent of all
> those mighty Revolutions, that have happened
> in *Empire*, in *Philosophy*, and in *Religion*.
> *Tale* 171

To encounter clinical experiment, anatomy, empiricism, and sophisticated understanding of object relations in the Digression on Madness is to be introduced to Paracelsus,[1] the father of modern medicine, and one of the *Tale*'s major targets. Paracelsus epitomized for Swift the rise of modern science and millennial movements, in lock step with both Luther's Reformation and Calvin's Puritanism. In the process of advancing modern medicine, science, and Christianity, Paracelsus connected them to Neoplatonism, chemistry, astrology, alchemy, the occult, white magic, demonology, and the Book of Genesis—all subjects of the *Tale*. His ideas have won diverse and far-flung disciples ever since, and his cosmology remains at the center of the modern Jungian unconscious and twentieth-century holistic medicine.

In the fifteenth century Marsilio Ficino's Florentine Academy rearranged the alliance between classical learning and Christianity; Plato replaced Aristotle with profound implications for the rise of science, the north European Reformation, and the modern European world. In medicine, the momentous Renaissance changes in learning and religion pitted the four humors tradition of the rationalist Galen against the holistic medicine of the Neoplatonic empiricist Paracelsus in a philosophical clash that has continued to divide medicine to the present.

For Swift, satire and medicine were closely allied and humoral diseases of the mind could be treated as effectively in literature as those of the body were in medicine. Thus to challenge Galen's medical cosmos was to challenge the classical satirist's. But the changes in humoral medicine and literature were symbolic of an entire reformation in the European world; and Swift pitted his genius against the modern configuration. Plato's man as microcosm,

---

[1] Philippus Aureolus Paracelsus (1493?—1541). His real name was Theophrastus Bombastus von Hohenheim.

Paracelsus's astral psyche, and Calvin's inward light were all one to the satirist. The ideas of an inner-directed human attuned to cosmic forces were moving inexorably on a millennial course toward a new theosophy, marked by optimism and faith in linear human progress. Within the framework of both humors traditions, however, the modern movement underestimated and self-servingly misinterpreted the spiritual, animal, and mortal aspects of human nature. In the *Tale*'s cosmos—and reemerging in the postmodern world—a contest exists between opposing views of the human condition. The *Tale* addresses the interrelated issues, employing a profound knowledge of medicine and of Paraclesus. Swift single-handedly intended to combat the combined influence of Neoplatonism, Paracelsus, and Calvin by assuming the role of the primitive satirist as physician. Responding to the ghost of Thomas More, Swift set down the priorities of the Renaissance humanist: "God's servant first," classical ideals, the humanities, lasting human values, the reflective life, and nobility of soul.

Swift considers the influence of Paracelsus on this awesome macrocosmic scale. Among the *Tale*'s select list of "the [six] great Introducers of new Schemes in Philosophy" (166), Epicurus, Diogenes, Apollonius, and Lucretius are his ancients. Only the relatively modern Paracelsus and Descartes deserve comparable ranking in his company of those who have advanced new systems. These latter-day world changers represent the chemical and mechanical givens in seventeenth-century natural philosophy. The satirist gives the two extravagant innovators macrocosmic significance and also evaluates their contributions within the empirical vocabulary of anatomy—that is, at the microcosmic level—used in Paracelsus's own clinical examinations. Paracelsus's critical Neoplatonic terminology referred to *faculty, soul, seeds* or *semina,* and *qualities.* Imitatively, the *Tale* asks "What Faculty of the Soul" causes mortal man to advance new systems? "From what Seeds" does this disposition spring? "And to what Quality of human Nature" are these great innovators "indebted for their Number of Disciples?" (166).

An analysis of the specifics of Paracelsus's mystical-medical cosmos, both clinically and theoretically, helps to answer Swift's large rhetorical question about what pathological abnormality best defines the four ancient and two modern systematizers and myth makers:

> For, what man in the natural State or Course of Thinking, did ever conceive it in his Power, to reduce the Notions of all Mankind, exactly to the same Length, and Breadth, and Height of his own? (166)

Paracelsus had moved significantly in this direction. He redefined medicine by looking imaginatively at the supernatural in the psyche and in all matter.

Blending alchemy, Neoplatonism, Genesis, and the book of nature, he propounded the modern myth of a new dispensation between God, the macrocosm, and his human legate, the microcosm. It was this theosophical position that determined a major direction of modern medicine. Correspondingly, his seventeenth-century disciples, the Paracelsians, revolutionized—intellectually, politically, and socially—learning, governance, and religion in northern Europe.

In his satiric preoccupation with the disease of madness in moderns, Swift adds Genesis, another Paracelsian fundamental, to the notion of air as the predestined element or *Quinta essentia* in modern madmen. As Allen G. Debus has shown, Paracelsus assigned equal authority to the Scriptures and the sacramental book of nature: "Rather than embracing Aristotle and Galen, Paracelsus turned to chemistry and natural magic. In a deliberate spirit of reform he sought a new medicine and a new natural philosophy based upon the Holy Scriptures and nature rather than Greek [rational] philosophy" (*The Chemical Philosophy* 2: 540).

Within this framework, Paracelsus had pronounced a new pantheistic and Neoplatonic genesis. Debus has described

> a high proportion of sixteenth- and seventeenth-century Paracelsians who were wandering scholars in their student years. While encouraged to study the world through observation, they were also told to read and reread the early chapters of Genesis as a proper basis for their new knowledge. Here the story of the Creation was to lead them quickly to the problem of the elements. (2: 541)

Debus also found that late seventeenth-century science was "dependent upon an earlier world view . . . and even Boyle insisted that the adoption of a corpuscular philosophy did not rule out the acceptance of a natural philosophy based on Genesis" (2: 545).

In Section VIII of the *Tale,* Swift aligns the creation story of Genesis with the new creation of that "renowned *cabalist* Bumbastus" and his learned Aeolist sect.[2] In the *Tale*'s new dispensation, however, the learned Aeolists not only reinterpret Genesis in Neoplatonic, medical, and occult terms but they replace God and the *logos.* God in Genesis gave man dominion over all living creatures and inspired into man's "nostrils the breath of life" (Gen. 1:26; 2:7; 7.22). "What," asks the *persona* of the *Tale* rhetorically, "is Life itself, but as it is commonly called, the *Breath* of our nostrils?" (151). (Cf. *Paradise Lost* 7. 524–28: "This said, he form'd thee, *Adam,* thee O Man / Dust of the ground, and in thy nostrils breath'd / The breath of Life; in his own

---

[2] References to Paracelsus [Theophrastus of Bombastus von Hohenheim] and kabbala [cabala, cabbalah] appear in Walter Pagel 212–217, 284 ff., 299 ff.

Image hee / Created thee, in the Image of God / Express, and thou becam'st a
living Soul.") The persona continues. Wind, therefore, "had the Master-
Share, as well as Operation in every Compound" (151):

> THIS is what the *Adepti* understand by their *Anima Mundi;* that is to say, the
> *Spirit,* or *Breath,* or *Wind* of the World: Or Examine the whole System by the
> Particulars of Nature, and you will find it not to be disputed. For, whether you
> please to call the *Forma informans* of Man, by the Name of *Spiritus, Animus,*
> *Afflatus,* or *Anima;* What are all these but several Appellations for *Wind?* (150–51)

As Paracelsus had revered Genesis as the Divine Word, so the persona in
his Paracelsian frame of mind uses Genesis arbitrarily to reassign God's
powers to Paracelsus and his learned Aeolists. Like God, man himself now
proposes and disposes, being

> in highest Perfection of all created Things, as having by the great Bounty of
> Philosophers, been endued with three distinct *Anima's* or *Winds,* to which the Sage
> *Aeolists,* with much Liberality, have added a fourth of equal Necessity, as well as
> Ornament with the other three; by this *quartum Principium,* taking in the four
> Corners of the World; which gave Occasion to that Renowned *Cabbalist,*
> *Bumbastus,* of placing the Body of Man, in due position to the four *Cardinal*
> Points. (151–52)

Paracelsus and the *Tale* have looked at the macrocosmic level for the
unifying world soul; it follows that the medical reformer and the satire must
search for its microcosmic correspondence within the human soul (*Tale*
152–53). Since Paracelsian medicine depended on Neoplatonic correspondences, all objects or substances were understood to contain both spirit and
matter. In its cosmology, the four elements only incidentally related to the
surface of objects. Paracelsus provided a new spiritual perspective on the
world around us by endowing it with more profoundly ingrained patterns,
providing the search for empiric knowledge with an entirely new field of
operation. Walter Pagel has brilliantly synthesized this revolutionary modern
epistemology:

> Paracelsus leaves no uncertainty as to what really matters concerning the essential
> difference between natural objects, i.e., their specificity as individuals and
> members of a species. The decisive factor is the immanent, specific, soul-like
> force rather than the—visible—chemical components of an object. The substances
> which we handle in daily life are but crude covers that envelop and disguise a
> pattern of spiritual forces. It is this pattern and not the corporeal cover which is
> responsible for the composition of matter. (83)

Paracelsus's emphasis on the spiritual makeup of bodies as central to
medicine and disease did not rule out the corporeal qualities of bodies; rather

it is the individual arrangement of these qualities or properties in a specific body that directs the physician-alchemist-philosopher to its spiritual makeup or signature. "To be a body at all, an object has to display certain properties such as moisture, dryness, heat, cold and also structure, solidity and function" (Pagel 84). The first four properties refer to the elements earth, water, fire, air; the last three properties refer to sulphur, salt, and mercury—Paracelsus's three principles. These four elements and three principles are the archetypes of qualities. Most critical are

> the spiritual forces which are the true elements and principles, whereas empirical objects such as the "elements" of the ancients and the chemical substances in nature are, as it were, crystallised deposits—the results of an interaction of spiritual forces which causes these forces to become more and more condensed, "qualified," specialised and thus limited in power. (Pagel 84)

Predominant for Paracelsus's philosophy and medicine, and important for Swift's satire

> is the idea of the "*Predestined Element*" or "*Quinta Essentia.*" In each object one of the elements acquires a power superior to that of the others—and it is this element which forms the kernel of the object. It embodies all its specific power and virtues [arcana] and thereby marks the essential difference of one object from another. (Pagel 83)

The satirist exploits these principles. Paracelsus's argument for the *Quinta essentia*—ironically, the quintessence of his own doctrine—fascinates Swift. Having apportioned his discussion in the Paracelsian mode equally between the books of Genesis and nature, Swift arrives simultaneously at Paracelsus's, the persona's, and his own *Quinta essentia:*

> Man brings with him into the World a peculiar Portion or Grain of *Wind,* which may be called a *Quinta essentia,* extracted from the other four. This *Quintessence* is of a Catholick Use upon all Emergencies of Life, is improvable into all Arts and Science, and may be wonderfully refined, as well as enlarged by certain Methods in Education. . . . Upon these Reasons, and others of equal Weight, the Wise *Aeolists,* affirm the Gift of BELCHING, to be the noblest Act of a Rational Creature. (152–53)

In the *Tale,* air or wind, one of the four elements, becomes the *Quinta essentia* of the Aeolists, or the moderns. This air, wind or gas in the alimentary canal, may be "disembogued" from the anus of the teacher into the mouth of his disciple. Or the air or wind may ascend to the brain from the digestive tract and wander to any part of the body, the misdirection leading to madness and other dire consequences to the individual and his environment.

Swift finds a satiric organizing principle in Paracelsus's Neoplatonic macrocosm-microcosm key: the chemical search for the unifying soul of the world. Pagel's definitive work on *Paracelsus* offers an important clue to the *Tale*'s focus on modern medicine, madness, and the Dark Authors:

> The search for the hidden invisible spirit which governs and moves visible bodies is the keynote of Paracelsus' natural philosophy. In this it followed one of the main tenets of Platonism as revived by Ficino: that all corporeal activity derives from a non-corporeal vital principle joined to matter. This principle owes its power to the immaterial soul which subordinates corporeal life to uniform and persistent order. The soul in its highest form is the Soul of the World, followed by the souls of the celestial spheres and finally the soul of all creatures alive. The world is full of souls and demons. (218)

What is nature's or the divine organizing principle of the world and does this macrocosmic principle have a correspondence with the microcosm of the human soul? It is the fundamental nagging question and source of wonder for all *rationis capax* on the planet. The question can be phrased theosophically referring to the *soul* or psychologically to the *psyche*. Paracelsus and other adepti have variously referred to this vital principle as the *Anima Mundi, Forma informans, Spiritus Anima, Afflatus,* and *Animus* from which each object extracts its *Quinta essentia.*

The satirist uses all the Paracelsian terms and more (150–54) to ridicule Paracelsus's cosmology and medical methodology. Swift equates this occult-Christian-Platonic-alchemical medicine and its search for the world-soul with his own satirico-medical "discovery" of the redundancy of air, one of the four key elements, in the alimentary canal of the moderns. Swift reduces Paracelsus's critical linkages of the Platonic correspondences between the unifying soul of the world and the human soul to the *Tale*'s macro-micro correspondences of the stomach and the brain, with the digestive system having pre-eminence:

> Now, I would glady be informed, how it is possible to account for such Imaginations as these in particular Men [Epicurus, Diogenes, Apollonius, Lucretius, Paracelsus, Descartes and others], without Recourse to my *Phenomenon of Vapours,* ascending from the lower Faculties to over-shadow the Brain, and thence distilling into Conceptions, for which the Narrowness of our Mother-Tongue has not yet assigned any other Name, besides that of *Madness* or *Phrenzy.* (167)

In the opposing discourses between Swift and Shaftesbury in the Digression on Madness, the interchangeable terminology is confined to *mind, brain, understanding, senses, body,* and *happiness.* But when we come to Paracelsus and Calvin, the *Tale* provides a thesaurus of synonyms for madness. The cognates include *spirit, inward light,* the Platonic *microcosm,* the Paracelsian *quinta essentia, vision, wind,* the *grain of wind,* the *four winds, air, pneuma, belching, anima, afflatus, spiritus mundi, inspiration, breath of man's life, primordium, world soul, ruling element, influence of the stars* (Paracelsus's *astral psyche), turgidus, forma informans, words, learning, man's highest perfection,* and *Vapours.* Miriam Starkman has added that you can also read, for all these terms, *God, universe, soul,* and *body* (45–49). Hugh Ormsby-Lennon has reduced *spirit* and *pneuma* in the *Tale* to Henry More's *spermaticall power* (42).[3] Swift diagnoses the patient as suffering from a profound psychosomatic disturbance. His term *my Phenomenon of Vapours* is a wicked one in this context since it confounds matter and spirit and the empirical observation of sense data with an inner psychic process. Swift has deliberately and literally conflated spirit and matter, mind and body, religion and learning, divine and secular, phenomenology and ontology, and satire and medicine.

Swift is using the Neoplatonism of Paracelsus to oppose an optimistic divine order implicit in Plato's philosophy, the reformations of Christianity since Ficino, Luther, Calvin, and the composite modern myth. In the Kronos myth, no new dispensations are forthcoming from a god that interacts dialectically with human expectations; there is no astral psyche to hook on to. The satiric voice, therefore, serves as physician, registering diagnostic concern. As satirist-physician, it seeks to draw in both Galen's humoral medicine and Paracelsus's building upon it with iatrochemical, alchemical, Neoplatonic innovations. On one hand, Swift accepts Galen's presuppositions, which Owsei Temkin informs us

> rested in the dietetic orientation of ancient Greek medicine, which gave its attention to man's food and drink and the air surrounding him as necessities for the maintenance of physical and mental life, as causes of disease, and as factors in preserving and restoring health. (*Galenism* 154)

On the other hand, for purposes of the *Tale,* Swift accepts Paracelsian concerns for autopsy and other anatomical exercises, clinical practice and experience, chemical cures over academic medicine, the divine secrets of nature, alchemy, astronomy, visions, and the occult. Swift himself believes in a soul as an organizing principle governing each individual with divine intimations, but he rejects the modern variations on this medico-theological

---

[3] In "Swift and Spirit," Ormsby-Lennon examines the *Tale* solely as a sexual playground wherein the sublimating author indulges in an orgy of *double entendres* and cognates for the male organ. His "psycho-sexual conjectures" (9) are revealing on the history of religious fanaticism in the *Fragment [Mechanical Operation]* where *spirit* and *pneuma* are "nothing more or less than sperm" (51). For both the Puritan enthusiast and the modern scientist, "a sexual interpretation of 'spirit' remains germane" (11).

principle, particularly the astute Paracelsus's, as literally beyond human understanding. His history of fanaticism explains Calvin's inward light, Ficino's Neoplatonic microcosm, and Parcelsus's astral psyche as occult aberrations. These European world changers are a race apart. "The Commonwealth of *artificial Enthusiasm*" composed of "your commonest Pretender to a Light *within*" enjoys qualities "other mortals seem to want" (282):

> There must be a sort of preternatural *Spirit* possessing the Heads of the Modern Saints; and some will have it to be the *Heat* of *Zeal* working upon the *Dregs* of Ignorance, as other *Spirits* are produced from *Lees* by the Force of Fire. (282–83)

Preternatural, *heat, dregs, lees,* and *fire* belong to alchemical discourse. After the manner of Paracelsus's alchemical medicine, therefore, Swift's "history of Fanaticism" will look for some "great Seed or Principle of the *Spirit*" (283). From this survey, the satiric voice discovers the great physiological-psychological thread that runs through his history of enthusiasm: compelling messages—sexual and stomachic—from the lower body, placing the brain under chaotic siege. The satiric voice presents this discovery with parodied medical detachment:

> I am apt to imagine that the Seed or Principle which has ever put Men upon *Visions* in Things *Invisible,* is of a Corporeal Nature; for the profounder Chymists inform us, that the Strongest *Spirits* may be extracted from *Human Flesh*. Besides, the Spinal Marrow being nothing else but a Continuation of the Brain, must needs create a very free Communication between the Superior Faculties and those below; and thus the *Thorn in the Flesh* serves for a *Spur* to the *Spirit*. I think it is agreed among Physicians that nothing affects the Head so much as a tentiginous Humor, repelled and elated to the upper Region, found by daily practice, to run frequently up into Madness. (287)

Swift's use in this passage of *seed* or *principle, visions invisible, corporeal, profounder chemists, spirits,* and *flesh,* the Neoplatonic correspondences of above-below, pathology, psychology-physiology, and *physicians* resonates with Paracelsus as keenly as with purely sexual imagery. It also echoes the religious fanaticism of which the post-Reformation sects, the Paracelsians, and the Puritan utopian commonwealthsmen became part and parcel. Not only does the satirist combine them; earlier in the century, they had already merged. Swift has used medical images elsewhere. For example, the metaphor of *the dispensatory* for Lady Bess's government appears in his condensed history of Britain. Apothecaries and surgeons like Paracelsians, Neoplatonists, Christians, and Harvey dealing with blood had contributed to dethroning Galen and academic medicine. Similarly, his history of religious fanaticism in the *Mechanical Operation* yokes Calvin's inward light and the astral psyche of Paracelsus's alchemical medicine. Modern religion, governance, and learning intercommunicate; animal appetites interpenetrate.

Within a century after Ficino, Paracelsus, and Calvin, their followers combined their particular claims for the primacy of the spirit. At the time of the Puritan Revolution, the mystery of inward light was the major claim of the dissenting sects; the Neoplatonic microcosm informed Cambridge Platonism, occult gnosticism, the Rosicrucians, the Royal Society, and the astral psyche animating Paracelsian medicine. Swift blends them all. Not only in his 1725/6 *Sermon* and his 1711 proposed *Additions* to the *Tale,* but also in the *Tale* itself he associates the new inward light with the new Neoplatonic medicine. These developments in the seventeenth century are the suspect modern mysteries that have replaced the equally suspect modern Christian ones. Jack, in devotion to the Scriptures, "his Father's Will,"

> began to entertain a Fancy that the Matter was *deeper* and *darker,* and therefore must needs have a great deal more of Mystery at the Bottom. *"Gentlemen,"* said he, *"I will prove this very skin of parchment to be Meat, Drink, and Cloth, to be the Philosopher's Stone, and the Universal Medicine."* In consequence of which Raptures, he resolved to make use of it in the necessary, as well as the most paltry Occasions of Life. He had a Way of working it into any Shape he pleased, so that it served him for a Nightcap when he went to Bed, and for an Umbrello in rainy Weather. He would lap a Piece of it about a sore Toe, or when he had Fits, burn two Inches under his Nose; or if any Thing lay heavy on his Stomach, scrape off, and swallow as much of the Powder as would lie on a silver Penny. They were all infallible Remedies. (190–91)

The seventeenth-century world of the *Tale* thus unites sixteenth-century reformers and their instruments of change, Calvinist inward light and Paracelsian occult medicine, just as on a larger scale the *Tale* unites satire and medicine.

Satire and medicine have common roots in the classical humors tradition, but scriptural interpretation had reinvigorated each discipline in the Renaissance. Similarly, the unifying of classical and biblical traditions since the Renaissance has informed modern European intellectual history, including satire and medicine. The *Tale* resonates with both traditions, both disciplines. In a single sentence of the Preface, the satirist intones "that we live in the very Dregs of Time"; the Golden Age has "fled with Astraea," the goddess of justice, and in the words of the Psalmist "all are gone astray"; black bile (Horace's *Splendida bilis*) flows from the satirist's spleen. Meanwhile, he issues generalized indictments of foppery and fornication, pride and dissimulation, and bribery, rapine and injustice, avarice, hypocrisy, and extortion. These charges receive a polite hearing in modern Britain, but change nothing:

"'Tis but a Ball bandied to and fro, and every Man carries a Racket about Him to strike it from himself among the rest of the Company" (Preface 51–2).

To descend from the divine Astraea of the Golden Age to the melancholic spleen of Horace in the same sentence is to introduce the two faces of Saturn and satire, with satire's immemorial relationship to diagnostic medicine. The universal myth of the Golden Age or a Biblical Eden brings to every human consciousness remembrance of an original serenity, peace, and eternal spring. Robert C. Elliott, the preeminent historian of satire, finds the positive face of satire existing in the "preliterary as well as the subliterary" language of carnival and festival. Besides the Saturnalia, he cites rites of reversal in the Apo ceremony of the Ashanti, the Sacaea in Babylon, the Cronia in Greece, the Kalends in Rome, the Feast of Fools in France, and the Lord of Misrule in England.[4] Elliott might have explained that these ancient sacrificial rites were annual purgations in which role reversals allowed the participants to break the binding social contract and conventions for a single day or festival and laugh at their patriarchs for fellow human frailties. New Greek and Roman comedy and *comedia dell'arte* echo these rites. And in Sigmund Freud's ego psychology, Elliott uncovers "a clue to what the Golden Age actually is: a time or a condition in which limitation and renunciation do not exist."[5]

Elliott finds that "it is a mighty leap from the festivals, which have the structure of ritual, to the literature of satire and utopia" (*The Shape* 16). Still satire and the Golden Age are functionally linked in festival, and the "curious doubleness" of Kronos-Saturn as represented by Hesiod informed European satire from Greek New Comedy to Swift. In addition to being king of the Golden Age, god of agriculture, and deliverer of civilization to Italy, Saturn has a "fearsome and dark side" in the myth: "Kronos-Saturn castrated his father and ate his children" (19). Secularized,

> utopia and satire are ancestrally linked in the celebration of Saturn, a god who reigns over the earthly paradise, but who also by reason of his concern with melancholy, disease, and death becomes the patron of snarling Renaissance satirists. . . . Satire and utopia are not really separable, the one a critique of the real world in the name of something better, the other a hopeful construct of a world that might be. (*The Shape* 24)

In the classical and Judaic myths, the gods and God controlled the destinies of man in and outside the isles of the blessed and paradise. According to Biblical eschatology, the millennium—that blessed state—will come again in

---

    4 See also Samuel L. Macey, *Patriarchs of Time*. Macey traces the ambivalence in the gods of time and their rites from the Indo-Iranian and the Saturnalia to the Christian Christmas.
    5 *The Shape of Utopia: Studies in a Literary Genre*, 14–15. Elliott refers to Freud's, *Group Psychology and the Analysis of the Ego*, 18:131.

God's good time. By the Renaissance, however, satirists like Thomas More were not the only ones envisioning an ancient Golden Age or a modern Eden. In the wake of the classical Renaissance and the Protestant Reformation, the millennium or new divine dispensation seemed imminent. From the end of the sixteenth to the middle of the seventeenth century, this Latter-day Glory prompted the optimistic Puritan eschatology of Thomas Brightman, Henry Finch, William Gouge, John Cotton, John Owen, Joseph Mede, and others.[6] Since the Old Testament merely foreshadowed the Christian dispensation, however, the Fall had been cancelled. In the wake of the Reformation and confirming Renaissance Neoplatonism, Johann Andreae's *Christianopolis* and Francis Bacon's *New Atlantis* imagined nonsatirical and secular ideal states. The reconstructed classico-Christian and secular mythology of the modern European world encouraged human beings to create their own bliss. Indeed, with the rise of the new learning and the rule of reason, man himself assumed the role of creator in nonsatiric utopias; and his role steadily increased in his less ironic, more euphoric imagined worlds. The synchronized modern world was one of megatrends that would secularize and literally materialize as man moved closer to co-sponsorship with the divine Creator. The wistfully contrived Golden Age of the satirists became the province of the relativistic moderns and the goal of the future.

The ideal worlds of satire—the Golden Age past and More's Utopia, figments of the artistic imagination—differ vastly from the optimistic modern utopias that emerged in the seventeenth century. Satire has no place for moral relativism. The positive face of satire is always balanced by the negative aspects of Kronos and man: vices, follies, a corrupt and diseased nature, and built-in imperfections leading to the dream state and mortality. The modern vision not only clashed with the old satiric reality but it embittered the traditionally melancholy satirist. The new positive vision borrowed from his imagined ideal and from his treasured terminology (*utopia*) and, from his point of view, it attenuated satire's important power—its role as physician to attend the psyche in the body politic.

There is another, corresponding, clash. Satire is a therapeutic, a branch of medicine; and when Paracelsian medicine challenged the Galenic humors, the literary humors tradition also came under siege. The observer of the *Battle of the Books*, anticipating the subject matter of the *Tale*, allegorized the confrontation:

> Paracelsus, at the Head of his *Dragoons*, observing *Galen* in the adverse Wing, darted his Javelin with a mighty Force, which the brave *Antient* received upon his Shield, the Point breaking in . . . the second fold. (243–44)

---

6 See Peter Toon, Katharine R. Firth, and William Lamont.

Not only is the modern utopia mute about human bestiality, human evil, human limitation, and an uninvolved divine but it conjures up optimistic combinations of God's plan, nature's bounty, man's grace, reason, prelapsarian goodness, latent virtues, relativism, and beneficent control over the total environment. How could the therapeutic role of satire find a voice in these "dregs of time," the modern world?

The modern myth of a divine spirit within erases the reality of inner human imperfections. Modernism, for Swift, rests on denial of human bestiality, reflecting an immature desire to return to a collective Eden and a private womb. Relative values replace absolutes. Within these frameworks, all modern societies look for something relatively better, between amelioration and perfection. No less than in primitive societies, moderns assign evil to some convenient antichrist or devil, the beast that is the other. By pasting all villainy on the other, a form of projection, the individual and his society defend against addressing the vicious and the mortal ingrained in their own human natures. Like the fate of Swift's satire, man's real nature becomes a ball bandied away as a defense.

The *Tale* presents the two faces of satire—vicious reality and the virtuous ideal, as well as the divided legacy of modern medicine—the rationalist Galen and the empiricist Paracelsus with their mutual concern, disease and mortality. All Swift's satiric victims envision some utopian commonwealth, some new Golden Age, but suffer from "my Phenomenon of Vapours" which reaches epidemic proportions. To diagnose their madness satirically, Swift mischievously unites Galen's pathology with Paracelsian symptomatology.

We should not wonder at the profusion and profundity of medical allusions in the *Tale*. The extent of his medical library suggests that Swift and his *Tale* could participate knowledgeably in the historical empiricist-rationalist medical conflict.[7] His books in 1715 and in 1740 included the works of Aristotle and Hippocrates in Greek and Latin, Galeni in 3 volumes and an *Epitome*, Paracelsus complete in 2 volumes, Celsus, Gibson's *Anatomy*, Fuller's *Pharmacopaea*, and Highmore's *Anatomy*, as well as titles by Avicenna, Cardan, Casaubon, and Fernel.[8]

Schematic histories of medicine extending to the late twentieth century illustrate Swift's extraordinary mastery and prescience. In 1934, Arturo Castiglioni's article on the "Neo-Hippocratic Tendency of Contemporary Medical Thought" attempted to show some of this, recognizing the continuing

---

[7] See Harold Williams's lists of the books in Swift's library and T. P. Le Fanu's catalogue of his library in 1715, with an inventory of his personal property in 1742.

[8] His medical library was so extensive that, to avoid breaking up the corpus in 1740, it was presented intact to Dr. Richard Helsham.

polarization into our time between the medicines of Aristotle and Hippocrates and of Galen and Paracelsus. The rational and empirical traditions represent opposing attitudes of mind and opposing psychological temperaments that have extended into every field of endeavor in most recorded cultures. According to Castiglioni, the two poles of the dichotomy are the "technico-morphological, chiefly analytical" and the "cosmical, vitalistic, and synthetical." He classifies Galen and the nineteenth-century German physiological school as representative of the analytic, rationalist trend, Hippocrates, Paracelsus, and Samuel Hahnemann as representative of the synthetic medical thinkers, the empiricists. To be sure, it must be added that conflicts have always existed within the two precincts, with borrowings and assimilations from the other. Some historians have argued that Castiglioni's important article made the distinctions neater than they actually are. Nevertheless, the basic separation seems valid. And it clearly is a separation that Swift exploits by setting Galen and Paracelsus against each other to achieve much of the satire of the *Tale.*

Harris L. Coulter's three-volume *Divided Legacy: A History of the Schism in Medical Thought* (1975) expanded on Castiglioni's premise of the two oscillating traditions in the history of medicine to the present. The resulting thesis may be summarized as follows: history shows that the primary data of the physician's experience can be interpreted either by emphasizing the paramount significance of the sensory data or by looking for a higher order of reality assumed to exist behind the observed data. This dichotomy or conflict between particular facts and general laws has been expressed in many ways in various fields in many eras. The two mind sets have been distinguished as rationalism and empiricism—the fox knowing many things or the hedgehog knowing one big thing, analytical or synthetical, Aristotelian or Platonic, medieval nominalism or medieval realism. In medicine, the first of these tendencies looks for local symptoms, considers the infection of each organ separately, uses a local treatment based on the assumption of a cause, and leads to mechanistic thinking generally. The second tendency attributes the origins and functions of life to a superior vital energy such as the *physis* of Hippocrates. Man is bound to a cosmos of immutable laws; in this universal, unitarian conception, disease strikes the whole organism and has its origins in a perturbation of natural harmony.

Over time the influence of each way of treating human illness has alternated with and modified the other: the conflict of rationalist and empirical doctrines seems to be based on enduring differences in psychological orientation. The conflict is in the Hippocratic Corpus itself. Causal analysis of the organism is at the nub of the rationalist school; the empiricists reject that school's concern for logical consistency in favor of a holistic medicine administered by a physician who feels sympathy and love for his patient. According to Coulter, "The therapeutic philosophy of Paracelsus makes even more explicit the tie between a holistic medicine and the physician's charity or Christian love for his patient" (1: xv).

For empiricists, "symptoms are the signs of the curative effort of the *physis* and must be interpreted as positive or beneficial phenomena, not morbid," Coulter explains. Theory and practice are fused. Instead of "contraries,"

> the Empirical tradition has tended to espouse a theory of "similars"—meaning medicines which further and promote the inherent self-healing effort of the organism. (1: xviii)

On the other hand, from classical times to the late nineteenth century, the rationalist school separated theory and practice. Beginning with Aristotelian logic, rationalists described diseases in terms of opposite qualities and prescribed remedies of opposites. Coulter leans toward the clinically oriented empiricists Hippocrates and Paracelsus and their homeopathy over the theoretically oriented rationalists Aristotle and Galen and their allopathy. His history of medicine, however, records the changes, oscillation, and interaction between these poles to the present day, including the effects of social, economic, and political factors on medical thought.

In his conclusion to the last volume, Coulter finds the rationalist school still dependent on Aristotelian logic and the Galenic idea of "contrariety." He argues for empiricism, partly because of "the primacy of symptomatology over pathological knowledge" (3: 489–90). Since symptoms are chronologically prior to pathology (the condition of the disease itself), they should be prior in importance:

> The appropriate form of treatment all along was the effort to strengthen the habitat, the organism, by the specific medicine, and then the organism would itself dispose of the pathogen.
>
> More than 400 years ago the great empirical thinker, Paracelsus, observed that "the physician must cure the disease in the way it wants to be cured, not in the way he wants to cure it." Paracelsus meant that the physician should be careful not to assume that the pattern of physiological relationships is identical with abstract patterns drawn from other sources, and he had especially in mind Galenic or Aristotelian logic. (3: 504–5)

Swift argues for balance and the golden mean and repose of mind. He attacks extremes and excesses and believes that, by their emphasis on spirit over matter, the empiricist Paracelsus and his heirs are appropriate satiric victims. But by their emphasis on matter over spirit, the rationalist Royal Society and their mechanistic systems also qualify as victims. As empiricists and rationalists find common cause and confuse spirit and matter, Swift pronounces them collectively mad and modern.

As histories of satire from Saturnalia to *Gulliver's Travels* and of medicine from Hippocrates to the present prepare modern readers for Swift's treatment of the modern world in the *Tale*, so too will an awareness of still another Renaissance marriage of classical and Christian traditions: Neoplatonism and the medieval occult. In the *Tale*, illumination and enlightenment come, ironically, from dark authors. The 1973 *Oxford* edition of the *Tale* produced "Notes on *Dark Authors*" as an appendix (353–60) because, the editors acknowledged, Swift's satire on "Mysticism, Cabbalism, Alchemy and Rosicrucianism" had been neglected. They might have added hermetics, gnosticism, magic, chemical medicine, psychic disorders, typology, and apocalyptic tradition to the list of modern mysteries satirized by Swift in the *Tale* but until then researched only in isolated studies by historians and by literary critics hardly at all. However, when chronologically rearranged, the notes for the 1973 *Oxford* edition, establish a direct line of influence from the alchemist-physician Paracelsus (1493–1541) to the pietist Jacob Boehme (1575–1624); Sendivogius (d. 1636 or 1646); one of the anonymous *Rosicrucian Manifestos, Fama Fraternitatis* (1614); Thomas Vaughan's *Anthroposophia Theomagica* (1650) and *Anima Magica Abscondita* (1650); and John Heydon's *The Rosie Crucian Infallible Aximata* (1660) and *Holy Guide* (1662).

In most Swiftian studies, allusions to the dark authors have been treated essentially as satire on the esoterica of seventeenth-century occult enthusiasts. Still, the darkest and most occult of all is Paracelsus himself, their spiritual ancestor. Swift's history of the occult in the *Tale*, from the sixteenth century to the seventeenth-century Rosicrucians and the Royal Society, gives prominence to that prime mover. The *Tale*'s history of medicine constructs oppositions between Galen and Paracelsus centrally and Aristotle and Hippocrates tangentially.

Paracelsus may be said to have rejected all forms of rationalism. He especially confronted the ancient rationalist and assigner of causes, Galen, rejecting Galen's relating the four elements to the four humors. Earth, Water, Fire, and Air, however, "occupy a prominent place" in Paracelsus's medical philosophy (Pagel 82). The divergent use of the elements by Paracelsus and Galen enables Swift to satirize the former's philosophy, on one hand, and to reaffirm the Galenic theory of humoral balance, on the other. Antonia McLean has spelled out the specifics in this theoretical clash:

Paracelsus, therefore, abandoned the accepted association of the four elements [earth, water, fire, air] with the four corresponding qualities [dry, moist, hot, cold] which lay at the basis of the Galenic theory, and substituted a system which was based on the chemical reaction of the elements with the [his three added] principles [sulphur, salt, mercury], and which, once the true nature of matter and its interactions was discovered, proved essentially more correct. Disease for Paracelsus was no longer an imbalance of humours which could be corrected by a remedy of the contrary quality, but a chemical reaction within the body, which could be treated by chemical means [similars]. As a result, the only possible method of diagnosis was clinical examination. (191)

Swift, of course, did not agree with these judgments. Instead he exploits the radical Paracelsian departure from Galenic medical theory and in the climactic Section IX of the *Tale* analyzes the chemical components of contagious madness in the modern commonwealth. In this satire, as we have seen, moderns suffer from an excess of wind in the alimentary canal. One of the four elements accepted by Galen and adapted by Paracelsus, the redundancy of wind—or air or gas—is disseminated anally and orally among modern disciples, who distribute madness abundantly throughout European society. Swift sees this chemical disease as having originated with Paracelsus's theory of the four elements and the three principles; but he prescribes treatment according to the Galenic theory of humoral imbalance. Paracelsus cures by similars; looking at the symptoms, the Paracelsian mode, Swift sees contagion spreading by the similarities of redundant Vapours among disciples of modernism. But Galen cures by contraries; looking at the pathology, the Galenic mode, Swift opposes the calm but truly critical satiric voice to the fanatic enthusiasm of his millenarian modern persona. Thus the universal modern malady has a symptomatic Paracelsian source, but Swift ironically offers a Galenic pathological diagnosis and treatment by contraries. By examining Paracelsus's Neoplatonic medicine, readers may recognize the source of Swift's personally fashioned occult medicine in the *Tale*, "my *Phenomenon of vapours*" (166). Swift's medicine serves as both an ingenious parody and satire of Paracelsian medicine and a diagnosis and commentary on the epidemic madness among moderns who have followed in the wake of Paracelsus.

Paracelsian medicine is satirized in the *Tale*, and the Galenic concept of *pneuma* or air serves to define Swift's seventeenth-century fanatics in religion and learning. On the subject of *pneuma*, Galen in the second century A.D. argues with the founder of Pneumatism, Erasistratus of Chios (c. 300–250 B.C.). Charles Singer and E. A. Underwood explain that, influenced by the atomism of Epicurean philosophy, Erasistratus believed the phenomena of life are associated with the existence of a subtle vapour, *pneuma* or spirit, which permeates the organism, and causes its movements. This subtle vapour is held to have some affinities with the air we breathe. Pneumatism is, in fact, a primitive attempt to explain the phenomena of respiration. (49)

For Erasistratus, air was taken in by the lungs and passed to the heart where it was converted to the *pneuma,* the vital spirit, and sent to various parts of the body. But Leonard G. Wilson reports that Galen challenged this thesis:

> The fundamental change which Galen made in the physiology of respiration was to show that neither the left ventricle of the heart nor the arteries contain air (that is, *pneuma*), but that they invariably contain blood. In making these steps forward Galen necessarily destroyed the whole of the beautifully articulated Erasistratean theoretical structure. (300)

In correspondence, Marianne Winder, an authority on Paracelsus, contributed additional information to the two-millennia discourse about the spiritual properties of the essential element:

> The idea of *pneuma* existed already before the Stoics, and you may find it in the Presocratic philosophers. But when it gained importance in the sixteenth and seventeenth centuries among religious movements, this may be due to their having practised breathing exercises or having repeated prayers or incantations which set off trances. [These,] in turn, were accompanied by physiological changes, such as change of heart rate, rate of metabolism, etc., which were attributed to the action of pneuma or wind which, in turn, was regarded as connected with the soul. (11 February 1987)

Having distinguished elements of Paracelsian and Galenic medicine Swift used to diagnose and treat modern madness as "my Phenomenon of Vapours," we can return to the satirist's major preoccupation, the moderns' claim of inner light. Here we must separate the author's satiric distortion of reality from what he believes to be the actual distortion of reality in the modern mind. For the purpose of his *Tale's* satire, Swift distorts Paracelsian medicine to diagnose the disease of mad moderns as redundancy of wind; at the same time, for the same end, he considers what the dark authors—i.e., "the true illuminated"—have themselves distorted as their claimed legacy, inward light:

> 'TIS true, indeed, the Republick of *dark* Authors, after they once found out this excellent Expedient of *Dying,* have been peculiarly happy in the Variety, as well as Extent of their Reputation. For, *Night* being the universal Mother of Things, wise Philosophers hold all Writings to be *fruitful* in the Proportion they are *dark;* and therefore, the *true illuminated* (that is to say, the *Darkest* of all) have met with such numberless Commentators, whose *Scholiastick* Midwifry hath delivered

them of Meanings, that the Authors themselves, perhaps, never conceived, and yet may very justly be allowed the Lawful Parents of them: The Words of such Writers being like Seed, which, however scattered at random, when they light upon a fruitful Ground, will multiply far beyond either the Hopes or Imagination of the Sower. (186)

To convince the *Tale*'s readers that inner light is mere illusion, Swift decides to look inside using Paracelsus's experimental medicine. Paracelsus recognized the corporeal qualities of bodies, but looked at their arrangement in a specific body to detect its spiritual pattern, signatures, or astral psyche. Swift uses this methodology to undermine Paracelsus's vision. First, P. M. Rattansi tells us that Paracelsus believed that Aristotle and other ancient naturalists

> were powerless to explain the irreducible specificity and individuality manifested by everything that existed. Their explanations dwelt only on the surfaces of things, never penetrating the visible and tangible, which was only the outward "signature," to reach the immanent soul-like power and force. (*Art and Science* 51)

Believing, however, that no spiritual correspondences or microcosmic patterns lurk inside natural objects, Swift attacks anatomists like Paracelsus and recommends that "cutting, and opening, and mangling, and piercing, offering to demonstrate" (173) be dispensed with. One will not find inside a great organizing principle or immanent inner light, either Neoplatonic or Christian.

> Now, I take all this to be the last Degree of perverting Nature: one of whose Eternal Laws it is, to put her best Furniture forward. And therefore, in order to save the Charges of all such expensive Anatomy for the Time to come; I do here think fit to inform the Reader, that in such Conclusions as these, Reason is certainly in the Right; and that in most Corporeal Beings, which have fallen under my Cognizance, the *Outside* hath been infinitely preferable to the *In*. (173)

To refute further Paracelsus's epistemology—as we saw earlier (above, pp. 104–7)—Swift then satirizes the ghoulish clinical procedures of "him who held *Anatomy* to be the ultimate End of *Physick*" (174):

> Yesterday I ordered the Carcass of a *Beau* to be stript in my Presence, when we were all amazed to find so many unsuspected Faults under one Suit of Cloaths. Then I laid open his *Brain*, his *Heart*, and his *Spleen*; But, I plainly perceived at every Operation, that the farther we proceeded, we found the Defects encrease upon us in Number and in Bulk. (173–74)

Here again a reading of Rattansi elucidates Swift's veiled reference to Paracelsian anatomy. "His [Paracelsus's] work is replete with allusions to 'anatomy,' but it signified either chemical anatomy, which revealed the true nature of things, or the study of the concordance between the greater and lesser worlds" (*Art and Science* 55). While Paracelsians looked for the spiritual, the inner light, the signatures in the corporeal body, Swift's satirical examination locates only the guts and an inhumane experimenter bent on testing his occult theory. For Swift, if moderns must deny the bitter human truth of human imperfection, mortality, and the lapsarian soul, better then to settle for the surface of things than to pretend to have probed and come upon inward light.

F. R. Leavis's commentary on the "Carcass of a Beau" passage reveals what can happen on the literary side of the gulf separating medicine and literary criticism. Leavis concludes that Swift's writing on this occasion displays "probably the most remarkable expression of negative feelings and attitudes that literature can offer—the spectacle of creative powers (the paradoxical description seems right) exhibited consistently in negation and rejection" (28). "What the savagery of the [this] passage from the *Digression* shows mainly," Leavis finds,

> is Swift's sense of insecurity and of the undisguisable flimsiness of any surface that offered.
>   The case, of course, is more complex. In the passage examined the 'surface' becomes at the most savage moment, a human skin. Swift's negative horror, at its most disturbing, becomes one with his disgust-obsession: he cannot bear to be reminded that under the skin there is blood, mess, and entrails; and the skin itself, as we know from *Gulliver,* must not be seen from too close. (27)

Leavis's coda to this opinion proclaims his arbitrary decision to throttle Swift's "negative" genius by limiting the satirist's sphere to the *literati.* Interlopers from other scholarly provinces need not apply:

> No doubt psychopathology and medicine have an interesting commentary to offer, but their help is not necessary. Swift's genius belongs to literature, and its appreciation to literary criticism. (27–28)

The relentless power of Swift's satire has provoked many such readings that defend against it. The nonpracticing psychologist launched by credentials as a literary historian reduces the totality of a work of art to what he considers the author's damaged psyche to justify denying the authority of his passionate argument.

For the most part, Swift's readers have recognized neither Paracelsus's vital importance to the modern world nor the satirist's suprisingly profound understanding of Paracelsian medicine and cosmology. Consequently, readers and critics alike have not understood the medical core of Swift's grim indictment of the modern world. As moral thinker, classical satirist, Galenic

humorist, and orthodox divine, Swift asks for psychic balance in the individual and his society. With moderns pridefully assuming they could experimen-
tally locate and measure the divine spirit and simultaneously reject their
mortal nature, Swift, like his fellow Tory satirists, prophesied the rise of the
modern utopian wilderness. In the empirical modern world, the illusion of
virtue in the holistic man, now larger than life, provides the widest facade and
rationale for rampant vice.

Swift will not accept the new myth. The modern magi begin with
recognition of the force of the nomadic-agrarian compromise in the Genesis
myth. But in their search for a new dispensation, a new genesis—an agrarian-
urban myth—modern natural philosophers and Protestant theologians have
added their own compromise. To relieve the gloom of the Fall and to
centralize man's control of his universe and destiny, moderns have empha-
sized man's goodness and partnership in the divine creation. They find God
still flowing into man His "inward light." In this new genesis, modern man
has created a self-defining learned elite claiming an egocentrically perceived
inward light and offering its own personally interpreted divine dispensations
to the world at large. Primary among prospects in this utopian future is
exclusion of the discourse on human mortality and other frailties. But to
ignore our fatal dualism will not eradicate it. The *Tale* contrasts the confident
composure of the modern apostles and their seductive myth of a modern
genesis with the gloom of its prophetic vision.

CHAPTER NINE

NEWTON: MILLENNIAL MECHANICS

> Words; which are also Bodies of much Weight
> and Gravity, as it is manifest from those deep
> *Impressions* they make and leave upon us.
>
> *Tale* 60

In 1703, one year before the *Tale* was published, Sir Isaac Newton became president of the Royal Society. Though this chapter's inscription is Swift's jest, it seriously takes on the challenges of Newton's interconnected physical and theological systems and the associated motto of the Royal Society, *Nullius in Verba,* with their joint underpinnings of reason and revelation. Swift is willing to pit the "Weight and Gravity" of Kronos satire against the two-pronged scientific millenarian myth.

The persona's opening argument in the *Tale* is ostensibly about how the rhetorical value of different platforms, the "engines of orators" (59)—the pulpit, the stage, and the gallows—depends on their positioning over the heads of the masses for maximum effects. The reader may believe that he is listening to a technically valid plea for superior information-delivery systems when the modern persona announces that the words "must be delivered from a due Altitude, or else they will neither carry a good Aim, nor fall down with a sufficient Force" (60); yet any reader aware of the story of Newton's apple should not miss the deliberate comparison and contrast between the mechanical force of falling bodies and the spiritual force of cascading satiric words.[1] In the beginning was the Word, the Logos, the divine organizing principle. From this mythic root stemmed all the law and the prophecy in the Greco-Roman and Judaeo-Christian worlds until the rise of science and the Reformation. Together, Newton's mechanical laws of gravitation (1665–6) and motion (1687) and the Royal Society's dictum ignoring all save experimental actions modulated the myth of an awesome, divinely inspired, and mysterious world to reasonable and humanly controlled rules for a manageable universe. Though God may have proposed, it is humans who dispose. But to revise the divine contract, vitiating its gift of verbal facility to humans, appalled Swift.

---

[1] See Maurice J. Quinlan, "Swift's Use of Literalization as a Rhetorical Device."

There can be little doubt that a literary-scientific split developed in seventeenth-century Europe as a result of this theological change. The new myth challenged absolute governments, traditional church-state alliances, the classical humors in medicine and literature, and Aristotelian scholasticism. In the 1680s the Dublin Philosophical Society provided Swift with a local image of the fateful European split, and especially of the faith and deeds of its illustrious pioneering parent, the Royal Society. Its antihumanist motto, *Nullius in Verba,* at once defined the Royal Society's own tasks and threw down the gauntlet—enthusiastically accepted by Swift—to literary men. This motto, according to K. Theodore Hoppen,

> expressed the ideal [read, myth] which its founders hoped would underlie the scientific work of future generations. [Sir William] Petty insisted that the crucial difference between his statistical research and that which had gone before, lay in his exclusive use of "arguments of sense and . . . such causes as have visible foundations in nature," as opposed to the earlier reliance on "mutable minds, opinions, appetites, and passions of particular men." Molyneux too considered that the essential and novel characteristic of the new philosophy was that it realized itself "in actions, not in words."[2]

For the early seventeenth-century John Donne, "new philosophy calls all in doubt. . . .'Tis all in pieces, all coherence gone."[3] Not so, the Royal Society, energized by a mythic replacement that almost literally fell into place. It does not go too far to find a mythical given in the intellectual pride and zeal of Marsh, Temple, Shaftesbury, Bentley, Wotton, Toland, and Browne that still controls the mind sets, premises, and conclusions of modern research and professional documentation. The mythical apparatus that encases, indeed enshrines, scientific language leads the most objective examiner to respect that language and what the discipline it supports may do to ameliorate the human condition. But by a Swiftian irony, the process of negating other knowledge systems diminishes the scientific epistemology itself. The myth makes the would-be objective scientist a subjective enthusiast, and thus unwittingly one of Swift's enthusiastic modern priests.

The scientific myth, energizing and stabilizing the modern world, had beginnings that the *Tale* satirizes and cultural historians now readily verify. However they phrase it and whatever their social or political leanings, modern cultural historians agree that a basic conflict today began in the early seventeenth century between the dedicated partisans of revelation and of reason. This divergence among world changers may be discerned in modern

---

2 Hoppen quotes from Petty's *Political Arithmetick* and from the Preface to W. Molyneux's *Sciothericum Telescopicum.* 76.

3 *The First Anniversary: An Anatomy of the World,* ll. 210, 213.

understandings of the slippery term *enlightenment,* most often applied to a period, as in the Rosicrucian Enlightenment of the seventeenth century, the High Enlightenment of the eighteenth century, and the Radical Enlightenment that slipped covertly between them. In these three instances *enlightenment* refers originally to forces newly discovered within the individual, of either divine or rational origins. If the Reformation directed learned attention to the inner light of the Holy Spirit, Descartes and Locke reoriented that attention to the altogether different light of reason. The irony of the conflict between these opposing forces in the larger theaters of modern European institutions is that the same argument occurred within the seminal minds that defined the two enlightenments.

Whether one accepts Charles Webster's analysis of continuity and change in his *From Paracelsus to Newton* (1982) or Margaret C. Jacob's opposite appraisal of the shorter period from Boyle to Newton, one recognizes that both historians are aware that their three major figures found equal inspiration in the revelatory and rational lights.[4] Similarly, all the major natural philosophers of the religious and scientific enlightenments—like the cultural historians who have recorded their differences but themselves adopt similar opposing stances—were cognizant of the revolutionary implications of each of the new lights for learning, religion, and governance. Each light in its own right provides a compelling, mind-changing, world-changing argument for individual autonomy and liberty of conscience against all the old world tyrannies. Of course, new tyrannies are imposed by the self-anointed modern priesthoods, themselves now institutionally ensconced to govern the achievement and allocate the distribution of the separate lights. Choosing sides in the argument over the two inner forces—the holy spirit and reason—occupied Newton and the Boyle lecturers such as Samuel Clarke, Richard Bentley, and William Whiston and their opponents, who included radical sectaries and such freethinking deists as Toland, Matthew Tindal, and Anthony Collins between 1688 and 1710. But heterodoxy in one age becomes orthodoxy in another.

The problem of myth, even in a world dominated by facts and information, is its necessity. Quoting Rousseau and Durkheim, Lester G. Crocker has no doubts "that social stability depends on solidarity, which in turn depends on the prevalence of myths bound up with ritual and ceremonial, symbols and traditions. Myth creates a structure that mobilizes our wills and emotions, and gives purpose to what we do and are; without it the individual feels isolation and anxiety, a situation productive of lawlessness and social chaos" (28). Fifteen years after Crocker's presidential address on myth to the Fourth International Congress on Enlightenment (1976), the anarchic specter he

---

4 Jacob, *The Cultural Meaning of the Scientific Revolution.*

raised for a postmodern environment still seems a real eventuality should the myth of the lights fail.

Scientific millenarianism is the modern term that describes the myth of the twin inner lights of reason and revelation. Richard H. Popkin precisely defines our scientific millenarianism as "a vital intellectual and spiritual force" that brought about "the union of the new science and a defense against religious skepticism" in his Foreword to James E. Force's *William Whiston: Honest Newtonian* (xviii). That the movement's original defense of religion has become a defense of secular materialism can be seen in the mythic promise of material or earthly salvation as paramount above eternal salvation in the purposes and priorities of every twentieth-century national state. As millenarianism became secularized, as Swift understood it would be, the defense against religious skepticism was expanded to include arguments against the satirist's lonely skepticism about the reality of the modern myth of linear human progress—or as the full title of the *Tale* and its persona ironically promised—*The Universal Improvement of Mankind.*

In his Foreword Popkin states the case succinctly.

> To try to appreciate the enormous intellectual journey that Western man made between 1600 and 1800 without taking account of the rise and transformation of millenarianism is to miss some of the crucial dynamics of what happened—and to misunderstand where we are today and how we got here. (Force xiv)

One cannot venture far into the scientific *millenarian* myth without weighing Newton's contributions to it. Popkin has devoted scholarly energies to redressing the balance between the consistent overconcentration on Newton's physical theories at the expense of his theological ones; his research recognizes that each Newtonian system, the physical and the theological, vitally supports the other. And speaking of his agreement with Force, Popkin says that "We share an intrepretation of the centrality of theological and religious ideas to Newton's thought and to Newton's seriousness as a Millenarian which can only be understood by examining the intellectual and theological context of the time."[5]

Force summarizes the matter this way in his own essay:

> Amidst the raging tumult of party, sectarian, and intellectual strife which characterizes his society before and after the Glorious Revolution of 1688, Newton calmly goes about the business of illustrating the true nature and extent of God's dominion in theology, in science, and in politics for those who have eyes to see and ears to hear. He is secure in his view that in the latter days such knowledge

---

[5] Introduction to *Essays on the Context, Nature, and Influence of Isaac Newton's Theology* by Force and Popkin, viii.

will increase even while 'many will run to and fro' (Daniel 12:4). ("Newton's God" 93)

Force also cogently crystallizes Newton's physical and theological principles at the same time that he separates them from differing contemporary positions:

> Matter does not move, as it generally does, in accord with mathematically precise laws of nature such as those described in the *Principia* because of any Neo-platonic overflow of God's being into the world or because of any Hobbist, Cartesian, or Leibnizian notion of necessary rational order intrinsically immanent within matter or imposed once and for all long ago by a deity who long since has absented himself from the daily operations of creation. . . . Both matter and natural law originate in the will and power of God. God's dominion is the funda-mental first metaphysical principle underlying Newtonian mechanics. ("Newton's God" 84)

Reversing the customary priority of Newtonian physics, Popkin puts it succinctly that "if one starts from Newton's religious views, then perhaps it is not so strange that one with his prophetic vision could see nature and history as unfolding to the same climax" ("Newton's Biblical Theology" 94).

In tracing the lineage of "the millenarian dimension in our intellectual history" from the Reformation to the present, Popkin finds it emblematic that Whiston, a contemporary and natural satiric victim of Swift, won the confi-dence and backing of Sir Isaac Newton:

> Newton was pleased with this [Whiston's] union of the scriptural account of God's way of running the world and the physical system presented in the *Principia,* and when he retired from the Lucasian Chair of Mathematics [at Cambridge], he had young Whiston appointed to it. (Force xiii[6])

Newton and Whiston are links in a continuum of interacting millenarians, often as consecutive instructors, pupils, or disciples of one another that stretches from the sixteenth-century Marian Exiles through John Napier, Thomas Brightman, Henry Alstead, Joseph Mede, Milton, Samuel Hartlib, Comenius, John Dury, Henry More and his Cambridge Platonists, Robert Boyle, John Wilkins, William Petty, the invisible college, the Boyle lecturers, and the Parisian avant-garde La Peyrere, Gassendi, Mersenne, Grotius, and

---

6 See Force on Whiston and Swift. "Whiston paradigmatically typifies the overt linkage between pride in the achievements of Newtonian science and Whig political attitudes, as well as the radical religious heterodoxy that was so distasteful to Jonathan Swift. Swift's antiscientism was of a piece with Atterbury's persecution of Whiston; both were anti-Newtonian. Swift, not incidentally, personally detested Whiston; and he and the other Scriblerian Tories such as Arbuthnot took every opportunity to ridicule Whiston and his 'projects'" (94).

Hobbes. Swift's *Tale* attends to them all. But Popkin's Foreword offers a short course on the profound "scientific-millenarian view," not only up to 1704 as Swift treats it in the *Tale* but throughout its subsequent integration in the modern world. The underlying world view shifts from theological to secular convictions, as Swift had predicted it would and Popkin records it:

> The scientific-millenarian view continued after Newton and after Whiston in the writings of the founder of modern psychology, David Hartley, and those of the great physicist-chemist Joseph Priestley, who carried on this tradition up to the time of the French Revolution, which Priestley interpreted as the beginning of the end of this world. (Force xi)

In the early seventeenth century, the growth of scientific knowledge was seen "as part of the fulfillment of the prophecies about the events leading up to the actual reign of Jesus Christ on earth for one thousand years" (Force xi). The Puritan Revolution was decisive in England—where fleeing ideological fugitives of the Thirty Years War found a political and intellectual haven. But as we have seen in the lamentations of Milton and those of other classical republicans, as well as of the Royal Society and the radical sects, the 1660 Restoration stalled the gaining of Paradise, submerged scientific-religio-philosophical-political alliances, and turned workers in the vineyard of the New Eden into trimmers, tackers, and futurists:

> During Newton's most productive period as a scientist, he was also working continuously with [Henry] More in unraveling the prophecies in Scripture, and More was telling him of the latest treasures he had found in the cabalistic manuscripts coming from Palestine. Newton, as we know, long delayed publishing the principle of universal gravitation because he was so involved with More in millennial research. (Force xiii)

By 1696, the year Whiston offered his cosmology in *The New Theory of the Earth* and the ostensible beginning of the *Tale,* intellectuals used reason and the new epistemologies of natural philosophy, embracing such subgroups as empirical probabilities, to support and "prove" Biblical prophecies. The same epistemologies were used by Gassendi, Hobbes, and Spinoza among others to develop skepticism about the Bible's accuracy and relevance;[7] liberal Anglicans like Henry More—as Swift well knew—were caught, as Bacon had been earlier, between subscribing to Cartesian-Hobbesian skepticism and the Paracelsian-Rosicrucian empiricism *cum* occult theories of Genesis and Revelation. More and the other Cambridge Platonists taught the latitudinarians

---

[7] See Robert H. Hopkins, "The Personation of Hobbism in Swift's *Tale of a Tub* and *Mechanical Operation of the Spirit.*"

Stillingfleet, Wilkins, and Tillotson to craft a religion midway between radical dissent and secular skepticism while avoiding the shoals of deism and natural religion. "The latitudinarians," Popkin says, "sought to show that it was reasonable to accept the text of the Bible as accurate and to accept its account of the early history of the world"; he concludes that "millenarian theorizing was a most important element in the course of 'the making of the modern mind' that can only be ignored at one's peril" (Force xiv, xvi).

Millennial ideas have since delineated the role of modern secular states. "The outpouring of millenarian interpretation of the two [American and French] revolutions and the Napoleonic age is immense, much of it long forgotten and unstudied" (Force xvii). Yet, following on these ideologically sponsored cataclysms, the nineteenth and early twentieth centuries have seen the states influenced by the European culture, including the United States and Russia, armed with equally energizing myths of manifest destinies challenging each other's secular prophecies while vying for ideological, political, and material controls and geopolitical space in what is now euphemistically known as the Third World. That the United States and the French Republic have become "secular states with secular destinies," Popkin believes, "has blinded us to the force of a major way of understanding events" (Force xviii).

As Popkin's Foreword traces the lineage of "the millenarian dimension in our intellectual history" (Force xix), Jacob's Epilogue to her comprehensive 1988 study of *The Cultural Meaning of the Scientific Revolution* just as astutely examines other parts of our scientific dimension. Although her critics have seen her use of Toland as standard bearer for attacks on the origins of modern capitalism as less than objective, Jacob's extensive research and summary contributions to understanding of what she calls Radical Enlightenment and the cultural underpinnings of the European twentieth century command the highest respect.[8] Her Epilogue sums up precisely the conditions that Swift predicted for the modern world, although she freights this conclusion with her strong scientific and political convictions. Like many other cultural historians, Jacob apparently feels sure that she has been asked to don the mantle of a new priesthood:

> At this moment in human history historians concerned with Western science are being asked increasingly to make ethical or normative statements about the

---

[8] See G.C. Gibbs's review of Jacob's *The Radical Enlightenment:* "But what is Professor Jacob's thesis? Briefly, it is this. The early Enlightenment is to be perceived in terms of two cultures, the Newtonian and the Radical. . . . Whereas the Newtonian Enlightenment was mildly deistic, the Radical Enlightenment was pantheistic or materialistic. . . . The Radical Enlightenment cherished, disseminated and sought to establish a republican ideal by propaganda and intrigue, and was intent upon subverting the prevailing order in church and state" (68).

historical meaning of scientific inquiry—in effect, about how we got to where we now are. It is also true that in the postwar era a new history of science in our culture is being written by a generation of historians capable of standing back, as it were, from our science largely because the once unassailable claim that its progress equals human progress can no longer be assumed. (251)

True enough, chinks are appearing in the brave modern world. Hers is a fair reassessment, with Swiftian overtones. But then the question arises: Just how far back do such scientific believers as Jacob intend to stand? Stated simply, the heroic burden, the social mission, of these new "citizen historians"— Jacob's own heroic phrase—like that of Toland and the freethinkers or the Newtonians and the ascendant Whigs earlier, finally carries a uniform acceptance of the scientific epistemology and the millenarian myth of progress as givens, superseding the humanistic epistemology or any and all other possible myths.

Her Epilogue recognizes that "when we think as social scientists or historians we are doing so with socially focused methodologies derived from the very methodology of the new science" (253). Looked at historically, this "scientific history" derives from the nineteenth century and "cannot be separated historically from the method and metaphysics of early modern science" (253). Universal human welfare is her fine goal, the scientific language her way, and the scientific millenarian myth the rudder for her missionary course. She carries the torch high:

> The language of science must be capable of absorption, and indeed creation, by thought processes that also express other elements of the human experience. The systematic experience of nature and the codification of that experience into laws cannot be divorced from social experience. In that sense the language of science is also socially anchored, and true creativity is rooted in social experience as transformed by ingenuity. (254)

Jacob's apparent crusading aim is to redistribute the language of science to a universal population and apply it as assiduously to social issues and social research as it had formerly been applied, exclusively by a white male elite, to the narrower interests of the physical sciences. But if this language of science has created acknowledged impediments to human progress by overconcentration on the physical world, with benefits accruing with vicious selectivity, why should it be reassigned where it has no facility to solve many of the very social problems its inappropriateness helped spawn in the first place?

The weaknesses in the social sciences, long recognized by physical scientists, have resulted from an inordinate dependence on measurement, usually statistical, to understand issues, values, and human predicaments that cannot accurately or efficiently be reduced to quantifiables. The dynamic interplay between verifiable clinical experience and testable theoretical hypothesis simply does not occur in these areas. When the social findings in this mistaken language prove meaningless, as they usually do, the convenient and comforting fall back statistical position is, of course, *consensus*. The force of public opinion whatever its scientific weaknesses, as Jacob clearly sees, is viewed as a result greatly to be valued over its social and political alternatives: arbitrary hierarchical authority, traditionally Western white male oligarchies, or pure absolutism. Hence the new goals of the citizen historian. Modern mass media, demagogues, ideologues, and other evangelists and enthusiasts increasingly exploit—and indeed, manipulate—the consensus. Yet Jacob uses her vast learning circuitously to arrive at the statistical panacea, the pretense of scientific language, for the modern social scientist.

It should be noted that Jacob acknowledges two major arguments that Swift embedded in the *Tale:* modern faith in "scientific inquiry" since the eighteenth century has, first of all, tempted us "to ignore culture, to quantify the past." More egregiously, scientific inquiry has cultivated allegiance to the myth that it can "dominate the material order through knowledge . . . with a host of other assumptions about nature and power, men and women, science and the state, which appear increasingly to endanger not simply our progress but also our survival" (253).

Jacob's analysis of cultural history has convincingly illustrated that science and religion have effectively excluded women and non-whites from their discourses, thus contributing much to European political domination by white male elites since the seventeenth century. But her conclusion, unlike Swift's, is not to question the language of science and its accompanying millenarian myth, but to enlist everyone in this scientific discourse, especially those Western and non-Western peoples most beguiled by its three centuries of "false promises." All of her history of scientific culture and of culture *per se* serves to undergird her primary "principle": "the widest possible dissemination of scientific knowledge, that is the democratization of learning, will . . . foster an indigenous creativity in matters of application or innovation" (253–54). The *Tale*'s persona, "a most devoted Servant of all *Modern* Forms" (45), would applaud at the same time that the *Tale*'s satiric voice would remain highly skeptical of a new self-anointed heroic priesthood—Toland revisited.[9] When uncontaminated with zeal for the modern myth, Jacob's researches succinctly and dramatically reinforce Swift's fundamental positions. Contrarily, when faith in the salutary results of the language of science

---

9 "Why, from Bacon forward, is science adored by democratic societies when it is clearly ministered by an elite and usually incomprehensible priesthood? Democratizing science—if that is possible—would only have the result of increasing the number of zealots." Frank T. Boyle, in correspondence.

(i.e., *its* epistemology) approaches mythic proportions and the sense of missionary vocation becomes overwhelming, it produces the very zeal Swift warned us about.

To summarize, Jacob's cogent arguments and the comprehensiveness of her bibliographic materials support Swift's attacks against the same entrenched oligarchic elites in learning, religion, and governance that were anathema to her radical enlightenment. However, when she celebrates her own radical and countervailing priesthoods of British and Dutch activists with Toland as bridge, then her critics respond with the same disfavor that Swift heaped on Temple, Shaftesbury, Locke, and Toland for their alliances with the same Dutch republicans. Jacob's 1988 study unwittingly supports Swift's more balanced attack on both the incumbent and moribund priesthoods she abhors and the radical modern priesthoods she approves: his allied horrors.

Turning from the comprehensive implications of the scientific revolution considered in the cultural histories of Popkin and Jacob to Charles Webster's 1982 essays *From Paracelsus to Newton,* one is again struck by correspondences between twentieth-century cultural assessments and Swift's ideas about his contemporaries and predecessors. Webster confirms Swift's finding that Paracelsian and other Neoplatonic views permeated the learning, religion, and governance of his age:

> It is clear that there were remarkable elements of continuity [personal salvation, Neoplatonism, reformation theology, cosmology, Genesis] sufficient to indicate an important degree of contiguity between the worldviews of the early sixteenth and late seventeenth centuries. . . . The revolution towards which they [Paracelsus (1493–1541) and Newton (1642–1727)] worked was firmly rooted in the search for means of reviving the wisdom possessed by Moses, or Adam before the Fall.
> [In the period between Paracelsus and Newton] Francis Bacon [1561–1626] also acknowledged a philosophical ancestry among the pre-Socratics and based his whole approach on the scriptural idea of return of man's dominion over nature, which was finally to counteract its sacrifice at the Fall. (1–2)

Jacob's and Webster's social and political aims part company here. From Jacob's perspective Bacon, "a precise contemporary of Galileo, offered the new science as one of the avenues by which that millenarian reformation might be achieved. But he did so in language that specifically repudiated any association between millenarianism and the culture of the people, or between science and the contemporary opponents of church and state" (Jacob *Cultural Meaning* 20).

As historian of science Webster looks panoramically at the broad sweep for continuity among world views, whereas Jacob uncovers the continuity of coteries and alliances among politically powerful elites and their radical adversaries. What Swift does is trace the centennial continuity of public and private deception among intellectual elites—the moderns—whose limited epistemology by definition must eschew the nonmeasurable and more disturbing realities of human nature.

Webster's broad view suggests a remarkable affinity with Swift's. He records "the persistence of the influence of figures such as Paracelsus" and notes that the humanist "attempt to discredit Paracelsus . . . was totally unsuccessful at the time. . . . [and in no way interfered with] the virtually unimpeded rise of the influence of the medical reformer" (3). He concludes that "the first major confrontation of the Scientific Revolution was between Paracelsus and Galen, rather than between Copernicus and Ptolemy" (3–4); and he asserts that "In view of the self-evident kinship between hermetic, alchemical, and scriptural sources, the deciphering of alchemical texts was an exercise that no scientific exegetist [in Newton's age] could resist" (10). Webster quotes F. E. Manuel, a twentieth-century historian with whom Popkin would agree, that Newton "saw himself as the last of the interpreters of God's will in actions, living on the eve of the fulfilment of times" (11). Webster's introductory essay ends with a thesis that the *Tale* assumed:

> In reality the worldview of the Scientific Revolution should be viewed as a diverse phenomenon, the result of a dynamic interplay of forces [*e.g.* mechanical philosophy, natural magic, alchemy, hermeticism] which emanated from many different directions. All of these forces contributed to the process of creativity and change, and none of them deserves to be written off *a priori* as a useless intellectual encumbrance from a discredited magical past. (12)

Webster's essay on spiritual magic points out linkages between the Reformation and the Scientific Revolution—between spiritual, occult, and secular forces. In contrast with the concerns of Jacob for radical ideological-intellectual-political movements in the real world, Webster is concerned with how evolving new cosmologies, prophecies, and belief in "the restoration of an earthly paradise" became energizing forces on seminal minds. As we have seen, Swift's satire joins both fields of reference.

Webster supports the views of Ernest Tuveson, Manuel, Jacob—and Swift—that the imagery of the millennium, as either optimistic or pessimistic prognostication, "was if anything increased by the hot pace of scientific progress in the later part of the [seventeenth] century" (67):

> Although called a "Sabbatical Reign," "New Kingdom" or "New Evangelical World," the new order as conceived by Burnet, Edwards, Evelyn, or Whiston seemed to consist of precisely the same economic and social order nourished by the latitudinarians and consolidated by them after the Glorious Revolution. Fifth Monarchism was thus stripped of its magical and subversive elements, and the residuum subsumed into the discipline of the church. (68)

While Webster and Swift agree on the fantastic elements, they disagree on the destiny of the scientific revolution. What Webster sees as the positive results of many interacting dynamic forces, Swift reads as cumulatively destructive. In contrast to Webster's and Jacob's interpretations of modern cultural history, Swift's satiric thrust is to forewarn of a continuum—not of a positive scientific revolution and religious reformation, not of vying reforming, revolutionary, and entrenched politico-intellectual forces—but a continuum of disparate intellectual, religious, and political interests coalescing, because of a universally seductive one-dimensional epistemology and the exotic myth seeming to guarantee authority and perpetuity, into a mad modern world.

Three seminal influences are blended in the seventeenth-century natural philosophy that undergirds this modern myth, each since assimilated into our science: the fact-laden and systematic Baconian information program for the advancement of learning; the imaginative Paracelsian empiricism modified by Van Helmont and ultimately purged of its occult spiritualism, but retaining faith in Genesis and Neoplatonism; and the precise Cartesian mechanical philosophy followed by the Newtonian synthesis. These influences correlate with the aims of the Dublin Philosophical Society to promote experimental philosophy, medicine, and mechanics, and taken together they provide the satire on modern science in the *Tale*. Swift divides his satire on modern learning into these three categories and attacks the fathers of each—Bacon, Paracelsus, and Descartes—and their disciples. At the same time, the influences overlap and combine in the *Tale* as they did in the Royal and Dublin Societies and in the thought of Boyle and Newton. (As we discovered earlier, Homer was no match for the rising power of these combined forces and ironically comes across very badly indeed in the modern world, and therefore in the satirized judgment of the *Tale*.)

Although Swift focused on the European re-formation achieved by these meshing but diverse intellectual currents in the seventeenth century, the mass of Swift studies deals with eighteenth-century English literary matters. Despite some caveats, the few ventures taken into the more encompassing Swiftian world have been especially valuable in deciphering his complexities. In 1936, for example, R. F. Jones's *Ancients and Moderns* treated the *Battle of the Books*, the companion piece to the *Tale*, within the larger seventeenth-century historical context. Historians of science recognized Jones's work then as a signal contribution, but have since found it necessary to correct serious weaknesses in its approach. One such historian, P. M. Rattansi, credits him for being "among the earliest to appreciate the importance of Paracelsian and Helmontian currents and the way in which their proponents could join hands with 'Baconians' in urging a new approach to the study of nature" (Rattansi Review 250–51) but questions Jones's sweeping dictum that "our modern scientific utilitarianism is the offspring of Bacon begot upon Puritanism" (Jones 91; Review 251). Rattansi, like Swift implicitly, argues against the exclusive influence of Bacon here. Among the complexities introduced by midcentury, Rattansi—like Swift—recognized the scientific and sectarian use of Scripture, especially the book of Genesis, to stress grace and illumination, combined with emphases on Neoplatonic schema, the mechanical philosophy from Descartes, and Paracelsian medicine.

Swift would approve Rattansi's other cautions about Jones's work, particularly as they apply to the *Tale* and the *Battle of the Books*. Jones limits the New Science to Bacon's study of natural phenomena by observation and "experiment"; he limits his setting to England instead of considering Europe an intercommunicating whole; and he fails to take into account that while the thrust of modern science has been to achieve secular goals, neither Bacon nor Newton viewed progress in the purely secular, materialist framework it later assumed. (They also were not so immune to European cross-fertilization as Jones suggests.) For Rattansi, Jones misses, as Swift does not, the fundamentally religious and apocalyptic idea of progress. The bulwark of modern secular mythology, the idea of progress underlies seventeenth-century natural philosophy and the influence of Channel-crossing reformers in religion and learning. Swift satirizes "the basis for Bacon's programme, the dream of using a new science of nature to repair the effects of the Fall of Man" (Review 254). Rattansi finally points to Jones's overemphasis on the ancients-moderns antithesis.

In *Swift's Satire on Learning in A Tale of a Tub* (1968), Miriam K. Starkman acknowledges her "great indebtedness" to Jones and also draws attention to the seventeenth-century background. She credits Temple's moral philosophy more than his controversial *Essay upon the Ancient and Modern Learning* as influencing the *Tale* (13), and she recognizes that William Wotton's "pride and millenarian enthusiasm . . . evoked some of Swift's sharpest satire" (17). She finds Swift "subverting modernity" and persuading man to virtue (22–23). She also finds him attacking Temple's and Newton's "Epicurean imperturbability" on moral and psychological grounds. Her discussion of the faculties of the mind, the early psychology, underscores Swift's fundamental belief that the whole rational system is "constantly imperilled by another complex system, the appetitive powers of the soul, the emotions," or lower faculties (34–36).

Starkman is particularly searching on Swift's sartorist system in the *Tale*. In this mock Neoplatonic system, the universe being "a large suit of clothes which invests everything . . . Man himself is but a Micro-Coat" (60):

What links man now to his deity, the tailor, is the body of his body, the "outward" dress of his outward dress, his clothes. And since clothes officiate for man in the nature of a soul, in effect they become his "inward dress"; and such little real soul as he may have left becomes his least important, outward dress, his body. "By all which it is manifest, that the outward Dress must needs be the Soul." Thus depraved man, depraved for having lost his soul, is properly linked to the macrocosm, the "large *Suit of Cloaths* which *invests* everything." For *clothes* have modified *man so* completely that they have become *man.* Man, having lost his soul, which distinguishes him as man, is no more. (62)

Turning to the new science, Starkman lists the salient aims of the Royal Society as utilitarian, systematic, encyclopedic, mechanical, and universally beneficial—all modern and all anathema to Swift. The *Tale* satirizes all these aims. They represent aspects for the satirist of the optimistic and therefore false myth that, whether the human is divorced from or allied with the Creator, omits the essential givens of human nature: it is vicious and mortal.

With an irony he would have savored, after her trenchant analysis Starkman concludes that Swift's satire on science "is scarcely just or perceptive" and "principally of antiquarian interest to us" (85, 86). Since Starkman's insights on Swift's discovery of mythical fallacies governing modern man stand up to searching scrutiny, her disclaimers of his twentieth-century applicability offer reassuring evidence from the world of literary criticsm of the imperturbably self-sufficient modern dogma Swift exposes.

Until very recently, some literary critics were loath to tamper with the prelapsarian myth of scientific progress. Ironically, their felt need to produce disclaimers, their resistance to the acute connections they themselves have uncovered, serves to reinforce Swift's compelling epochal power and his understanding of the tenacity of the modern myth even in light of contradictory facts. Swift wanted to challenge the pious yet self-aggrandizing aims underlying modern science: his humanistic challenge discomforts confident moderns enough for them to disavow the quality of their own discriminations. Faith in reason *per se* has created a new learning that allows the entry of a new religion, Neoplatonism, which spawns an old governance with new facades. Neoplatonism, a melange of correspondences, Christian and pagan inner lights, the books of nature and Genesis, information systems and the occult, pastes over—as Starkman's analysis rightly concludes—the loss of the human's true spiritual nature, integrated object relations, and ego psychology. The human animal has been turned, like the modern world, upside down with all the bodily appetites and predatory aggression compellingly fantasized, visually enhanced, powerfully sponsored, and universally transmitted in fidelity to this mythical warp.

To reach the polar positions of Swift and Clarke or Swift and Toland or Swift and Marsh, chronology is important. When Swift attacked the Puritan Revolution and its legacy of dissenting sects, he also satirized the Neoplatonic origins of Anglican rationalism and the deism and natural religion evolving from Bruno and the Socinians. Similarly, intertwining the thought of Paracelsus, Bacon, and Descartes provides clues to the midcentury enthusiasms of Thomas Vaughan's Rosicrucianism, Henry More's Cambridge Platonism, and Hartlib's "Invisible College" and the Royal Society. As one of the founders of the Oxford Philosophical Society in the late 50s and the Dublin Philosophical Society in the early 80s, Narcissus Marsh provides the bridge to Swift's Oxford and Dublin of the 90s, with Neoplatonism the binding force. This intertwined legacy supplies clues also to the seemingly contradictory rational and revelatory philosophical positions taken by Robert Boyle and Isaac Newton over the latter half of the century.

When old myths die, new learning and new myths accommodate each other. The overthrow of Aristotelianism and the attacks on the Christian mysteries sponsored by the Church of Rome left a mythical vacuum in sixteenth-century learning, religion, and governance soon filled by Christianized Neoplatonism. Articulated originally by Plotinus and revived by the Florentines Marsilio Ficino (1433–99) and Pico della Mirandola (1463–94) in the late fifteenth century, Neoplatonism became the mythical cornerstone of Paracelsus's empirical chemical philosophy. Paracelsus joined Neoplatonism with alchemy, natural magic, cabbala, hermetics, and Scriptures; and by the end of the sixteenth century, Paracelsians believed that the prelapsarian state would be restored as the millennium approached (Rattansi *Scientific background* 212).

According to Iago Galston, Paracelsus was among the last of the learned men "who attempted to amalgamate the ancient and modern learnings" ("Psychiatry" 408). For Galdston as for Charles Singer and E.A. Underwood, Paracelsus foreshadowed belief in the "new instauration" (*From magic* 105). The Renaissance reoriented man's attention to the fundamental dichotomy between delight in the miracle of life and horror at still having to deal with certain physical disintegration and mortality. The new optimism had to deal with rooted pessimism. If man indeed were to become the Renaissance measure, he needed to be linked with the immeasurable, the eternal. Neoplatonism, when wedded to Christianity and alchemy, opened a way for Paracelsus to discover new correspondences between God and man, life and death, health and disease, spirit and matter, the astral and human psyches. Neoplatonism linked the reasonable aspects of medieval medicine, alchemy, hermetics, cabala, magic, and gnosticism with Paracelsus's new chemical empiricism. Long before the terms *holism* and *Gestalt* gained currency, Paracelsus perceived man integrated within himself and in relation to the whole world. His profound faith in Genesis suggested to him an impending new dispensation between God and man, a new myth moving from the nomadic-agrarian to the agrarian-urban European societies. The original separation of the divine from the human would be healed.

In the esoteric subculture of the occult, Swift discerned the theological motivation underlying the new myth for modern man. Discoveries and inventions, indeed all scientific progress and spiritual reformation since the Renaissance, subserve the quixotic search for some way to get around Adam's Fall resulting in mankind's imperfect and fatal nature. To be sure, in 1572 Erastus had defended Galen against the Paracelsians and in 1606 Libavius had claimed Paracelsus's work to be full of illegitimate and demonic magic and his macrocosm-microcosm analogy false. Yet in all modern reformulations, reformations for regeneration, no innovation has appeared more alluring than the celestial prospects of Neoplatonism. When united with the accessible grace of Christ in the agrarian New Testament and the magic of alchemy transmuted to the gold of modern chemistry and the notion of exponential progress in natural philosophy, the Platonic correspondences of macrocosm-microcosm exalted man while rearranging his mundane authorities and tyrannies.

This gnostic route to surmount evil and return to a prelapsarian good remains the sturdy myth of modern science, Protestant Christianity, and European societies.[10] Empiricists and rationalists unite in its cause. The mythological belief and astrological search for a mystical world somewhere in space continues the irrational alloy in the scientific epistemology.

In postulating a macrocosmic world soul vibrating throughout the infinite, the Neoplatonists believed that the microcosmic human soul must needs establish links with the divine macrocosm. Consequently, Paracelsus emphasizes the psyche. For Paracelsus, separation and individuation are forged in its celestial fire. P.M. Rattansi has precisely analyzed this vision:

> The theme of separation had a deep and poignant significance in Paracelsian thought. Creation itself, as described in the Genesis account, was a separation. But since it was a disruption of the primal unity, it implied a fall and degeneration. . . . Separation and conflict was a transient state. All nature tended toward its own primitive state and would one day return to it. ("Art and Science" 53)

For Paracelsus, separation from the divine macrocosm forces the individual to reestablish correspondences with the divine nature that are there in potentia.

---

[10] For Swift's attacks on gnosticism, see Ronald Paulson.

While individuation in psychoanalytic object relations theory specifically refers to a circuitous, but necessary psychic separation for the baby in its first year from its undifferentiated union with the natural mother, individuation for Paracelsus and his modern disciple Carl Jung is the individual's lifelong quest to discover his or her specific astral element or individual identity that will reestablish linkage with the severed primal unity. Unity with the astral psyche, divine force, or earth mother must be forged in the celestial fire of the human psyche. Paracelsus felt that he had pierced the covers of matter to discover the divine inner light, the microcosm within.

Swift too recognizes the psyche as the center of organization or chaos of body, mind, society, and the surrounding natural world. His search too is for unity and harmony. But he sees few magi among the moderns; instead, he finds "an increase of contradiction" making for anarchic, rather than disciplined, individualism. New divine and secular priesthoods proliferate without the divine connection being made. He thus disagrees fundamentally with Paracelsus, and even more with the philosopher's seventeenth-century disciples. Swift denies their organizing principle that the reconnection of astral and human psyches will return the fallen human to a primal unity with the creator. For Swift, the moderns instead promote centrifugal separation from mortal and immortal human destiny, society, traditional and self-knowledge, and maturity of the species. The utopian republicans infiltrate governance while the two opposing branches of natural philosophy, the Paracelsian mystical empiricists and the Cartesian mechanical rationalists, battle for preeminence in learning. Moreover, these factions have united their forces with the religious enthusiasts. For Swift, classical republicans and natural philosophers differ not one whit in their modernism from the Quakers, Anabaptists, and Family of Love, the latter-day radical believers he equates with other dissenting sects bent on appropriating Christianity. He lumps them as optimists whether they subserve the Christianized Neoplatonism of Paracelsus or the millennial mechanics of Newton or the rational natural religion of the deists.

Evil vanquished is no part of the Kronos-Saturn myth. In the naive desire to eliminate any serious consideration of evil, we witness modern attempts to neutralize Kronos as the Newtonian Watchmaker God or the Shaftesburian—benevolent—Father Christmas. Samuel L. Macey's *Patriarchs of Time* traces the chronology of the myth from the Indo-Iranian gods of finite and infinite time through Kronos-Saturn with his castration of his father Uranus to his own castration at the hands of the modern priests. Macey can't help quoting Swift's commentary in the *Tale* on Kronos emasculated and the consequent masking and mutilation of the bitter truth—Truth being Kronos's daughter—about ourselves and our destiny (62):

UNDER the *Stage-Itinerant* are couched those Productions designed for the Pleasure and Delight of Mortal Man; such as *Six-peny-worth of Wit,* Westminster *Drolleries, Delightful Tales, Compleat Jesters,* and the like; by which the Writers of and for GRUB-STREET, have in these latter Ages so nobly triumphed over *Time;* have clipt his Wings, pared his Nails, filed his Teeth, turned back his Hour-Glass, blunted his Scythe, and drawn the Hob-Nails out of his Shoes. (63)

The 1973 *Oxford* edition includes an appendix, "Notes on Dark Authors," that includes the *Tale*'s allusions to Paracelsus and the Paracelsians. Much has been uncovered in the last quarter-century concerning the Paracelsians and the Rosicrucians in the German states and their catalytic influence on The Thirty Years War and the Civil War in England.[11] In both wars, the *Rosicrucian Manifestos* turned the Reformation and the new learning into an occult utopian myth generating enthusiasts who assaulted the establishments of religion, governance, and learning throughout northern Europe. The Paracelsian vanguard included chemical philosophers, magi like John Dee, mystics like Jacob Boehme, Dutch publishers and engravers, propagandists, and militant activists. Their utopian myth might be summarized as follows: Adam had no bestial passions; rather he drew his strength from God's emaning—that is, flowing—into all of nature including His masterpiece and deputy, the human. The most intricate self-knowledge, therefore, provided means to recross the abyss caused by original sin and to realign the soul for infusion of the Holy Ghost—the light within. Such a pilgrimage back to Paradise could confer spiritual leadership and priest status to guide others to that original harmony with God. We are not far removed from Milton's liberty of conscience and professional revolutionaries.

Swift believed profoundly that modern writers threatened the time-honored foundations of society. He believed their motivation to overthrow moribund absolute states rested on their unconscious desire to erect tyrannies of their own mythical devising. He granted that moderns like Toland had found out "the Art of exposing weak Sides, and publishing Infirmities" (*Tale* 172) in their zeal to tear down established institutions. But moderns did not rest content to overthrow the tyranny and dry rot of outmoded ideas and authorities; these "Grand Innovators" (*Tale* 166) sought to fill the vacuum with new institutions erected on shakier theosophical foundations tempting them to enlarge their new precincts with schemes and systems, myths and mysteries, if anything, more suspect, more elaborate and infinitely more popularly seductive than those they replaced. Swift collectively categorizes these refinements "as, *long Schemes in Philosophy, dark and Wonderful Mysteries of State;*

---

[11] For further discussion, see Frances Yates, *The Rosicrucian Enlightenment,* Hugh Trevor-Roper, "The Paracelsian Movement" in *Renaissance Essays,* Allen G. Debus, and Walter Pagel.

Laborious Dissertations in Criticism and Philosophy, Advice to Parliaments,
and the like" (*Tale* 262).

The leap from the old Genesis to the new became a major preoccupation of
Paracelsus and the Reformation, the Rosicrucians, the Instauration, the Inter-
regnum, Toland, the *Tale*'s persona, and the *Tale* itself. It links the twin
sixteenth-century pillars of the modern revolution, science and reformation. In
going beyond the Phalaris and Dublin controversies, Swift in the *Tale* sees the
modern genesis as having emanated from Paracelsus. Though Paracelsus's
mystical cosmos remains the inspiration of Aeolist wisdom in the *Tale,* Swift,
forever yoking his victims, the historical and the contemporary, again borrows
from Toland to illustrate pervasive continuity.

Frances Yates has linked the Renaissance vitalist Giordano Bruno to
hermeticism, magic, and Neoplatonism. In turn, both Robert E. Sullivan and
Stephen H. Daniel, biographers of Toland, have documented the influence of
Bruno's metaphysics on their subject from 1698 onward. As Daniel has noted,
Bruno had a fascination for the infinite power and activity of the universe that
led to Toland's profound conviction that the essential activity of matter is
motion (195–96; 200–03). Changing material forms reinforced the hermetic
tradition and the Biblical dictum that whatever was will be again.

Toland's *Amyntor; or a Defence of Milton's Life* (1699) discussed the
legitimacy of the Canon of Scriptures in hermetic terms. By pursuing Toland's
irenic argument on the Scriptures, Swift finds still another inconsistency in his
position on the mysteries: the great rational opposer of Christian mysteries
cannot resist the pedantic opportunity to purvey his own illuminist mysteries.
By way of Irenaeus and Bruno, he has accepted the Paracelsian celestial
cosmology and the Genesis myth. "*Irenaeus* the famed Successor of the
Apostles," Toland wrote,

> positively affirms, that there cannot be more, nor fewer than Four Gospels: "For,"
> says he, "there be Four Regions of this World wherein we live, with Four
> principal Winds, and the Church is spread over all the Earth: But the Support and
> Foundation of the Church is the Gospel, and the Spirit of Life: Therefore it must
> follow, that it has Four Pillars, blowing Incorruptibility on all sides, and giving
> Life to Men." (50–51)

In his description of the mad Aeolists in the *Tale,* Swift plays with Toland's
thought. His phenomenon of vapours is temporarily transferred from its
obvious humoral associations to an allusion to *Genesis* and Irenaeus, to divine
inspiriting of life into man. "The Breath of Man's Life is in his Nostrils" (154)
serves as a reprise of his earlier linking of the beginnings of the Aeolist sect
and the modern world with Genesis 2.7 (151): "And the Lord God formed man
of the dust of the ground, and breathed into his nostrils the breath of life: and

man became a living soul." Having reminded his readers of the Old Testament formulation of man's creation by God and his re-creation by the moderns, Swift turns to the New Testament version of the divine gift according to Irenaeus and Toland. In the telling, he allows the persona to glorify the moderns' new genesis. Using Toland's comment on the regions of the four winds, the *Tale* assures us that

> THEIR [Aeolists'] Gods were the four *Winds,* whom they worshipped, as the Spirits that pervade and enliven the Universe, and as those from whom alone all *Inspiration* can properly be said to proceed. (154)

Swift then modulates from the mystical number four to the chief wind blowing from the "almighty North," Scotland or the "Land of Darkness." By these allusions, he shifts from the "dark authors" to his despised "land of darkness"; further, he moves from the Paracelsian occult medical philosophy and faith in Genesis to Milton, Toland, and the zealous Presbyterian sectaries. The latter invaders from the North "have brought over their choicest *Inspiration,* fetching it with their own Hands, in certain *Bladders,* and disploding [Milton's word] it among the Sectaries in all Nations" (154–55).[12]

Thus in presenting his array of moderns, Swift modulates from the Paracelsian-Rosicrucian-Miltonian-Tolandic mystery of a New Eden to his own reading of the seventeenth-century reformation as a Galenic humoral imbalance in modern learning, the phenomenon of vapours, a new madness, a new darkness, a new chaos passed off as inner illumination, the divine inspiration vouchsafed to modern man by the Reformation. In the *Tale,* he links notions of the celestial forces within with his phenomenon of vapours in the digestive tract. He uses odious vapours in the digestive tract as his private substitution for the modern's egocentric notion of man's "inward light," his unifying myth. He sees in this myth an elaboration of Paracelsus's search for astral signatures in the microcosmic psyche. He recognized that even the most rational of mechanists such as Descartes, Boyle, and Newton, the most militant of republicans such as Milton and Sidney, and the most rational of Anglicans such as Henry More and Locke acknowledged a divine or mystical source of inspiration within underlying modern reforms. The vitalist Neo-platonic notion of correspondences had led to the conviction that man, the microcosm, possesses "inward light" flowing from God, the macrocosm. Chemical philosophers adapting Paracelsian doctrine had reinforced Christian sects in exalting the notion of the spirit within, the microcosm mirroring the macrocosm of God in nature. With all these enthusiasts claiming "inward

---

12 Cf. *Paradise Lost,* vi.605.

light" as the mystical principle undergirding modern institutional change, Swift could reorganize the modern forces in the *Tale* under his own satiric modern myth—the rubric of madness, a communicable gastroenterological humoral disease of epidemic proportions, bordering on a universal intellectual plague. That is, the *Tale* reduces the myth of illumination or inward light to epidemic indigestion: too many natural philosophers had eaten the forbidden fruit from the tree of knowledge in Genesis and come up windy.

Swift uses Paracelsian medicine in the *Tale* alongside the Galenic humoral tradition. If stomachic vapours ascending translate to inward light satirically, they also indicate an epidemic form of melancholy medically and psychologically. Indeed, the conflicting variations of melancholy underlie the *Tale* and define its satiric victims, on one hand, and the nature of a satirist, on the other.[13] As a case in point, he finds a valuable midcentury psychosomatic clue in *Enthusiasmus Triumphatus* (1662), Henry More's attack on the Rosicrucian Thomas Vaughan's *Anthroposophic Theomagica* (1650) attributing modern enthusiasm to pathological melancholy. More's satiric conceit was apposite, since it enlists the psycho-pathological rational theorist Galen and the humors tradition to diagnose the Paracelian disciples. Swift's most basic satiric motif is a single universal modern purpose, reentering an optimistic utopian world; he attributes obsession with it to a single pathological modern condition, an epidemic humoral imbalance or madness mistakenly thought to be inward light.

Michael V. DePorte has thoughtfully treated the links between melancholic vapors, madness, the imagination, and enthusiasm in the *Tale* and in More's *Enthusiasmus Triumphatus*. He explains that in More's jest the Rosicrucian enthusiast Vaughan suffers from an overheated imagination, a disease in which the corrupted melancholic humor of black bile rises to the brain as a vapor. This type of melancholy DePorte describes as "hypochondriacal or 'windy' melancholy, and More, in a witty play on one of the meanings of 'inspire' ('to blow or breathe into'—*O.E.D.*), seizes on it as the specific source of the enthusiast's much vaunted inspiration" (Introduction iv). DePorte attributes More's disparagement of imagination to his Platonic conviction that it is delusive in distorting the world of appearances. Both John Phillip Harth and DePorte recognize that the *Tale* uses More's model of vapours rising from the "lowest region" of the body to infect the brain as the single affliction of Swift's modern Aeolist sect, kin to More's Rosicrucian Vaughan. In his essay on the *Tale*, DePorte discusses the later Augustan view of the imagination as the anarchic faculty.

---

[13] For a full analysis of the diametric pathological and philosophical melancholy central to the *Tale*, see below, pp. 214–18.

Swift's use of Henry More's device of attacking enthusiasm as melancholy madness exposed him to the very label of Anglican reactionary that he had registered against More and the Cambridge Platonists. More's Neoplatonism, when combined with the mechanistic thought of Descartes at the time of the Restoration, supports the science of the Royal Society and Newton, as well as Anglican rationalism; these concerns admit both More and Descartes to the *Tale*'s Aeolist sect. In what Rattansi calls a novel restatement of Renaissance Platonism, More

> held that Cartesianism and Platonism were once part of a "Mosaic Cabbala"—
> hinted at in the Book of Genesis—of which the physical part alone passed to the
> "atheistic" Greek atomists, while the metaphysical one was taken over by Plato.
> Mechanical explanations . . . could only be explained by invoking the "spirit of
> Nature," a new version of the Platonic World-Soul. ("Scientific Background"
> 235–36)

Swift's persona similarly lacks any principle of order or restraint. DePorte comments that, "Through the persona of the narrator, then, Swift is able to continue the attack on that insistent subjectivity which for him constitutes insanity and which is consistently seen as the chief feature of 'modernity'" ("Digressions" 48); and in his book on madness in the *Tale* he pursues the Stoic syllogism that "knaves and fools are mad, because every deviation from reason is a deviation into madness" (*Nightmares* 55). For DePorte, the Digression on Madness gives definitive expression to that syllogism by using the "vapours" image to illustrate how the intellect may be crippled by passion. As we have seen, Swift extends the "vapours" image to all tyrants, innovators, and world changers. This sweeping indictment leads DePorte to affirm the thesis also developed here: The reader of the Digression is compelled

> to recognize how warped the world's values are apt to become. Radical innova-
> tions, new conquests, new philosophies, new religions, are insane because they
> ignore the central realities of man's condition—his weakness and his fallibility.
> (*Nightmares* 65–66)

The myth of a modern genesis held that rational and virtuous men would institute millennial progress toward a better world simply by releasing the forces of nature and inhibiting the sources of absolutism. Amelioration of the human condition was the earnest cooperative goal. Swift, however, interpreted this ideal of progress back to Eden as socially restrictive and morally degenerate: a highly sophisticated means for erecting more seductive facades for more invasive tyrannies. Behind the towering theosophical facades, he found, ready to dominate the modern world, a conspiracy of enthusiastic rationalists, pious frauds, demagogic opportunists, corrupt hedonists, and the certifiably insane—all of them exalted by the acquiescent modern learned community and reverenced by the trailing obedient masses.

The millenarian aspects of science have been buried as so deep a given in the modern unconscious that it would be a prodigious labor to raise them to consciousness. Were this accomplished, however, the validity of most modern institutions would be seriously challenged by aesthetic, humanistic, and psychiatric epistemologies—and by the scientific epistemology itself that undergirds these institutions. The ensuing breakdown of encrusted and entrenched political-scientific hierarchial alliances in religion, learning, and governance, with their networks of mass controls, might then create a profound reorientation of human energies, thought, and values, re-directing them from the tyrannies of so-called reality principles and pat interpretations of the major European revolutions since printing and the Reformation. We might then arrive at a viable postmodern age at the end of a journey charted by Swift. If Swift challenges the misreading of human nature by those setting forth the ark of the modern covenant, then even though he pleaded for stability his *Tale* remains a revolutionary document, enhanced by the almost three centuries since its creation.

Though twentieth-century assumptions and the *Tale*'s commentaries on the scientific forces propelling the modern world suggest a conflict of discourses worth the most serious attention, the intellectual credentials of the infidel Swift storming the establishment gates have been questioned. The myth preservers have seen fit to level the *ad hominem* charge against Swift as either an extreme radical or an extreme reactionary or a poor manager of his career. Ironically, Swift's definitive twentieth-century biographer Irvin Ehrenpreis looks dismally at Swift's learning in the light of what he is sure should have concerned any learned writer most: his livelihood. Ehrenpreis dismisses his subject's "uniformitarianism, anti-intellectualism, negative philosophy of history, and his rejection of the [rising] middle class merchants and financiers" as evidence that his epistemology interfered with a more vital modern consideration, good business sense; he concludes that, "A vision turned early, firmly, nobly, and mistakenly to the past, ruined his career."[14] Ehrenpreis uses modern standards of success, wealth, and power more appropriate to commerce and governance than learning and wisdom. The biographer's own mythical standard may be congenial to insouciant professionals, but Swift was ready to pay any price including damage to his career to make his profound statements about the modern world and its rejection of fundamental truths.

---

[14] "Swift on Liberty," 73.

Moderns with modern priorities cannot comprehend that the well-balanced Swift is attacking their entire construct.

But the issue is not whether we turn to the past or live in economic and virtuous safety while voicing civic concern and living with material comforts in the present. The question is which vision of the past governs that present and its future. Is it viable? Swift finds that the scientific millennarian myth in his time accommodated the Neoplatonic soul of the world, the dominant Judeao-Christian God in heaven and on earth, and Epicurean atomism of pure chance. It accommodated both revelation and reason, and he understood that it would transform millennial expectation to a secular materialism.

Edmund Halley's 1687 Ode on Newton's *Philosophiae naturalis principia mathematica* along with its source, Lucretius's *De rerum natura,* finds in Newtonian physics a keystone of the Epicurean revival. All three works are Swiftian targets for the bodies of thought they carry.[15] Neither Newton's classical philosophy nor his mechanics nor his millennial theology mattered to the *Tale*'s satiric voice. If Kronos-Saturn's unsettling words "of much Weight and Gravity" as opposed to Newton's apple fall "from a due Altitude . . . [and] carry a good Aim . . . with a sufficient Force" (60), the reader might do better to track their celestial source than observe their terrestrial thud.

---

[15] See Charles Scruggs, "Swift's Use of Lucretius in *A Tale of a Tub.*"

CHAPTER TEN

SWIFT: SATURNINE MELANCHOLY

> Thus Human Life is best understood by the
> wise man's Rule of *Regarding the End.*
> (*Tale* 145)

By attacking all modern persuasions, the 1704 *Tale* subjected its anonymous author to the spectrum of indignant criticism—from the learned within the established church and state to deists and freethinkers outside the establishment. To come to terms with such a negative consensus, despite the strong interest in the work shown by the numbers of its readers, Swift took on the difficult task of mending his political fences without compromising a word of the *Tale*'s intricate and deliberate moral discourse. Subsequent readers have been in the more fortunate position of observing how, between 1707 and 1711, Swift extricated himself from the dilemma of defending the discomfiting tenets of his discourse and salvaging his career in church and state. The 1709 Apology appended to the 1710 Fifth Edition of the *Tale* served the latter end. But it is the neglected and misunderstood 1707 *A Tritical Essay upon the Faculties of the Mind* (*PW* 1: 246–51)—published in 1711—that provides at once a truthful explanation of the thrust of the *Tale* and a chart of the direction of Swift's life.

As Swift points out in his Apology for the *Tale*, he had "never yet been in want of an enemy," either from "the weightiest men in the weightiest stations" or from "common answerers" (6,9). In the course of this politic defense, he alleges that "we are taught by the tritest maxim in the world" (7) that the best are likely to be the worst corrupted.[1] Such a reference directs attention to his more profound defense of the *Tale* dated August 6, 1707 and published in 1711, the *Tritical Essay.*

With the title, the reader encounters a problem of definition, compounded by Swift and his scholarly interpreters. *Tritical,* a word Swift added to the language, the *O.E.D.* defines as "of a trite or commonplace character." The editors of the standard edition of Swift's works recognize it as an obvious compounding of "*trite* with play on *critical*" and in their Introduction have

---

[1] *Corruptio optimi pessima.* 7n1.

taken this coinage as a pejorative. They believe that Swift was parodying a still undiscovered essay of the period because of his congenital dislike of commonplaces, dullness, banalities, and stale topics (1:xxxv).[2]

The point about a commonplace is that it is devoid of anything new or original: it is well-worn by time, possibly becoming stale and trite but possibly to its advantage. Swift plays on the moderns' interest in what is new and their passion to reject what is not, but his interest in the essay is to find advantages in the commonplace. His motivation in the *Tale* and, by extension, the *Tritical Essay* is the satirist's desire to get mankind's attention by using his "utmost rhetoric." To see how skilfully he satirically links three unrelated uses of the elusive word *commonplace*—the new, the well-worn, and the eloquent—it is useful to refer to the *O.E.D.*'s A.1. definition of *commonplace*, in which the word takes on its eloquent sense—the premise of a discourse: "With the ancient rhetoricians: A passage of general application, such as may serve as the basis of an argument; a leading text cited in argument." Within this learned context the argument, or discourse, of the *Essay* challenges the exotic disarray of newfangled, modern discourses. The basic opposition in the *Tritical Essay* is between the conceits of modern philosophy and the bedrock of ancient rhetoric.

Where in this whirl of ironies is truth? Readers are left to test their own faculties of mind; but they will do well not to accept Swift's new word *tritical* at its face value, for then they will miss the moral decisiveness in well-worn, tried, and true maxims. If this slow accretion of the *consensus gentium* defines the hard-won truths of human experience, then its antithesis is found in the flashy modern mysteries propagated by the *Tale*'s persona. The satiric voice in the *Tale*, on the one hand, believes that "the Brain, in its natural Position and State of Serenity, disposeth its Owner to pass his Life in the common Forms" (171). Partly because the obsessive ideas and agendas of the *Tale*'s persona, dissenting Jack, Toland, Milton, Marsh, Shaftesbury, and their new institutions are far from common forms and commonplaces, for the satirist they express modern madness. To read the *Tritical Essay* in this positive context is to uncover his commentary on the truths Swift upholds in the *Tale* against the onslaught of modernity. As in the *Tale*, in the *Tritical Essay* he finds increasing contradiction but asserts the need for unity and concord.

Before we can perceive the parallels between the discourses of the *Tritical Essay* and the *Tale*, we must follow Swift as he combats contradiction with contradiction in his characteristically deceptive fashion. He addresses the *Tritical Essay* to an unknown "Lover of Antiquities" who "would be very

---

[2] Ehrenpreis is no less dismissive. "In his *Miscellanies* of 1711 was 'A Tritical Essay', which is a compound of clichés" (3: 839).

much obliged with any Thing that was new" (1: 246) and soon accuses many current writers of composing superficial moral discourses loaded with "stale Topics and thread-bare Quotations." The author of the *Tritical Essay*, however, reports that he has carefully avoided these errors and offers here a model for young writers:

> The Thoughts and Observations being entirely new, the Quotations untouched by others, the Subject of mighty Importance, and treated with much Order and Perspicuity: It hath cost me a great deal of Time: and I desire you will accept and consider it as the utmost Effort of my Genius. (1: 246)

The essay, like its title and like the *Tale,* thus goes off in opposite directions: while promising novelty at the surface in "broad daylight" for fools, it hides ancient commonplace truths and proverbial wisdom—these truths being proverbially "at the bottom of a [Truth's] well." To alert the wise reader, he buttresses his comments with references to Horace, Juvenal, and the Bible, playing exactly the same trick he uses in the *Tale*. In displaying his "utmost *rhetorick* against Mankind," the satiric voice quotes passages from the Bible and other well-worn truths to challenge the modern persona—and then passes them off as "Common places *equally* new and eloquent" (51–52).

Echoing the *Tale*'s reference to man as the microcoat, the essay's moral discourse begins by referring to the Neoplatonic philosophy of man as microcosm. Swift wrings from the Neoplatonic notion of correspondences his own psychological, social, and theological beliefs. First he hurls the Neoplatonic doctrine *in toto* against the modern Epicureans who hold the universe to be a random arrangement of atoms in contrast with Neoplatonism's assumed direct, interactive correspondences between man and his universe, man and nature, and man and God. Then he reduces the grand universal myth of "as above, so below" to the questions of individual sanity and order in society. Swift asserts that "In my opinion, the Body Natural may be compared to the Body Politick" (1: 246). This reprise from his earlier judgments is neither the voice of an unknown parodied author nor Neoplatonic orthodoxy. Rather Swift has adapted Neoplatonism to his own commonplace truth. The body politic, the larger collective entity, is no more than an extension of the body natural of many individuals. Woe to society if men in the "weightest stations" suffer from psychic disorder. We recall that in the *Tale*'s Digression on Madness in a Commonwealth the absolute monarchs Henry IV and Louis XIV of France set their worlds into internal panic and international upheaval for reasons no more earthshaking than purely private, psychosomatic disorders.

If order in society reflects a natural order in the human body, it is easier to identify with Neoplatonism than with the Neo-Epicureans. Both the *Tritical*

Essay and the *Tale* argue against the atomism of Epicurus in similar terms. When the essay asks, "How can the *Epicureans* Opinion be true, that the Universe was formed by a fortuitous Concourse of Atoms?" (1: 246–7), it echoes the *Tale:*

> *Epicurus* modestly hoped, that one Time or other, a certain Fortuitous Concourse of all Mens Opinions, after perpetual Justlings, the Sharp with the Smooth, the Light and the Heavy, the Round and the Square, would by certain *Clinamina,* unite in the Notions of *Atoms* and *Void,* as these did in the Originals of all Things. (167)

John Phillip Harth has suggested that this attack is based in Anglican polemics against the atomism of Epicurus and Lucretius revived by Thomas Hobbes (138). But the passage is directed as much against Halley's *Ode on the Principia,* linking Epicurus and Lucretius with Newton.

Swift asks, in effect, Which philosophy will gain modern ascendancy: Neoplatonism or Neo-Epicureanism? Which mythical reading of the universe is more pleasing for modern man—divine order or blind chance? Epicurean philosophy suits modern European states, for "this is an Opinion fitter for that many-headed Beast, the Vulgar, to entertain" (1: 247). But the Epicureans, like the modern European society, have built on a weak foundation; therefore, they and we move from error to error, lose substance in gaping at the shadow, and embrace clouds instead of Juno. Gambling that the universe is pure chance, we are doomed, like Nebuchadnezzar's image, to break into pieces.

If we are thus caught between the philosophical extremes of man as a microcosm in a divine system or man and the universe as chance atoms, and if we have been ruled in the past by absolutists projecting their psychic and physical infirmities as universal policy, then where may lost modern man turn? Swift again calls on the commonplaces, the wisdom that cries in the street. If we but know the disease and understand that truth may live at the bottom of a well, we may cease groping in open daylight like blind men.

But why should his readers listen to this iconoclast and mocker of modern orthodoxy? The tritical author distinguishes his qualifications from those of "so many far more learned men," including Aristotle. The same Swift who boldly introduces his moral discourse as "the utmost Effort of my Genius" in the next breath would humbly "offer my Mite [a pun?], since a Stander-by may sometimes, perhaps, see more of the Game than he that plays it" (1: 247). Here Swift delineates his unusual role among his contemporaries. He is a keen observer and analyst of a society whose institutions in church, learning, and state are moving away from the blind and arbitrary authority of the past toward an optimistic, new world with its own forms of blindness and arrogance. Within the conflicting frameworks of Epicurean atomism and

Neoplatonic concepts of progress and benevolence, man can end with a pessimism far more virulent than medieval *contemptus mundi.* Within his adopted framework of the *consensus gentium,* these are the tritical author's considered opinions. He has stated his complaint against readers with utmost clarity in the *Tale:* There "hath been a superficial Vein among many Readers of the present Age, who will by no means be persuaded to inspect beyond the Surface and the Rind of Things. . . . the transitory Gazers have so dazzled their Eyes, and fill'd their Imaginations with the outward Lustre, as neither to regard or consider, the Person or the Parts of the Owner within" (66).

Meanwhile proverbial "Wisdom after long hunting will cost you the Pains to dig out"; "the deeper you go, you will find it the sweeter." Its coat is "thicker," "homelier," and "courser" than the modern world has any time or use or patience for (*Tale* 66). His moral discourse thus places Swift in rhetorical isolation from his learned contemporaries—but, by the same token, within our hearing now.

For Swift, the proverbial, ancient melancholy of the satiric tradition and the golden mean of the humors tradition in European literature are the rhetorical paths to wisdom about to be cut off. Of the first of these waning traditions, he had already provided the clue that informs the *Tritical Essay* in his "serious" and crafted Apology to the *Tale:* "for we are taught by the tritest Maxim in the World" (7).

No one has written more acutely about the tradition of proverbial wisdom than James Obelkevich. Obelkevich defines proverbs conventionally enough as "traditional popular sayings which offer wisdom and advice in a brief and pithy manner" (44). They employ a "wide range of poetic and rhetorical resources" including metaphor; they are "moral and didactic" and formulate "part of a society's common sense, its values and way of doing things" (44). In pre-industrial Europe "it was the peasants, the majority of the population, who used proverbs most" (45). "Sceptical of official pieties, though it [the proverb] rarely called for anything resembling political action, it was by turns cynical, amoral, coarse, and obscene" (49). "Realistic, unsentimental, sus-picious of idealism and heroism, they [proverbs] call for a recognition of limits as the key to survival" (52). The commonplaces and proverbial wisdom in the *Tale* and the *Tritical Essay* share these characteristics.

In Elizabethan England, the proverb was venerated not only by the peasants but by all classes, especially the educated. But Obelkevich reports that it "fell foul of virtually every major development in learned culture between 1660 and 1800; Renaissance humanism, which in some sense had been based on proverbs, was replaced by a culture—whether Augustan, enlightened or Romantic in emphasis—which was constructed on their rejection and absence" (59):

Rhetoric as the guide to writing was replaced by grammar; metaphors were attacked, notably by the Royal Society, as emotional and untruthful. . . . And when the bias of learned culture passed from wisdom to knowledge and from the Ancients to the Moderns, proverbs were left stranded. The Enlightenment did not venerate the past but wanted to break free from it; in the *Encyclopédie*, that compendium of progressive thought, there was little room for musty proverbs. . . . Static, stereotyped, incurably earthbound, they had no point of contact with the new conception of life as the unfolding of an individual destiny. (58)

Obelkevich finds that "Swift pillories [proverbs], along with the trite witticism and banal small talk of the day" (57) in *A Complete Collection of Genteel and Ingenious Conversation*. But it should be clear by now that Swift never abandoned this rhetorical tradition. The *Tritical Essay*, like the *Tale*, meant to close the sluice gates protecting the rhetorical arts and the *consensus gentium* from the tidal wave of modern philosophy.

In the *Tritical Essay*, Swift digresses briefly on Aristotle and philosophy. The stander-by does not account for every phenomenon in nature, a task that obsessed the peripatetic philosopher. In the *Tale* the satiric voice had suggested that philosophers who attempt to encompass all knowledge should instead shape their "Understanding by the Pattern of Human Learning." This humbler approach instructs them in their "private Infirmities, as well as in the stubborn Ignorance of the People" (171).[3] The tritical author assents to one of the tritest of maxims, that nature does nothing in vain:

She is chiefly admirable in her minutest Compositions, the least and most contemptible Insect most discovers the Art of Nature, if I may so call it; although Nature, which delights in Variety, will always triumph over Art. (1: 248)

That triumphant nature is never spent leads the author to expand on the contrary results attending "the various opinions of philosophers." They

have scattered through the World as many Plagues of the Mind, as *Pandora*'s Box did those of the Body; only with this Difference, that they have not left Hope at the Bottom. And if Truth be not fled with *Astraea*, she is certainly as hidden as the Source of *Nile*, and can be found only in *Utopia*. (1: 248)

Astraea and *Utopia*, the two contrasts with the philosophic plagues of the mind, are key terms in the *Tale*. The former invokes satire, rhetoric,

---

[3] Swift's attack here is more on modern attempts to outreach Aristotle than on the ancient himself. Cf. *PW* 2: 97: "But it hath been a fashion of late years to explode Aristotle, and therefore this man [Tindal] hath fallen into it like others, for that reason and without understanding him. Aristotle's Poetry, Rhetorick and Politicks are admirable, and therefore, it is likely so are his Logicks." Similarly, his *Character of Aristotle* admits "We have not all his works. . . . He seems to be a person of the most comprehensive genius that ever lived" (*PW* 5:345). A. P. Bos has attempted to reconstruct those lost theological works on the Kronos myth so dear to Swift.

commonplaces, melancholy.[4] The *Tale*'s satiric voice, resorting to a string of commonplaces, complains that in Britain nowadays

> you may securely display your utmost Rhetorick against Mankind, in the Face of the World tell them, "That all are gone astray; That there is none that doth good, no not one; That we live in the very Dregs of Time; That Knavery and Atheism are Epidemick as the Pox; That Honesty is fled with Astraea"; with any other Common places *equally* new and eloquent, which are furnished by the *Splendida bilis*. (51–52)

This splenetic interlude inveighing against the evils of the times is quickly silenced by the *Tale*'s persona, who confesses to "having neither a talent nor an inclination for satire":

> On the other side, I am so entirely satisfied with the whole present Procedure of human Things, that I have been for some Years preparing Materials towards *A Panegyrick upon the World;* to which I intended to add a Second Part, entituled, *A Modest Defence of the Proceedings of the Rabble in all Ages.* (53–54)

If, however, the melancholy reference to the Golden Age of *Astraea* provokes the *Tale*'s persona to return to his modern optimism, the similar reference in the *Tritical Essay,* unrestricted by a modern persona, provokes Swift to inveigh against the overweening pride of philosophers and the bootless invective of his critics and witlings. Philosophers, in an allusion to Plato and Diogenes, are, like the *Tale*'s TRUE—false to Swift—critics, able to "see the Faults of each other, but not their own" (1: 248). The *Tale* had defined the TRUE critic as *"a Discoverer and Collector of Writers' Faults"* (95). Swift devotes one-fifth of the *Tritical Essay* to the TRUE critics who have emerged against the *Tale,* identifying their myopia with the arrogance of philosophers and the learned. Here, for the first time in his literary career, he raises himself to full stature above them as the aloof, unique, and lonely genius his works reveal, the worthy heir of Juvenal and Horace.

In his high disdain, Swift invokes the commonplace image of flies burning their wings about a candle. "They rail at what they cannot understand." In the words of Juvenal, they are tormented with envy. He mocks all his witless witlings by first alluding to Browne's contribution to Irish philosophy, an idea he will offer again in *Gulliver's Travels:*

> I must be so bold, to tell my Criticks and Witlings, that they are no more Judges of this, than a Man that is born blind can have any true Idea of Colours. (1: 249)

---

4 For the classical and European Renaissance backgrounds on Astraea, see Frances A. Yates's *Astraea The Imperial Theme in the Sixteenth Century.*

The *Tale* had used the same image: "Men in misfortune, being like men in the dark, to whom all colors are the same" (134). Swift similarly will not relent against such critics as William Wotton, William King, and Samuel Clarke, declaring "I value their lashes as little, as the sea did when *Xerxes* whipped it" (1: 249). Their vessels are empty, their heads, vacuums. Because they are the drones of the learned world devouring the honey and not working themselves, "A Writer need no more regard them, than the Moon does the Barking of a little senseless Cur" (1: 249).

Having reduced the divine exaltation of the Neoplatonists, whipped Epicureans for exploiting the opportunities of chance, denounced all philosophers for plaguing the minds of men through overweening pride, and scorned his critics for their sounding brass, the *Tritical Essay* next attacks orators for prizing action over contemplation. Like Demosthenes, who saw oratory as action, the modern virtuosi have achieved perpetual motion in their tongues. As in the *Tale,* the *Tritical Essay* moves easily from the virtuosi of the Royal Society to men who "admire Republicks" in the mid-seventeenth-century vein:

> Orators flourish there [in republics] most, and are the great Enemies of Tyranny: But my Opinion is, that one Tyrant is better than an Hundred. Besides, these Orators inflame the People, whose Anger is really but a short Fit of Madness. (1: 250)

Then in an old legal proverb, Swift simultaneously delivers the *coup de grace* to the civic virtue of the classical republican discourse and punctures the "rights" discourse of modern European liberalism: "After which, laws are like cobwebs, which may catch small flies, but let wasps and hornets break through" (1: 250).[5]

Along with his attacks on the two discourses in modern vogue, Swift uses the essay to sound again a theme from the *Tale* that he would use again in the later *Gulliver's Travels*—and throughout his moral discourses and his career. He does so in a series of commonplaces: contemplation exceeds action; a wise man is never less alone than when he is alone. *Numquam minus solus, quam cum solus.* This private renewing of one's mind to realize one's sacrificial role in our predestined pattern of life and death (Romans 12:2) is the guarantee of Swift's melancholy in Hamlet's, not Timon's, manner (*Corr.* 1: 103). But the challenged life and challenging art faithfully serve each other. He adds another commonplace to ensure that his readers—if they would be disciplined for an

---

[5] In "The Legal Proverb in Defoe, Swift, and Shenstone," Robert C. Steensma found this classical proverb, used by Anacharsis in 600 B.C., taken up by Daniel Defoe and William Shenstone as well as Swift.

integrated life—will work as hard as he to detect the dimensions of the modern tragedy. "In oratory, the greatest art is to hide art. *Artis est celare Artem.* But this must be the Work of Time" (1: 250). It is, of course, the same triticism and the same covert and lonely art that only patience will unravel that pervades the *Tale,* as when Martin, desiring to rid himself of the gold lace in his coat, picked up the stitches "with much caution, and diligently gleaned out all the loose threads as he went, which proved to be—[like the toils of art] a work of time" (136).

To belabor a commonplace, time flies. Seizing the day means that we "lay hold on all opportunities and let slip no occasion" (1: 250). Swift accepts Locke's *tabula rasa* as the original condition of the mind of man. He adds, however, the psychoanalytic and mortal components, the alpha and omega of the mind. When soft it is capable of any impression, until time has hardened it. But, the *Tritical Essay* continues, in apparent mid-passage, death, that grim tyrant Kronos, the conqueror of the greatest conquerors "spares none from the Sceptre to the Spade" (1: 250). Swift loads commonplace on commonplace, truism on truism. All rivers go to the sea, but none return from it. He had used the same idea and phrase in the *Tale*'s Dedication to Prince Posterity—whose governor is Saturn-Kronos, Father Time, the lord of seas and ways of death. "Books, like Men their Authors, have no more than one Way of coming into the World, but there are ten Thousand to go out of it, and return no more" (36).

In concluding the *Tritical Essay,* Swift attacks the Neoplatonists' naive confidence in the ultimate triumph of virtue by observing that an inconstant modern world is governed purely by self-interest and has abandoned the Golden Mean for extremes. Even if Jupiter himself, day god of the moderns, should come to earth, he, like virtue, would be despised unless he arrived in a golden shower:

> For Men, now-a-days, worship the rising Sun, and not the setting. *Donec eris faelix, multos numerabis amicos.* (1:251)

It is against the backdrop of God's eternity, nature's infinity, and puny man's pride and sure mortality that the moral rhetorician in the *Tritical Essay* and the *Tale* asks the learned reader to judge his hopeless modern predicament—then cast aside modern philosophy with its arrogance and its violent swings between seductive hope and utter despair, between divine plan and chance atoms. Swift's undying allegiance was to the traditional humanism of Thomas More and the classical satirists Horace and Juvenal. He supported established institutions—as he did proverbial wisdom—so long as they served as repositories of truths and sources of social stability. He recognized them as sanctuaries of ancient learning that could be bastions of tyranny. His arguments for liberty are strictly within the classical frame of the *furor poeticus* of the melancholy temper.

In the continuity of attack on modern Europe by men of humor that has existed since the Renaissance, Swift's participation is pivotal. In the 175 years between Sir Thomas More's *Utopia* and the *Tale,* the European corruption that More delineated had become more universal; the world had turned upside down. The *Tale*'s vicious modern Europe is like More's dystopia, and Gulliver's England. Like More and like his own heirs, Laurence Sterne and Sterne's literary heirs, nineteenth-century Russian novelists, Swift spoke intimately to his readers about how the individual psyche is sure to confront old and new tyrannies in modern European states.

According to George M. Logan's *The Meaning of More's "Utopia"*, Machiavelli achieved what Aristotle had begun: severance of the link between politics and ethics. Both treated "actual constitutions apart from the ideal." But More went one step further, seeking to heal the breach between Plato's ideal of "what ought to be" and Aristotle's and Machiavelli's insistence on "what is": *Utopia* entered "the realm of what can be." For Logan, "the central meaning of *Utopia* lies in its advocacy of just such a humanist realism" (268–70). But in *A Tale of a Tub* Swift observes the progress of the advocates of "what can be" as they gained ascendancy, over the course of the seventeenth century, in learning, religion, and government. He records the ways of modern reformers and anticipates "what will be": the rise of populist European states led by madmen and knaves, and populated with fools.

Swift's *Tale* accords with More's *Utopia* and Erasmus's *In Praise of Folly* with respect to genre and rhetorical intention. More's "best-commonwealth exercise" compounded seriousness with jest, ideas with their social contexts, and political complexities with a sense of history. Logan points out that the skepticism and relativism of More, Erasmus, Rabelais, and Montaigne led "to the growing and increasingly complex use of ironic and fictive modes in their writing" (268). Using similar rhetorical paraphernalia, Swift's "worst-commonwealth exercise," the *Tale,* rises to its climax in the Digression on Madness.

The humanist authors under review favor the persuasion of rhetoric over systems of philosophy. The reason, Logan explains, is that philosophy is concerned with the universal, the unchanging, and the use of reason to discover truth whereas, "By contrast, rhetoric is concerned with the changing, the actualities of particular times and places" (264). He links humanism and rhetoric in their relation "to the characteristic historical sensitivity of humanist thought and to its civic and pragmatic emphases" (263). In ordering the classical heritage, rhetorical humanists accordingly consider "literary works [both] as wholes and within contexts" (263).

Of course, in their rhetorical exercises Swift has the advantage of historical hindsight over More. In the early sixteenth century, for example, Paracelsus and More represented the precursors of "what can be" in learning as Luther and Calvin did in religion; Henry VIII and the European republican city-states represented "what is" in governance. By the mid-seventeenth century on the Continent and in Britain, More's notion of "what can be" had become the integrated programs of the Rosicrucians, the fanatic sects, and the Puritan republican regicides.

Logan illuminates a major period of European intellectual history, but he does not consider the primitive role of the satirist as priest, prophet, and preserver of societal virtues. If More was a virtuous ideal for Swift, why did the personality Swift projected in his writings seem so scandalous to his contemporaries? His antic resistance against decorum and manners stems from primitive satire's role as the shocking reversal of perspective. Swift adopts this satiric role not only in his writings, but in his own persona much like Hamlet to confound his observers. His revelation of man in his satiric persona prefigures his fictive Yahoo in *Gulliver's Travels* and the offended Thackeray's lurid characterization of Sterne as the "foul satyr leering through the pages" as in a bacchanalian revel. Both Shakespeare and Sterne in his persona present Yorick as a fellow of infinite jest, and the *Tale's* satiric voice is not far from either in highlighting folly, frivolity, frolic, and fashion simply to contrast them with our somber destiny. If modern man will not heed primitive satire, the satirist will at least ask him to consider his own primitive nature: Look at your animal nature; do not preen yourselves on your overrated reason and developing ideal world.

Swift's harsh message may have caused some social upset and unease, but it did not retard the progress of modern optimism. What his view of human nature did was fuel his greatest conceit, that of *furor poeticus*. He maintained "the Privilege and Birth-right of every [Attick] Citizen and Poet, to rail aloud and in publick, or to expose . . . by Name, any Person they pleased, tho' of the greatest Figure" (*Tale* 51). The ideal of saturnine melancholy related to this conceit became for Swift both a basic part of his nature and also basic to a persona he sometimes assumed.

The misanthropy in some of his crafted correspondence reveals what Swift contrived. According to Craig Hawkins Ulman, "When he sends a carefully wrought satirical letter, or, more important, when he adopts the persona of the Dublin misanthrope, he still assumes that Pope will represent him—in one case by praising his wit, in the other by deploring his misfortune" (38).

Hidden behind the purposeful double vision in his satires and his public image is his real nature. As the *Tritical Essay* affirms, "he is least alone who is alone." Whether the *imago* is real or contrived or both, Ulman concludes that "the part he chooses is one which reinforces his satire: the role of the universal misanthrope" (40). But the distinction should be made between misanthropy and philosophical melancholy. Gulliver exhibits misanthropy "in Timon's manner." In contrast, and for good reason, Swift's studied private nature reveals a melancholy which fluctuates between contemplation and bile.

To understand Swift's melancholy and the melancholy he put into the *Tale,* a monumental scholarly work *Saturn and Melancholy* offers invaluable help. It traces the historical development of saturnine melancholy from Aristotle's Problem XXX,I in the *Problemata physica*[6] to Marsilio Ficino (1433–1499), including many recondite sources in medicine, natural philosophy, and art throughout the ancient, classical, Arabic, and medieval worlds. Although this prodigious research was undertaken primarily to elucidate Albrecht Dürer's *Melancholia I,* the work also contributes to a deeper understanding of Paracelsus's major contributions to modern medical and scientific thought and to understanding the Neoplatonic and classical sources of the melancholy that marked English literature from Milton to Thomas Gray and John Keats. Satirists are not given their due in this work, and Swift's name does not appear in it. Yet every major subject covered in *Saturn and Melancholy* is at the core of the *Tale,* including natural philosophy, religion, medicine, literature and art, myth, and the ancient-modern and the medieval-Renaissance dichotomies.

At the outset, a vast distinction must be made between the mad disease of melancholy and the divine melancholic constitution. The bile suffered by the *Tale*'s Aeolists is the mad disease of melancholy. The *Tale*'s satiric voice suffers with Horace from splenetic black bile, the divine melancholy disposition. In the *Tale,* Swift takes full advantage of what *Saturn and Melancholy* refers to as the achievement of the fourth century B.C.: "union between the purely medical notion of melancholy and the Platonic conception of frenzy" (17). Aristotle's Problem XXX,I had brought about this modulation of the idea of melancholy as governing two distinct states of mind affected by the black bile. Clearly influencing all disciplines and ages covered in *Saturn and Melancholy,* the Problem deserves analysis because of its use to define madness in the *Tale.*

The distinction between the melancholic constitution and the disease of melancholy is Aristotle's. Both conditions stemmed from the flow of black

---

6 The editors, Raymond Klibansky, Erwin Panofsky, and Fritz Saxl, provide the original Greek and an English translation of this work (18–29). They also provide references to Latin and English editions of the *Problemata physica* (18n54), as well as documentation of its attribution to Aristotle.

bile which either ennobles such great men as Hercules, Socrates and Plato or makes lesser men insane. In the disease "both the humor and the temperament produce air; wherefore the physicians say that flatulence and abdominal disorders are due to black bile" (21). The wise Aeolists in Section VIII of the *Tale* "affirm the gift of belching to be the noblest act of a rational creature" (153). Similarly the various inhabitants of Bedlam in Section IX, the Digression on Madness of the *Tale*, exhibit the same catalog of variable behaviors due to excessive heat or cold of the black bile described in Aristotle's Problem XXX. Swift finds "several dispositions and behavior" (176) among his melancholic madmen, just as Aristotle had found "straight away the greatest variety of characters, each according to his individual mixture" (24). Each of the *Tale*'s six Bedlamites has an excessive melancholic trait described precisely in Problem XXX,I. The first foams at the mouth (176), like Aristotle's type easily moved to anger (24); the second is eternally talking (176), like Aristotle's loquacious type (24); the third is a dissenter with foresight and insight (177), like Aristotle's divinely inspired soothsayer (24); the fourth will sing you a song for a penny (177), like Aristotle's melancholic who bursts into song (23); the fifth is a surly, gloomy, nasty, slovenly mortal (178), like Aristotle's type with paralysis, torpor, depression, and anxiety (23); and the sixth is a strutting orator (178), like Aristotle's type filled with exaltation and ecstasy (24).

Aristotle's catalog of melancholic types provides the *Tale*'s varieties of the vaporous disease of modern madness among the Aeolists and Bedlamites; it also describes the ideal natural constitution of the melancholic genius. The *Tale*'s satiric voice and Horace with their *Splendida bilis* (glittering [black] bile) represent the latter altogether different disposition from that of the persona and his fellow modern melancholics (52).[7] In Problem XXX,I, those with well-tempered melancholy are outstanding and extraordinary: "Those, however, in whom the black bile's excessive heat is relaxed towards a mean, are melancholy, but they are more rational and less eccentric and in many respects superior to others either in culture or in the arts or in statesmanship" (24–5). The balance, self-possession, and tranquility of spirit that Aristotle finds in the well-tempered melancholic constitution Swift advocates in the *Tritical Essay* as opposed to the qualities of mind of inflamers and unquiet spirits in the *Tale* and the *Discourse*. Here we see united Aristotle's vaunted golden mean with the Kronos myth central to his lost published dialogues that A. P. Bos is now endeavoring to reconstruct. As the authors of *Saturn and Melancholy* note, the temporary alteration of the melancholy humor by digestive disturbance leads to psychosomatic diseases, an acquired condition;

---

[7] *A Tale of a Tub and Other Works,* Ed. Angus Ross and David Woolley, 206n24.5.

the natural melancholic possesses a spiritual singularity permanently present (30). Both forms of melancholy are exploited in the *Tale*.

Swift is an expert on species of melancholy. Besides identifying types among the mass melancholia of his satiric victims, he distinguishes the melancholy in Timon's manner from the melancholy he himself shares with the melancholy Dane. Hamlet, in fact, demonstrates both the melancholy of madness and the melancholy of genius. He feigns melancholic madness "north, northwest" even as his pregnant soliloquies on man reflect Aristotle's ideal of melancholic genius. Shakespeare uses Hamlet's melancholy and his deliberate "north-north-west" madness (II.ii.369) to point out, as Swift does in the *Tale*, man's mortality and corruption and need for skepticism. At the same time, the Elizabethan dramatist understood man's new inclination to see himself as exalted. In apocalyptic language, Hamlet predicts "doomsday near" if it is proved "that the world's grown honest" (II.ii.234–6). Then in Galenic, Paracelsian, and Neoplatonic terms, Hamlet diagnoses his own and the world's condition:

> I have of late—but wherefore I know not—lost all my mirth, forgone all custom of exercises; and indeed, it goes so heavily with my disposition that this goodly frame the earth seems to me a sterile promontory; this most excellent canopy, the air, look you, this brave o'erhanging firmament, this majestical roof fretted with gold fire—why, it appeareth nothing to me but a foul and pestilent congregation of vapours. What a piece of work is a man, how noble in reason, how infinite in faculties; in form and moving how express and admirable, in action how like an angel, in apprehension how like a god: the beauty of the world, the paragon of animals! And yet to me what is this quintessence of dust? Man delights not me. (II.ii.292–305)

"Quintessence" is Paracelus's favorite word and Swift uses it with the same disparagement as Shakespeare. Shakespeare's tragic hero sees the mad world caught in the toils of passion, fashion, appearance, and corruption: surface disruptions. In the gravediggers' scene Hamlet finally contemplates the humbling mortality of Alexander and Caesar, just as the *Tale*'s satiric voice begins the Digression on Madness by describing the all-too-human madness and mortality of Louis XIV and Henry IV of France. Shakespeare's phrase "paragon of animals" wittily inflates and deflates man simultaneously, in the way that Swift's profane animal imagery for exalted moderns offended contemporary Anglicans and freethinkers alike.

Neither Swift's nor Hamlet's misanthropy is "in Timon's manner"(*Corr.* 1:103).[8] In fact, Shakespeare's hero's profound humanistic statement foreshadows Swift's kind of misanthropy—the love of individuals, but not the

---

[8] Timon swings wildly from benevolence to misanthropy like Gulliver.

species—and his own type of melancholy. Both the Elizabethan dramatist and the Augustan satirist attack Paracelsus's medicine, Neoplatonism, and the Protestant apocalyptic hope of a return to Eden. Their works show that the notion of the species as good provides license and opportunity to individual egocentrics, absolutists, and their time-servers morally and intellectually unequipped to make discriminations between good and evil. In sum, the benevolent tradition supports covert vice behind the facade of virtue, and the modern myth feeds on itself.

There is, of course, a polar distinction between the philosophic melancholy of the depressed Hamlet and the pathological melancholy of the enthusiastic Aeolists in the *Tale*. In the former case, the pestilential vapours have been induced by Hamlet's *pessimism* about "this quintessence of dust," reducing his psyche and sphere of action. In the *Tale*, the pestilential vapours were induced by modern *optimism* about human potential. The phenomenon of vapours is a matter of indigestion in the alimentary canal manifest externally as flatulence and belching from the digestive system and enthusiasm, disciple-ship, redundancy, lack of restraint, and madness when the vapours ascend to the brain—in the manner of Henry More's jest.

The Aeolists not only appear in the *Tale*'s text but have contaminated the air in Swift's real world. Their contagious disease has increased the number of disciples spreading modern influence. In his view, Paracelsus and the Paracel-sians, like Milton and the millenarians, are usurpers on the holy, humanistic ground of Kronos-Saturn and satire, melancholy, and genius. They contami-nate the classical legacy with Christian apocalypse and modern optimism and pervert the saturnine myth in the cause of Jupiter, the modern god of day. It is not surprising that the *Tale* sets the universal modern desire of men to return by action to a temporal Eden against the yearnings of satirists Thomas More, Joseph Hall, and Swift himself to return by contemplation to the divine Golden Age of Saturn and Astraea.[9]

Saturn and Melancholy traces the history of melancholy after Problem XXX,I as it merged over the centuries with the Stoic view, Galenic tradition, theology, moral philosophy, scholastic medicine, and natural philosophy to become part of a system of the four temperaments or humors, humoral pathology and characterology, and psychological classification. Reflecting this conglomeration of thought, the four humors were seen to correspond to

---

9 Angus Ross's study of *"The Anatomy of Melancholy* and Swift" offers an exhaustive "comparative assessment" of Robert Burton's voluminous work with the *Tale* and *Gulliver's Travels*. Among a host of findings, he notes that the text of the *Tale* "has a form of argument (parable and digressions), with citations and discussion, a form of mental ordering bred into Swift and Burton by their education and theological studies" (153).

the elements and the seasons and to harmonize with faculties of the mind, establishing relationships with moral significance (107).

To establish clearly that the doctrine of temperaments has survived, the editors of *Saturn and Melancholy* refer to Immanuel Kant's "aesthetic and ethical interpretation [of] the traditional doctrine of temperaments" (122). Kant's *Observations on the Sense of the Beautiful and the Sublime* endows the melancholy character with the sublime and interprets

> every trait of melancholy as the expression of a great moral consciousness. The melancholic and no other represented Kant's notion of virtue. . . . The "sadness without cause" was based on his possession of a moral scale which destroyed personal happiness by the merciless revelation of his own and others' worthlessness. (122)

Most of Kant's argument that the individual of sublime melancholy subjects his sensibilities to principles, depends on his own judgment, cares little for the opinions of others, guards secrets [!], turns his constancy to obstinacy, hates lies and deceit, finds truth sublime, and judges himself and others sternly appears as Swift's argument in the *Tritical Essay*. But Kant's romantic view misses another side of satiric melancholy. By allowing his ideal melancholic a deep conviction of human nobility and a hatred of external chains, he dismisses the darker, more sinister, and introverted side of the melancholy temperament.

Unlike German idealism, however, the seminal myth of Kronos-Saturn provides two sides for the satiric balance. Saturn, the planetary Star of Melancholy, opposes wickedness, force, and tyranny and governs long sea journeys like those in the satires of Thomas More, Hall, and Swift. But the Greeks knew him as Kronos, the dreaming Titan of Time who chastises as well as blesses, destroys as well as aids. His sickle dispatches the daily offerings of the *Tale*'s modern writers. Time in the *Tritical Essay* conspires with death to teach us our evanescence and mortality: the commonplace "ALL Rivers go to the Sea, but none return from it" (1: 250) reverberates with the myths of Saturn-Kronos as sea and river god controlling the ways of death. The *Tritical Essay* treats the Saturnian myth of the Golden Age and also alludes to the mental attributes of deep reflection and prophecy. The essay asserts that contemplation exceeds action, art requires the work of time, and virtue and God will not appear in the modern world while it is governed by self-interest.

Saturn and Melancholy follows the concept of Saturn through Arabic astrology, ancient mythical literature, astrophysics and astrology, Neoplatonism, early Christianity, moral theology, medieval mythography, astrological elements in scholastic natural philosophy, the oriental pictorial influence, and humanism; it notes that in rehabilitating the humanistic Saturn around 1500, Florentine Neoplatonism balanced "the two aspects of the Saturnine nature, the wicked and the mournful as well as the sublime and the profoundly contemplative" (209). A new humanist awareness of "the tragic and heroic disunity—the intellectual pattern of 'modern genius'" found its resonance in the saturnine and melancholic polarities:

> There was therefore a double renaissance: firstly, of the Neoplatonic notion of Saturn, according to which the highest of the planets embodied, and also bestowed, the highest and noblest faculties of the soul, reason, and speculation; and secondly, of the "Aristotlian" doctrine of melancholy, according to which all great men were melancholics. (247)

Even at the end of the fifteenth century, many centuries after Problem XXX,I, the Aristotelian question remained—"why men who were, innately, specially gifted, should always be melancholic by nature" (97). By this time, the Neoplatonic Ficino had tied the humoral temperament to a new art of healing subject to astral influences and general cosmic forces— correspondences developed further by Paracelsus. Born under the sign of Saturn, Ficino conjured up the idea of the melancholy man of genius "in the magic chiaroscuro of Christian Neoplatonic mysticism" (255). His system with its thorough assimilation of every major ancient and medieval discipline and influence covered in *Saturn and Melancholy* was epoch-making for modern medical and scientific thought, especially for Paracelsus. This system "contrived to give Saturn's 'immanent contradiction' a redemptive power" (271–72):

> As enemy and oppressor of all life in any way subject to the present world, Saturn generates melancholy; but as the friend and protector of a higher and purely intellectual existence he can also cure it. (271)

In the *Tritical Essay*, Swift contrasts the darkness of Saturn's truth with the futility of groping for it in Jupiter's daylight, asserting that "Although truth ... lives in the bottom of a well; yet we need not ... grope in open daylight" (1: 247). The *Essay* ends with an epitome of the evil of the modern time: "Men neglect the golden mean, Jupiter himself, if he came on the earth, would be despised. . . . For men, now-a-days, worship the rising sun, and not the setting" (1: 251). Ficino made these same distinctions:

> For just as the sun is hostile to nocturnal animals but friendly to those which are active in daylight, so is Saturn an enemy of those men who overtly lead a commonplace life, or who, though they flee the company of vulgar people, yet do not lay aside their vulgar thoughts. For he resigned common life to Jupiter, but

retained the sequestered and divine life for himself. Men whose minds are truly withdrawn from the world are, to some extent, his kind and in him they find a friend.[10]

Perhaps nowhere in English literature is there a greater contrast of saturnine melancholies than between Milton's poems *L'Allegro* and *Il Penseroso* and Swift's *Tale,* which mocks Milton throughout. While the authors of *Saturn and Melancholy* do not record affinities between satire and melancholy, they recognize Milton's thorough familiarity with the Italian tradition—which he knew at first hand—and his contribution to English "poetic" melancholy:

> This modern melancholy mood is essentially an enhanced self-awareness, since the ego is the pivot round which the sphere of joy and grief revolves. (231)

Milton revels "in the sweet self-sufficiency of the melancholy mood" (232) and blends the ecstatic and the contemplative into a unified melancholic, Saturnine picture, "mild on the whole rather than menacing" (231). This defanging, as it were, leads directly to the elegies and odes of the eighteenth and early nineteenth century, the night school of withdrawal, sentiment, sentimentality, and, ultimately, mockery of the mannered, ego-centered, gloomy mood.

With great insight, *Saturn and Melancholy* compares the melancholic with the humorist in English literature since the seventeenth century: "Melancholic and humorist both feed on the metaphysical contradiction between finite and infinite, time and eternity" (234). The melancholic suffers from the contradiction while the humorist, recognizing himself "fettered to the temporal," is "primarily amused":

> Hence it can be understood how in modern man "Humor" with its sense of the limitation of the self, developed alongside that melancholy which had become a feeling of an enhanced self. (235)

In discussing Ben Jonson's "fashionable melancholic" Stephen in *Every Man in his Humor* (235), the authors seem to forget their own insight, equating the "cheap ridicule of the *mere satirist*" [italics added] like Jonson with his character's "cheap means of concealing his own emptiness" (235). The denigration of the satirist by associating him with the humorist he satirizes reflects a profoundly distorted reinterpretation of the humors tradition while offering a protective shield to the Miltonian, sentimental, and romantic melancholy that the authors have exposed.

---

[10] Marsilio Ficino, *De vita triplici.* II, 15 in *Opera,* 522. Quoted in *Saturn and Melancholy* 272.

There are critical distinctions between the satirist and the humorist he satirizes and between the melancholy of Swift and that of the Milton he satirizes. In the Miltonian school of melancholy, the feelings of the poet and his persona are identical. This is not so in the literary humors tradition of Shakespeare, Jonson, Moliere, Swift, and Sterne. In that waning tradition, the fundamental opposition is between the authorial by-stander and the humorist he is observing; and this distinction measures the profound gulf between the melancholies of Swift and Milton. In their slight to satire and the humors tradition, the authors of *Saturn and Melancholy* have missed the fierce two-century struggle between two competing ideals of melancholy: ancient satire and modern gloom.

Satirists lay an immemorial claim on the two faces of Kronos-Saturn. His priests and his prophets have primitive roots in the origins of the myth with its authority to purge diseases of the mind—sometimes called evil—in all cultures except the modern European. Knowing these sacred origins, true satirists experience saturnine melancholy deeply. To the satirist Swift, Milton's lyric postures a fashionable modern feeling of melancholy, pedantically buttressed, basically a poetic conceit. In introducing the melancholy mood as a literary convention, Milton robs it of its mythic power. Further, his actions in the Civil War and his defense of the Stuart regicide and the Puritan Revolution, along with his unrelenting attacks on episcopacy, belie the contemplative life. Unlike satirists, Milton has renounced the Saturnine requirement of concealing the tragic face beneath the comic mask; and Swift is confident that Apollo will keep him away from Delphi.

Since reliance on proverbs was collapsing among the educated classes even as the melancholy of ancient satire had lost influence to the Miltonian modern gloom, it is not surprising that the humors tradition in European literature waned from the second half of the seventeenth century onward, to be replaced in a century by the ascendant benevolent tradition. The classical humors tradition finally closed down in the late eighteenth century with the final communal chorus of Mozart's *Marriage of Figaro;* it succumbed to the rise of Shaftesbury's more seductive benevolent tradition and works like *The Barber of Seville,* carrying Beaumarchais' personally aggrieved and Revolution-sparking social philosophy.

In *The Development of English Humor,* Louis Cazamian reminds us that the distinction between the man of humor and the humorist has "bewildered the critics" (409) since the plays of Ben Jonson, leading to "much ambiguity and confusion" (410) over the centuries. Humorist has basically two meanings. In Jonson's sense it is the person subject to a humor or fancy. But this sense itself required two meanings. In the seventeenth century, the humorist often was a vicious, dangerous, or violent obsessive suffering from a humoral imbalance, such as Jonson's Volpone and Moliere's Miser—and Swift's only slightly later Aeolists. By the eighteenth century, however, the humorist was likely to suffer from a milder passion, the obsession would be sillier and whimsical, the oddity and eccentricity endearing, as with Sterne's Uncle Toby or Dickens' Pickwick: the benevolent tradition rising.

The change in sensibility led to a European revolution in social norms away from conformity and the golden mean that had determined the humoral balance. Galenic medicine had determined that harmony or balance in the body natural; classical satire from Greek New Comedy onward had reflected it in the body politic. It became Swift's vocation to identify the emotionally disturbed, the Bedlam at large in changing times. The radical change to a modern concept of the individual in society has been summarized by Edward N. Hooker in "Humor in the Age of Pope." He explains that "Men were beginning to look upon diversity as a prime value, and the freedom of the individual to follow the peculiar bent of his nature became the Englishman's pride" (385). It can be argued that individual specialties define the commercial requirements of the modern state. The modulation toward diversity also reflects one component of the urban myth evolving to replace the agrarian myth of the New Testament in a new millennium, just as the New Testament itself had replaced the nomadic-agrarian myth of the Old Testament in the centuries before Christ. Hooker, who leans toward approving the newer world, acknowledges that learned values have been lost in the transition to individualism:

> True learning, to Fielding as to Swift, meant the illumination and wisdom culled from the experience of cultivated mankind, translated into prudent and generous social conduct. And without learning, Fielding insisted, even genius (the most splendid form of individualism) is an impertinence and a hollow mockery. (384)

Modern European societies have been diminished by the loss of men of genius committed to humane learning.

The vicious humorist and the foolish humorist must, of course, be distinguished; but another distinction is also essential. The modern world has come to accept the concept of a humorist as a person skilled in the literary expression of humor, but for three centuries it has posed some problems. When the authorial humorist or, as we shall call him here, the man of humor represents a humor, is it someone else's or his own? Corbyn Morris in 1744 and Jean Paul Richter in 1804 have offered the best clues. Morris's 1744 *Essay towards fixing the true standards of wit, humour, raillery, satire and ridicule* helps explain Swift's penchant for parodying moderns in his works and for insulting decorum and manners by profanity in both his works and his life:

A man of humor is one, who can happily exhibit a weak and ridiculous character in real life, either by assuming it himself, or representing another in it, so naturally, that the whimsical oddities, and foibles, of that character, shall be palpably exposed.[11] (15)

Helen Walden's dissertation on "Jean Paul and Swift" analyzes Jean Paul Richter's landmark study tracing the importance of humor *Vorschule der Aesthetik.* Richter recognizes that humor is the highest form of the comic and that it flourishes where there is an underlying seriousness: "Gloomy Ireland is the home of the masters of humor, Swift and Sterne" (Walden 50). Other humorists congregate at their feet. The humor the masters exhibit is the humor of genius, melancholy—that is, it is in a melancholy mode, but not in the Miltonian or romantic vein.

While they do not discuss Swift or other satirists, the authors of *Saturn and Melancholy* fittingly yield the accolade of true melancholy to Laurence Sterne, Swift's literary heir (237). A fundamental distinction can separate the exceptional man of humor and the ubiquitous humorist; but Sterne and Swift have the rarest of gifts among the few identified men of humor in that they can assume *both* roles. The man of humor in the melancholy mode positions the finite great alongside the finite small to show them both ridiculous against the backdrop of the infinite—that is, the sublime and the awe-inspiring. This is Richter's great concept (Walden 45). As shown in a lecture in his *Miscellaneous Criticism,* Coleridge "borrowed" Richter's theory of humor directly to describe Sterne's and Swift's genius in assuming a role subjectively and judging it objectively at one and the same time: "In short, to seize happily on those points in which every man is more or less a humorist" (123). Coleridge is correct in that, as the man of humor, Sterne steps back to watch Yorick, his humorous self, play out life's comedy. Swift's genius, however, assumes a role by *parodying* his humorist to perfection; but, as Richter notes, Swift's power is in his objective, dissimulating irony (Walden 53–57).

Even the most useful critical thought on humor, melancholy, and the sublime that we have been examining—from Morris, Richter, Kant, Coleridge, Cazamian, Hooker, and the editors of *Saturn and Melancholy*—judges Shakespeare, Jonson, Swift, and Sterne, alas, mistakenly, within the framework of the modern temper. Let us briefly look then at the saturnine affinities of three men of humor who seem clearly to oppose the modern tide: Swift attacked Milton's New Jerusalem, Sterne attacked the latitudinarian sense of goodness he had earlier preached, and Aleksander Pushkin attacked the romantic idealism in English and German literature that had seduced

---

[11] Dedicated to Sir Robert Walpole, the *Essay* drew favorable but slight comment.

contemporary Europe as far as Russia. Put differently, the satiric voice in the *Tale* suffers from the splenetic black bile in seeing the modern European world's corruption, Sterne created *Tristram Shandy* "against the spleen" (301), and Pushkin wrote *Eugene Onegin* "wherein I choke on my bile" (1: 69). Similarly, Swift's *Tale* contemplates time and death, *Tristram Shandy* argues that "time wastes too fast and life follows my pen" (610–611), and the author of *Eugene Onegin* realizes that "rushed by have many, many days . . . much, much has fate snatched away" (1: 308–9). In each of the major works of these three saturnine writers, a persona is deceived or a fool is deluded among knaves by the modern myth. The *Tale*'s persona is "the most devoted Servant of all *Modern* Forms" (45) while later Gulliver will present his England as Albion before his disillusionment. Sterne's more private persona, Yorick, deceived by the doctrines of innate goodness and moral sentiments— thanks largely to the Cambridge Platonists and Anglican rationalists— confronts a harsher, more valid reality in *Tristram Shandy* and *A Sentimental Journey*. Pushkin exposes the benevolent English novel and English and German romanticism—the European window Peter had opened—as they fatally entrapped the tragic Tatiana, the "winsome dunce" Lenski, and the Byronic Onegin. The loss was Russianness. What Henri Fluchère remarked of Sterne applies equally to Swift and Pushkin: "He seems to have sensed the infinite possibilities of a consciousness possessing at one and the same time an historical sense and the means of either enriching or escaping from it" (100). Herein is the supreme consolation of art, the touchstone of its immortality, the reason Homer lived for Swift.

Unlike Milton's, the melancholy temperament of the satirist Swift does not celebrate its own self-sufficiency but registers the truth of the literary humors tradition. That tradition does not offer a vouchsafed, apocalyptic vision or propose an appealing communal enterprise. Instead, its eternally consistent moral discourse seeks a deep human bond with the reader so that both may contemplate the deadly stakes, everyone's doomsday, the ineffable sadness, the cosmic humor, and the immortal triumphs concealed in the larger recesses of human destiny. Art for Swift, Sterne, and Pushkin represents a consummate mastery of an erring, humorous self that has been left playing on the stage of a haughty modern world. It represents the sublime and lonely victory of saturnine melancholy: the genius of humor must continue to challenge that world's narrow, false, and—thank Kronos-Saturn—divinely annulled expectations.

WORKS CITED

PRIMARY SOURCES

Andreae, Johann Valentin. *Reipublicae Christianopolitanae Descriptio.* Strasburg, 1619. *Christianopolis, An Ideal State of the Seventeenth Century.* Trans. Felix Emil Held. Oxford, 1916.
——. *Christianopolis.* Trans. and ed. Felix Emil Held. Diss. U of Illinois, Urbana, 1914.
Anon. *A Letter to the Author of Milton's Life. By a Divine of the Church of England.* London: John Nutt, 1699.
Anon. *Modesty Mistaken: or a Letter to Mr. Toland, upon his declining to appear in the ensuing Parliament.* London, 1702.
Anon. *Mr. Toland's Clito Dissected.* London, 1700.
Anon. *Remarks on the Life of Mr. Milton, As published by J.T. with A Character of the Author and his Party. In a Letter to a Member of Parliament.* London: J. Nutt, 1699.
Anon. *The Rosicrucian Manifestos: Fama Fraternitatis (1614) and Confessio Fraternitatis (1615).* Trans. Thomas Vaughan, 1652. Rpt. in Frances A. Yates. *The Rosicrucian Enlightenment.* Boulder, Colorado: Shambhala: 1978. 238–60.
Anon. *The Secret History of the Calves-Head Club, or the Republicans Unmasked* (London, 1703). *The Harleian Miscellany; or a Collection of Scarce, Curious and Entertaining Pamphlets and Tracts etc.* 12 vols. London: Robert Dutton, 1811. 12: 216–25.
Aristotle. *The Works of Aristotle transl. into English.* Ed. W. D. Ross. Trans. E. S. Forster. Vol. 7: *Problematica.* Oxford, 1927.
Bacon, Francis. *New Atlantis. Works.* Ed. Spedding, Ellis and Heath. 3: 130.
——. *The Advancement of Learning* (1605). Ed. William Aldiss Wright. 5th ed. Oxford, 1926.
Brightman, Thomas. *A revelation of the revelation . . . opened clearly with a logicall resolution and exposition etc.* Amsterdam, 1615.
Browne, Peter. *A Letter in Answer to a Book entitled Christianity not Mysterious as also to all those who set up for Reason and Evidence in Opposition to Revelation and Mysteries.* Dublin, 1697.
Campanella, Tommaso. *Civitas solis. The City of the Sun.* Trans. A. M. Elliott and R. Millner. London: The Journeyman Press, 1981.
Clarke, Samuel. *A Discourse concerning the Unchangeable Obligations of Natural Religion, and the Truth and Certainty of the Christian Revelation. Being Eight Sermons preach'd at the Cathedral Church of St. Paul, in the Year 1705, at the Lecture founded by the Honourable Robert Boyle, Esq.* London, 1706. Rev. and qtd. in *The History of the Works of the Learned. Or, An Impartial Account of Books Lately Printed in all Parts of Europe. With a Particular Relation of the State of Learning in each Country.* 8 (1706): 97–103.
Coleridge, Samuel Taylor. *Coleridge's Miscellaneous Criticism.* Ed. Thomas Middleton Raysor. London: Constable, 1936.
Cooper, Anthony Ashley, The Third Earl of Shaftesbury. *An Inquiry Concerning Virtue, in Two Discourses.* Ed. John Toland. London, 1699.
——. *An Inquiry Concerning Virtue, or Merit* (1699, 1714). Ed. David Walford. Introduction, A Selection of Material from Toland's 1699 Edition and Bibliography. Manchester: Manchester UP, 1977.

——. *Characteristics of Men, Manners, Opinions, Times, etc.* Ed. John M. Robertson. With an Introduction and notes. 2 vols. Gloucester, Mass.: Peter Smith, 1963.

——. *Standard Edition—Complete Works, Selected Letters and Posthumous Writings—In English with Parallel German translation.* Ed. and trans. Gerd Hemmerich and Wolfram Benda. Stuttgart:Frommann-Holzboog, 1981. Rev. by A. Owen Aldridge, *Arcadia* 18 (1983): 324–28.

——. *The Life, Unpublished Letters, and Philosophical Regimen of Anthony, Earl of Shaftesbury.* Ed. Benjamin Rand. London: Swan Sonnenschein, 1900.

[Day, Robert]. *Free Thoughts In Defence of a Future State.* London, 1700.

Foxe, John. *Acts and Monuments of these latter and perilous days etc.* London, 1563.

Hall, Joseph. *Mundus Alter et Idem. Another World and Yet the Same.* Trans. and Ed. John Millar Wands with an Introduction. New Haven: Yale UP, 1981.

Harrington, James. *The Oceana and Other Works of James Harrington, Esq; some whereof are now first publish'd from his own manuscripts. The whole collected, methodiz'd, and review'd, with an exact account of his life prefix'd, by John Toland.* London, 1697.

Heydon, John. *A New Method of Rosie Crucian physick: Wherein is shewed the Cause; and therewith their experienced Medicines for the Cure of all Diseases, Freely given to the inspired Christians.* London, 1658.

——. *Holy Guide.* 1662.

——. *The Rosie Crucian Infallible Aximata.* 1660.

Hobbes, Thomas. *Leviathan; or, the Matter, of a Common-wealth, Ecclesiastical and Civil.* London, 1651.

King, William. *Some Remarks on the Tale of a Tub.* London, 1704.

Locke, John. *An Essay Concerning Human Understanding* (1690). Ed. Peter H. Nidditch. Oxford: Clarendon Press, 1975.

——. *The Reasonableness of Christianity.* London, 1695.

Marsh, Narcissus. "An Introductory Essay to the Doctrine of Sounds containing some proposals for the improvement of Acousticks, as was presented to the Society of Dublin Nov. 12, 1683." *Philosophical Transactions* 14 (1683/4): 471–88.

——. *An Essay touching the Sympathy between Lute or Viol Strings. Natural History of Oxfordshire, being an essay toward the natural history of England.* Ed. Robert Plot. Oxford, 1677. 289–99.

——. *Institutio logicae in usum juventutis academicae Dubliniensis.* Dublin, 1679.

Mason, William Monck. *The History and Antiquities of the Collegiate and Cathedral Church of St. Patrick, near Dublin, from its Foundation in 1190, to the Year 1819.* Dublin, 1820.

Milton, John. *Complete Prose Works of John Milton.* Ed. Don Wolfe. Rev. ed. 7 vols. New Haven: Yale UP, 1980.

——. *The Works of John Milton.* Ed. Frank Allen Patterson. 18 vols. and 2 vols. Index. New York: Columbia UP, 1931–40.

Molyneux, William, John Locke *et al. Some Familiar Letters Between Mr. Locke, and Several of His Friends.* London, 1708.

More, Henry. *Enthusiasmus Triumphatus* (1662). Intro. by M. V. DePorte. *The Augustan Reprint Society Publication Number 118.* Los Angeles: U. of California Press, 1966.

More, Thomas. *Utopia.* 1527.

Morris, Corbyn. *Essay towards fixing the true standards of wit, humour, raillery, satire and ridicule.* London, 1744.

Orrery, John Boyle, Earl of. *Remarks on the Life and Writings of Dr. Jonathan Swift.* London, 1752.

Petty, William. *Essays in Political Arithmetick.* London, 1699.

Pushkin, Aleksander. *Eugene Onegin: A Novel in Verse* (1825–32). Rev. Ed. Trans. Vladimir Nabokov. 4 vols. Princeton: Princeton UP, 1975.

Rabelais, François. *The Histories of Gargantua and Pantagruel* (1523). Trans. J. M. Cohen. New York: Penguin Books, 1958.

Roper, William. *The Lyfe of Sir Thomas Moore, Knighte.* Ed. James Mason Cline. New York: The Swallow Press, 1950.

Sprat, Thomas. *History of the Royal Society.* 1667.

Sterne, Laurence. *The Life and Opinions of Tristram Shandy, Gentleman.* Ed. James Aiken Work. New York: Odyssey Press, 1940.

Swift, Jonathan. *A Discourse of the Contests and Dissentions between the Nobles and the Commons in Athens and Rome, with the Consequences they had upon both those States* (1701). Ed. Frank H. Ellis with an Introduction and Notes. Oxford: Clarendon Press, 1967.

——. *A Tale of A Tub, To Which is added The Battle of the Books and the Mechanical Operation of the Spirit.* Ed. A. C. Guthkelch and D. Nichol Smith with an Introduction and Notes. 2nd ed. Oxford: Clarendon Press, 1973.

——. *A Tale of a Tub and Other Works.* Ed. Angus Ross and David Woolley with an Introduction. *The World's Classics* edition. Oxford: Oxford UP, 1986.

——. *The Complete Poems.* Ed. Pat Rogers. New Haven: Yale UP, 1983.

——. *The Correspondence of Jonathan Swift.* Ed. Harold Williams. 5 vols. Oxford: Clarendon Press, 1963–65.

——. *Journal to Stella.* Ed. Harold Williams. 2 vols. Oxford: Clarendon Press, 1948.

——. *The Poems of Jonathan Swift.* Ed. Harold Williams. 2nd ed. 3 vols. Oxford: Clarendon, 1958.

——. *The Prose Works of Jonathan Swift.* Ed. Herbert Davis. 14 vols. Oxford: Shakespeare Head Press, 1939–68.

Temple, William. *Five Miscellaneous Essays by Sir William Temple.* Ed. Samuel Holt Monk. Ann Arbor: U of Michigan P, 1963.

——. *The Works of Sir William Temple, Bart. Complete in Four Volumes.* London, 1814.

Tindal, Matthew. *The Nation Vindicated from the Aspersions Cast on it in a Late Pamphlet.* London, 1711.

Toland, John. *Amyntor; or, A Defence of Milton's Life.* London, 1699.

——. *Anglia Libera: or the Limitation and Succession of the Crown of England explain'd and asserted.* London, 1701.

——. *Christianity not Mysterious: or, a Treatise Shewing, That there is nothing in the Gospel Contrary to Reason, Nor Above it: And that no Christian Doctrine can be properly call'd A Mystery.* The Second Edition Enlarg'd. London: Sam Buckley, 1696.

——. *Clito: A Poem on the Force of Eloquence.* London, 1700.

——. Letter of John Toland to [the Earl of Oxford], 7 December 1711. *Great Britain Historical Manuscripts Commission. Report of the Manuscripts of His Grace The Duke of Portland, preserved at Welbeck Abbey.* Vol. 5: 126–27. London, 1899.

——. *The Grand Mystery Laid Open: Namely, By dividing of the Protestants to weaken the Hanover Succession to extirpate the Protestant Religion.* London, 1714.

——. *The Life of John Milton, Containing, besides the History of his Works, Several Extraordinary Characters of Men and Books, Sects, Parties, and Opinions.* London: John Darby, 1699.

Vaughan, Thomas. *The Works of Thomas Vaughan.* ed. Alan Rudrum. Oxford: Clarendon, 1984.

Wotton, William. *A Defense of the Reflections Upon Ancient and Modern Learning, In Answer to the Objections of Sir W. Temple, and Others. With Observations upon The Tale of a Tub.* London, 1705. Rpt. in Jonathan Swift. *A Tale of a Tub, To Which Is Added the Battle of the Books and the Mechanical Operation of the Spirit.* Ed. A. C. Guthkelch and D. Nichol Smith. 2nd ed. Oxford: Clarendon, 1973. 313–28.

SECONDARY SOURCES

Adams, Robert Martin. "In Search of Baron Somers." *Culture and Politics from Puritanism to the Enlightenment.* Ed. Perez Zagorin. Berkeley: U of California P, 1980. 165–202.

——. "Jonathan Swift, Thomas Swift, and the Authorship of *A Tale of a Tub.*" *Modern Philology* 64 (1966–67): 198–232.

——. *Strains of Discord: Studies in Literary Openness.* Ithaca: Cornell UP, 1958.

——. "The Mood of the Church and *A Tale of a Tub.*" *England in the Restoration and Early Eighteenth Century: Essays on Culture and Society* Ed. H. T. Swedenberg. Berkeley: U of California P, 1972. 71–99.

228 BIBLIOGRAPHY

Albury, W. R. "Halley's Ode on the *Principia* of Newton and the Epicurean Revival in England." *The Journal of the History of Ideas* 39 (1978): 24–43.
Aldridge, A. Owen. "Shaftesbury and the Test of Truth." *PMLA* 60 (1945): 129–56.
——. "Shaftesbury's Earliest Critic." *Modern Philology* 44 (1946): 10–22.
—— "Two Versions of Shaftesbury's *Inquiry Concerning Virtue.*" *Huntington Library Quarterly* 13 (1949–50): 207–14.
Barnard, T. C. "Sir William Petty, Irish Landowner." *History and Imagination: Essays in Honor of H.S. Trevor-Roper.* Ed. Hugh Lloyd-Jones, Valerie Pearl and Blair Worden. New York: Holmes and Meier, 1981. 355–69.
——. "The Hartlib Circle and the Origins of the Dublin Philosophical Society." *Irish Historical Studies* 19: 56–71.
Belanger, Terry. "Publishers and Writers in Eighteenth-Century England." *Books and Their Readers in Eighteenth-Century England.* Ed. Isabel Rivers. New York: St. Martin's Press, 1982 5–25.
Berman, David. "The Irish Counter-Enlightenment." *The Irish Mind: Exploring Intellectual Traditons.* Ed. Richard Kearney. Dublin: Wolfhound, 1985. 119–40.
Biddle, John C. "Locke's Critique of Innate Principles and Toland's Deism." *The Journal of the History of Ideas* 37 (1976): 411–22.
Borkat, Roberta F. S. "Sir William Temple, the Idea of Progress, and the Meaning of Learning." *The Durham University Journal* 71 [N.S. 40] (1978): 1–7.
Bos, A. P. *Cosmic and Meta-Cosmic Theology in Aristotle's Lost Dialogues. Brill's Studies in Intellectual History.* Vol. 16. Leiden: E. J. Brill, 1989.
Boyle, Frank T. "Heresy in the Modern Empire of Reason: Swift, Deism, and Sir William Temple's Chinese Utopia." Diss. Trinity College, Dublin, 1989.
——. "Profane and Debauched Deist: Swift in the Contemporary Response to *A Tale of a Tub.*" *Eighteenth-Century Ireland* 3 (1988): 25–38
Cantor, Geoffrey. "Berkeley's *The Analyst* Revisited." *Isis* 75 (1984): 668–83.
Carabelli, Giancarlo. *Tolandiana: Materiali bibliografici per lo studio dell'opera e della fortuna di John Toland (1670–1722).* Firenze: La Nuova Italia Editrice, 1975.
——. *Tolandiana: Materiali bibliografici per lo studio dell'opera e della fortuna di John Toland (1670–1722). Errata, Addenda e Indici. Pubblicazioni Della Facoltà di Magistero Dell'Università di Ferrara.* Vol. 4. Università Degli Studi di Ferrara, 1978.
Cassirer, Ernst. *The Platonic Renaissance in England.* Trans. James P. Pettegrove. London: Nelson, 1970.
Castiglioni, Arturo. "Neo-Hippocratic Tendency of Contemporary Medical Thought." *Medical Life* 41 (1934): 115–46.
Cazamian, Louis. *The Development of Enlgish Humor.* 2 vols. Durham, North Carolina: Duke UP, 1951 (1930), 1952.
Coulter, Harris L. *Divided Legacy: A History of the Schism in Medical Thought.* 3 vols. Washington, D.C.: Wehawken Book Co., 1973–75.
Crane, R. S. *Critical and Historical Principles of Literary History.* Chicago: U of Chicago P, 1971.
——. "Suggestions Toward a Genealogy of the 'Man of Feeling'." *English Literary History* 1 (1934): 205–30.
——. "The Houyhnhnms, the Yahoos, and the History of Ideas." *Reason and the Imagination: Studies in the History of Ideas 1600–1800.* Ed. J. A. Mazzeo. New York: Columbia UP, 1962 231–53.
Crocker, Lester G. "When Myths Die." *Studies on Voltaire and the Eighteenth Century Transactions of the Fourth International Congress on the Enlightenment.* Ed. Theodore Besterman. Oxford: The Voltaire Foundation, 1976. 151:19–29.
Daniel, Stephen H. *John Toland his Methods, Manners, and Mind.* Kingston, Ontario: McGill-Queens UP, 1984.
Debus, Allen G. *The Chemical Philosophy: Paracelsian Science and Medicine in the Sixteenth and Seventeenth Centuries.* 2 vols. New York: Science History Publications, 1977.
——. *The English Paracelsians.* London: Oldbourne, 1965.

DePorte, Michael V. "Digressions and Madness in *A Tale of a Tub* and *Tristram Shandy.*" *Huntington Library Quarterly* 34 (1970): 43–57.

——. Introduction. *Enthusiasmus Triumphatus* (1662). By Henry More. *The Augustan Reprint Society* 118 (1966): i–vii.

——. *Nightmares and Hobbyhorses: Swift, Sterne, and Augustan Ideas of Madness.* San Marino, California: The Huntington Library, 1974.

Downie, James Alan. *Jonathan Swift: Political Writer.* London: Routledge and Kegan, 1984.

——. *Robert Harley and the Press: Propaganda and Public Opinion in the Age of Swift and Defoe.* Cambridge: Cambridge UP, 1979.

——. "Swift's *Discourse:* Allegorical Satire or Parallel History?" *Swift Studies* 2 (1987): 25–32.

Ehrenpreis, Irvin. *Swift: The Man, His Works and The Age.* 3 vols. Cambridge, Massachusetts: Harvard UP, 1962–83.

——. "Swift on Liberty (1952)." *Swift Modern Judgments.* Ed. A. Norman Jeffares. London: Macmillan, 1968. 59–73.

Elias, A.C. *Swift at Moor Park: Problems in Biography and Criticism.* Philadelphia: U of Pennsylvania P, 1982.

Elliott, Robert C. "Swift's *Tale of a Tub:* An Essay in Problems of Structure." *PMLA* 66 (1951): 441–55.

——. *The Literary Persona.* Chicago: University of Chicago Press, 1982.

——. *The Power of Satire: Magic, Ritual, Art.* Princeton: Princeton UP, 1960.

——. *The Shape of Utopia: Studies in a Literary Genre.* Chicago: U of Chicago P, 1970.

Ellis, Frank H. Rev. of *Swift at Moor Park: Problems in Biography and Criticism* by A. C. Elias. *Modern Philology* 81 (1983): 72–76.

Firth, C. H. "Dean Swift and Ecclesiastical Preferment." *RES* 2 (1926): 1–17.

Firth, Katharine R. *The Apocalyptic Tradition in Reformation Britain 1530–1645.* Oxford: Oxford UP, 1979.

Fisch, Harold. *Jerusalem and Albion: The Hebraic Factor in Seventeenth-Century Literature.* New York: Schocken Books, 1964.

Fixler, Michael. *Milton and the Kingdoms of God.* London: Faber and Faber, 1964.

Fluchère, Henri. *Laurence Sterne: From Tristram to Yorick: An Interpretation of Tristram Shandy.* Trans. and abr. Barbara Bray. London: Oxford UP, 1965.

Force, James E. "Newton's God of Dominion: The Unity of Newton's Theological, Scientific, and Political Thought." *Essays on the Context, Nature, and Influence of Isaac Newton's Theology* by James E. Force and Richard H. Popkin. Dordrecht: Kluwer Academic Publishers, 1990. 75–102.

——. *William Whiston: Honest Newtonian.* Cambridge: Cambridge UP, 1985.

Francis, Alan D. *The Methuens and Portugal 1691–1708.* Cambridge: Cambridge UP, 1966.

Furley, David J. and J. S. Wilkie. *Galen on Respiration and the Arteries.* Princeton: Princeton UP, 1984.

Galston, Iago. "The Psychiatry of Paracelsus." *Bulletin of the History of Medicine* 24 (1950): 205–18. Rpt. in *Science Medicine and History.* 2 vols. Ed. E. Ashworth Underwood. London: Oxford UP, 1953 1: 408–17.

——. *From magic to science.* London, 1928.

Gibbs, G. C. Rev. of *The Radical Enlightenment: Pantheists, Freemasons and Republicans* by Margaret C. Jacobs. *The British Journal for the History of Science* 17 (1984): 67–79.

Goldberg, Gerald Y. *Jonathan Swift and Contemporary Cork.* Cork: The Mercier Press, 1967.

Gunther, Robert William Theodore [R.T.]. *Early Science in Oxford.* 15 vols. Oxford: Oxford UP, 1920–67.

Harth, John Phillip. *Swift and Anglican Rationalism; the Seventeenth Century Background of Swift's Early Writings.* Chicago: U of Chicago P, 1961.

Heinemann, F. H. "John Toland and the Age of Reason." *Archiv Für Philosophie* 4 (1950): 35–66.

Heyd, Michael. "The Reaction to Enthusiasm in the Seventeenth Century: Towards An Integrative Approach." *Journal of Modern History* 53 (1981): 258–80.

Hinsie, Leland E. and Robert Jean Campbell, Ed. *Psychiatric Dictionary.* 4th Edition. New York: Oxford UP, 1973.

Holstun, James. *A Rational Millennium: Puritan Utopias of Seventeenth-Century England and America.* Oxford: Oxford UP, 1987.

Hooker, Edward N. "Humour in the Age of Pope." *Huntington Library Quarterly* 9 (1948): 361–85.

Hopkins, Robert H. "The Personation of Hobbism in Swift's *Tale of a Tub* and *Mechanical Operation of the Spirit.*" *Philological Quarterly* 45 (1966): 372–78.

Hoppen, K. Theodore. *The Common Scientist in the Seventeenth Century: A Study of the Dublin Philosophical Society 1683–1708.* Charlottesville: The UP of Virginia, 1970.

Hunter, William B., ed. *A Milton Encyclopedia.* 9 vols. London: Associated UPs, 1978–83.

Jacob, Margaret C. *The Cultural Meaning of the Scientific Revolution.* Philadelphia: Temple UP, 1988.

——. *The Newtonians and the English Revolution 1689–1720.* Ithaca: Cornell UP, 1976.

——. *The Radical Enlightenment: Pantheists, Freemasons and Republicans.* London: George Allen & Unwin, 1981.

Jones, Richard Foster. *Ancients and Moderns. A Study of the Rise of the Scientific Movement in Seventeenth Century England.* 2nd ed. Berkeley: U of California P, 1965.

Kelling, Harold D. and Cathy Lynn Preston, Ed. *A KWIC Concordance to Jonathan Swift's A Tale of a Tub, The Battle of the Books, and A Discourse Concerning the Mechanical Operation of the Spirit, A Fragment.* New York: Garland Publishing, 1984.

Kiernan, Colin. "Swift and Science." *The Historical Journal* 14 (1971): 709–22.

Klibansky, Raymond, Erwin Panofsky, and Fritz Saxl. *Saturn and Melancholy: Studies in the History of Natural Philosophy Religion and Art.* London: Thomas Nelson and Sons Ltd., 1964.

Korshin, Paul J. *Typologies in England 1650–1820.* Princeton: Princeton UP, 1982.

Landa, Louis A. "Swift, the Mysteries, and Deism." *Texas Studies in English* 24 (1944): 239–56.

Leavis, F. R. "The Irony of Swift." *Swift: A Collection of Critical Essays.* Ed. Ernest Tuveson. Englewood Cliffs, New Jersey: Prentice-Hall, 1964. 15–29. Rpt. from *Determinations.* Ed. F. R. Leavis. London: Chatto and Windus, 1934. 79–108.

Le Fanu, T. P. "Catalogue of Dean Swift's Library in 1715, with an Inventory of his Personal Property in 1742." *Proceedings of the Royal Irish Academy.* 37, Sect. C., No.13, 263–74.

Lloyd-Jones, Hugh, Valerie Pearl and Blair Worden, Ed. *History and Imagination: Essays in Honor of H.R. Trevor-Roper.* New York: Holmes and Meier, 1981.

Logan, George M. *The Meaning of More's "Utopia."* Princeton: Princeton UP, 1983.

Lund, Roger D. "Strange Complicities: Atheism and Conspiracy in *A Tale of a Tub.*" *Eighteenth Century Life* 13 (1989): 34–58.

McCarthy, Muriel. *All Graduates and Gentlemen.* Dublin: The O'Brien P, 1980.

——. "Swift and the Primate of Ireland: Marsh's Library in the early Eighteenth Century." *Dublin Historical Record* 27 (1974): 109–12.

Macey, Samuel L. *Patriarchs of Time: Dualism in Saturn-Cronus, Father Time, the Watchmaker God, and Father Christmas.* Athens, Georgia: U of Georgia P, 1987.

McLean, Antonia. *Humanism and the Rise of Science in Tudor England.* New York: Neale Watson Academic Publications, 1972.

Madsen, William G. *From Shadowy Types to Truth: Studies in Milton's Symbolism.* New Haven: Yale UP, 1968.

Montgomery, John Warwick. *Cross and Crucible: Johann Valentin Andreae (1586–1654) Phoenix of the Theologians.* Vol. 1 *Andreae's Life, World-View, and Relations with Rosicrucianism and Alchemy.* 2 vols. *Archives Internationales D'Histoire des Idées.* No. 55. The Hague: Martinus Nijhoff, 1973.

Moore, John Robert. "Milton Among the Augustans: The Infernal Council." *Studies in Philology* 48 (1951): 15–25.

Mossner, Ernest C. *Bishop Butler and the Age of Reason: A Study in the History of Thought.* New York: Macmillan, 1936.

Nicholl, H. F. "John Toland: religion without mystery." *Hermathena* 100 (1965): 54–65.

Nokes, David. *Jonathan Swift A Hypocrite Reversed: A Critical Biography.* Oxford: Oxford UP, 1985.

Obelkevich, James. "Proverbs and Social History." *The Social History of Language.* Ed. Peter Burke and Roy Porter. Cambridge: Cambridge UP, 1987. 43–72.

Olson, R. C. "Swift's Use of the *Philsophical Transactions* in Section V of *A Tale of a Tub.*" *Studies in Philology* 49 (1952): 459–67.

Olson, Richard. "Tory-High Church Opposition to Science and Scientism in the Eighteenth Century: The Works of John Arbuthnot, Jonathan Swift, and Samuel Johnson." *The Uses of Science in the Age of Newton.* Ed. John G. Burke. Berkeley: U of California P, 1983.

Ormsby-Lennon, Hugh. "Swift's Spirit Reconjured: das Dong-an sich." *Swift Studies* 3 (1988): 9–78.

Pagel, Walter. *Paracelsus An Introduction to Philosophical Medicine in the Era of the Renaissance.* 2nd Rev. Ed. Basel: Karger, 1982.

Paulson, Ronald. *Theme and Structure in Swift's "Tale of a Tub".* New Haven: Yale UP, 1960.

Pocock, J. G. A. *Virtue, Commerce, and History: Essays on Political Thought and History, Chiefly in the Eighteenth Century.* Cambridge: Cambridge UP, 1985.

Popkin, Richard H. Foreword. *William Whiston: Honest Newtonian.* By James E. Force. Cambridge UP, 1985. xi–xix.

——. "Newton's Biblical Theology and his Theological Physics." *Newton's Scientific and Philosophical Legacy.* P. B. Scheuer and G. Debrock, Ed. Dordrecht: Kluwer Academic Publishers, 1988. 81–97.

Quinlan, Maurice J. "Swift's Use of Literalization as a Rhetorical Device." *PMLA* 82 (1967): 516–21.

Rattansi, P. M. "Art and Science: The Paracelsian Vision." *Science and Arts in the Renaissance.* Ed. F. D. Hoeniger and J. Shirley. Cranbury, New Jersey: Associated UPs, 1985 50–58.

——. "The Intellectual Origins of the Royal Society." *Notes and Records of the Royal Society.* 23 (1968): 129–45.

——. "The Literary Attack on Science in the late 17th and 18th centuries." Ph.D. diss. University College London, 1961.

——. "Paracelsus and the Puritan Revolution." *Ambix* 11 (1963): 24–32.

——. Rev. of *Ancients and Moderns. A Study of the Rise of the Scientific Movement in Seventeenth Century England* by Richard Foster Jones. *British Journal of Philosophy of Science* 18 (1967): 250–55.

——. "The Scientific Background." *The Age of Milton: Backgrounds to seventeenth-century literature.* Ed. C. A. Patrides and Raymond B. Waddington. Manchester: Manchester UP, 1980. 197–240.

Riese, Walther. *Galen on the passions and errors of the soul.* trans. Paul W. Harkins. Columbus, Ohio: Ohio State UP, 1963.

Rosenheim, Edward. *Swift and the Satirist's Art.* Chicago: U of Chicago P, 1963.

——. "The Text and Context of Swift's *Contests and Dissentions.*" *Modern Philology* 66 (1968): 59–74.

Ross, Angus. "*The Anatomy of Melancholy* and Swift." *Swift and His Contexts.* Ed. John Irwin Fischer, Hermann J. Real and James Woolley. New York: AMS Press, 1989. 133–58.

Ross, Angus and David Woolley, Ed. *Jonathan Swift.* Oxford: Oxford UP, 1984.

Scruggs, Charles. "Swift's Use of Lucretius in *A Tale of a Tub. Texas Studies in Literature and Language* 15 (1973): 39–49.

Sensabaugh, George F. *That Grand Whig Milton.* Stanford: Stanford UP, 1952.

——. "Adaptations of *Areopagitica.*" *Huntington Library Quarterly* 13 (1949): 201–14.

Siebert, Frederick Seaton. *Freedom of the Press in England 1476–1775.* Urbana: U of Illinois P, 1952.

Singer, Charles and E. A. Underwood. *A Short History of Medicine.* Oxford: Clarendon Press, 1962.

Sirmans, M. Eugene. *Colonial South Carolina: A Political History 1663–1763.* Chapel Hill: U of North Carolina P, 1966.

Speck, W. A. "From Principles to Practice: Swift and Party Politics." *The World of Jonathan Swift: Essays for the Tercentary.* Ed. Brian Vickers. Cambridge, Mass.: Harvard UP, 1968. 69–86.

Starkman, Miriam. *Swift's Satire on Learning in A Tale of a Tub.* Princeton: Princeton UP, 1950.

Steensma, Robert C. "The Legal Proverb in Defoe, Swift, and Shenstone." *Proverbium* 10 (1968): 248.

Stokes, George T. *Some Worthies of the Irish Church.* London, 1900.

Sullivan, Robert E. *John Toland the Deist Controversy: A Study in Adaptations.* Cambridge, Massachusetts: Harvard UP, 1982.

Tanaka, Mitsuo. "Satire and *Satura:* A Thematic Study of Swift's Satire with Reference to Juvenal and Horace." Diss. Doshisha U, 1984.

Tave, Stuart M. *The Amiable Humorist A Study in the Comic Theory and Criticism of the Eighteenth and Early Nineteenth Centuries.* Chicago: U of Chicago P, 1960.

Temkin, Owsei. *The Double Face of Janus and Other Essays in the History of Medicine.* Baltimore: Johns Hopkins UP, 1977.

——. *Galenism: Rise and Decline of a Medical Philosophy.* Ithaca: Cornell UP, 1973.

Toon, Peter, Ed. *Puritans, The Millennium and the Future of Israel: Puritan Eschatology 1600 to 1660.* Cambridge: James Clarke & Co., 1970.

Trevor-Roper, Hugh Redwald. *History and Imagination.* New York: Oxford UP, 1980.

——. *Renaissance Essays.* 3rd Rev. Ed. London: Martin Secker & Warburg, 1985.

——. "Three Foreigners: The Philosophers of the Puritan Revolution." *Religion, the Reformation and Social Change.* 2nd ed. Macmillan, 1972. 237–93.

Ulman, Craig Hawkins. *Satire and the Correspondence of Swift.* Cambridge, Massachusetts: Harvard UP, 1973.

Venturi, Franco. *Utopia and Reform in the Enlightenment.* Cambridge: Cambridge UP, 1971.

Vickers, Brian. "The Satiric Structure of *Gulliver's Travels* and More's *Utopia.*" *The World of Jonathan Swift: Essays for the Tercentenary.* Ed. Brian Vickers. Oxford: Basil Blackwell, 1968. 233–57.

Vieth, David M. *Swift's Poetry 1900–1980: An Annotated Bibliography of Studies.* New Haven: Yale UP, 1983.

Walden, Helen. "Jean Paul and Swift." Diss. New York U, 1940.

Webster, Charles. *From Paracelsus to Newton: Magic and the Making of Modern Science.* Cambridge: Cambridge UP, 1982.

Weinsheimer, Joel. "Toland on Reason." Unpublished draft, November 1990.

Westman, Robert S. and J. E. McGuire. *Hermeticism and the Scientific Revolution.* Los Angeles: The William Andrew Clark Memorial Library, U of California, 1977.

White, Newport J. D. *An Account of Archbishop Marsh's Library, Dublin.* Dublin, 1927.

——. *Four Good Men: Luke Challoner, Jeremy Taylor, Narcissus Marsh, Elias Bouhéreau.* Dublin: Hodges, Figgis, 1927.

Williams, Harold. *Dean Swift's Library with a Facsimile of the Original Sale Catalogue and Some Account of Two Manuscript Lists of His Books.* Cambridge: Cambridge UP, 1932.

Wilson, Leonard G. "Erasistratus, Galen, and the 'Pneuma'." *Bulletin of the History of Medicine* 33 (1959): 293–314.

Winnett, Arthur Robert. *Peter Browne: Provost, Bishop, Metaphysician.* London: S.P.C.K., 1974.

Wolfe, Don M. *Milton in the Puritan Revolution.* New York: Humanities P, 1963.

Worden, Blair. "Classical Republicanism and the Puritan Revolution." *History and Imagination: Essays in Honor of H.R. Trevor-Roper.* Ed. Hugh Lloyd-Jones, Valerie Pearl and Blair Worden. New York: Holmes and Meier, 1981. 180–200.

Yates, Frances Amelia. *The Rosicrucian Enlightenment.* London: Routledge and Kegan Paul, 1972.

INDEX

BRILL'S STUDIES IN INTELLECTUAL HISTORY

26. JONES, R. *Learning Arabic in Renaissance Europe*. 1992. ISBN 90 04 09451 2
27. DRIJVERS, J.W. *Helena Augusta*. The Mother of Constantine the Great and the Legend of Her Finding of the True Cross. 1992. ISBN 90 04 09435 0
28. BOUCHER, W.I. *Spinoza in English*. A Bibliography from the Seventeenth-Century to the Present. 1991. ISBN 90 04 09499 7
29. MCINTOSH, C. *The Rose Cross and the Age of Reason*. Eighteenth-Century Rosicrucianism in Central Europe and its Relationship to the Enlightenment. 1992. ISBN 90 04 09502 0
30. CRAVEN, K. *Jonathan Swift and the Millennium of Madness*. The Information Age in Swift's *A Tale of a Tub*. 1992. ISBN 90 04 09524 1
31. BERKVENS-STEVELINCK, C., H. BOTS, P.G. HOFTIJZER & O.S. LANK-HORST (eds.). *Le Magasin de l'Univers. The Dutch Republic as the Centre of the European Book Trade*. Papers Presented at the International Colloquium, held at Wassenaar, 5-7 July 1990. 1992. ISBN 90 04 09493 8

DATE DUE

APR 27 1995			
MAR 20 1996			